I0817547

A HISTORY OF THE MODERN WORLD

A HISTORY OF THE MODERN WORLD

FROM 1950 TO THE PRESENT DAY

JEREMY BLACK

About the Author

Jeremy Black MBE is Visiting Professor to the Indonesian Staff College, Emeritus Professor of History at the University of Exeter, Distinguished Fellow in the Center for Military History and Strategy at Hillsdale College, Senior Research Fellow of the British Foreign Policy Group, and Senior Fellow of the Foreign Policy Research Institute. After leaving Cambridge with a starred first, he did graduate work at Oxford, and taught at Durham (1980–1995) and Exeter (1996–2020). In 2008, he won the Samuel Eliot Morison Prize from the Society for Military History. Recent books include histories of the Atlantic, Caribbean, Mediterranean, Pacific, US, Britain, France, Germany, Italy, London, Paris, Portugal, Spain, railways, cavalry, artillery, tanks, infantry, the British monarchy and British transport.

Acknowledgements

It is a great pleasure to thank those with whom I have been able to discuss the subject and who have commented on previous drafts, particularly Steven Fischer, Bill Gibson, Luigi Loreto, Nigel Ramsay and Richard Wylde. John Turing again has been an exemplary editor. It is a great pleasure to dedicate this book to William Thuillier, a sage friend.

For William Thuillier

This edition published in 2025 by Sirius Publishing, a division of Arcturus Publishing Limited,
26/27 Bickels Yard, 151–153 Bermondsey Street,
London SE1 3HA

ISBN: 978-1-3988-5493-2
AD012535UK

Printed in Malaysia

CONTENTS

Introduction

INTRODUCTION

The present is a fraction of time between past and future and the people in it a small percentage of those who have lived. The Romans called the dead 'the majority'. The present is bound up with the experience of the past and, paradoxically, also that of the future – the latter in terms of anticipations, hopes and fears. Written in 2024 and published in 2025, this book begins in 1950 and takes us up to the present day. It also indulges in a little speculation as to what may lay ahead in the near future. It's an account compounded of the past, present and future, their links, and the developments that give them meaning, however much that meaning is caught in the expectations of the present.

The scope here is global, because a modern history has to engage with all the world. A Western-centric account of world history is both flawed and redundant. This book will reflect a geographical landscape in which the majority of the world's population lives in Asia, and it will reflect a historical perspective in which most of those alive today have scant adult memory of the Cold War. To fail to do so, as indeed do most treatments of recent world history and most of modern world politics, is to produce work of limited value. It also flies in the face of the very things that we ought to be considering.

The late 1940s proved very important to Europe, with the war-ravaged continent divided into two rival blocs and only a few states left as neutral, notably Sweden and Switzerland.

BELOW: The occupation zones of Germany, 1945.

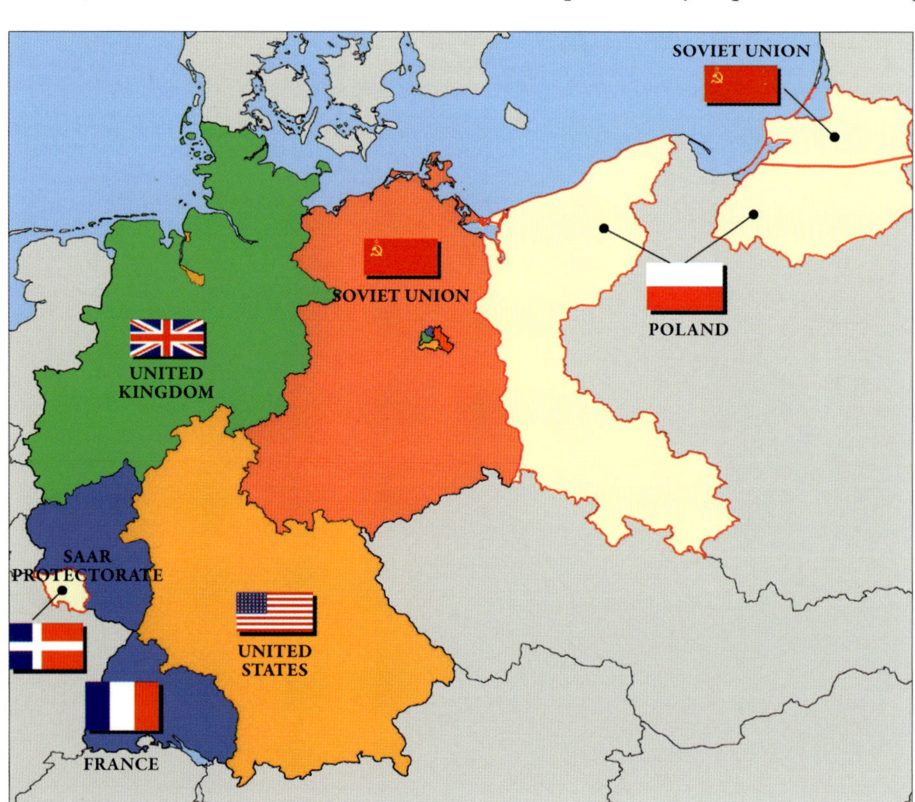

The division of Germany and Austria into zones of occupation by American, British, French and Soviet forces proved important to this process although was to be taken in different directions in 1955 when the occupation forces were removed from Austria, which was neutralized, whereas in Germany the division continued until 1989. Indeed, the Inter-German Border was a parallel to that created in 1953 between North and South Korea.

There was no such outcome in the remainder of Europe, but, instead, the establishment under the shadow of Soviet military power in Eastern Europe of Communist regimes. This was a violent process with force and

intimidation important, and opponents, imprisoned or killed. This use of force to impose a Soviet order spanned lands annexed to the Soviet Union, notably in the Baltic Republics and Poland, and those left under what became Soviet client states.

ABOVE: Truman signs the NATO agreement, 24 August 1949.

At the same time, starting in Yugoslavia, there was opposition to such status from some Communists, and this created a rift in the Communist system that was to be expanded when Albania followed the Chinese Communist line, and, separately, by autonomous moves by Communist states, notably Romania, although attempts to do so could be suppressed, most brutally in Hungary in 1956.

In Western Europe, there was no democracy in Portugal or Spain, which remained right-wing autocracies until the 1970s, but, elsewhere, there was an anchoring of anti-Communist politics, in which both conservative and left-wing parties followed democratic

ABOVE: Mao Zedong proclaims the establishment of the People's Republic of China, 1949.

means and advanced social welfarism to keep the working class from Communism. American financial assistance under Marshall Aid, military presence, and political action were all important to anchoring Western Europe in a Western bloc, a process cemented with the formation of NATO in 1949.

We start in 1950 because that decisively launches us into the modern world politically. While 1945 and the end of World War II might appear the obvious place to begin, with the final defeats of Nazi Germany and Imperial Japan, it was a year in which the fate of China was unclear, the US had a monopoly of nuclear weapons and Britain was still in control of India and dominant in the Middle East.

By 1950, all this had changed. China, for example, was under Communist control. Mao Zedong had taken power in 1949 and would remain the country's dictator until his death in 1976 – the longest period in office during that time for any leader of a major power. His reign over the world's most populous country helped provide a measure of continuity that contrasted markedly with the previous half-century of Chinese history.

By 1950, the US was no longer the sole nuclear power, the Soviet Union having produced its own atomic bomb. Soon, other nations would develop their own weapons of mass destruction. They continue to do so today. India in 1950 was no longer part of the

British Empire, and neither were Myanmar and Sri Lanka. New nations, not least Pakistan and Israel, now existed in formerly British-held territories, while Syria and Lebanon had gained their independence from France and the Philippines was free of US dominion. These developments – and more – help explain why it is better to begin a survey of recent world history with 1950 rather than 1945.

By 1950, as a reminder of the degree to which rapid change can occur, the challenge of the future was being reshaped away from the immediate aftermath of the world war, transformative as that had been. To start in 1945 is to look backward; to begin in 1950 is to look forward, and that is the approach taken here. It is to discuss how and why we got from then to now, and what this can tell us about the future.

The method adopted in this book is thematic. This is so it can show how developments in the present fit in a pattern involving the past and could lead us into the future. A thematic approach involves choices, notably of balance and emphasis. It is important that we do not lose sight of the significance of environmental, technological, social, economic

BELOW: Viceroy of India Lord Mountbatten declares India's independence in 1947.

ABOVE: The demilitarized zone between North and South Korea. Borders within what was once a single state have been a defining feature of the period since 1950, with life contrasting dramatically on either side of the divide.

and cultural themes in human history by focusing solely on politics. The latter, both international and domestic, is important, but so too are the other themes and we shall not crowd them out. Moreover, a narrative approach is inherently dated even before it is published, while a thematic one has the freshness of present-day issues and responses.

A thematic approach, however, does not provide guidance as to how much space should be devoted to particular subjects – or what should be covered within each subject and to what degree. Time, geography and context play their part. Religion, for example, will feature more heavily in the recent histories of Islamic countries than in, say, China or Japan.

The complexity of the world's current history owes much to the interaction of developments in many spheres, and readers should consider this when looking at this book. Each chapter does not stand alone but interacts with and relates to all the others. This complexity, moreover, is only to be expected of a global population that is larger, more literate, more politically engaged, more mobile and more affluent than ever before. India's election in 2024 saw the largest number of votes ever cast in a public ballot. There are many signs that these trends will continue.

Contrasts between states that were once part of one country, such as East and West Germany from 1945 to 1990, North and South Korea from 1945 to the present, India and Pakistan from 1947 to the present, China and Taiwan from 1949 to the present, or Israel and the Gaza Strip, indicate the centrality of politics to other aspects of life, notably society, economics and culture. This underlines a key point of this book: the need to read all the sections, and not to imagine that there is a simple linkage from one to the other, and certainly not a causative linkage.

At the most basic level of political causations, social experience is very different, individually and collectively, in states that have conscription, for example, which in 2024 included Algeria, Angola, Austria, Benin, Brazil, Belarus, Cyprus, Denmark, Egypt, Eritrea, Estonia, Greece, Iran, Israel, Latvia, Lithuania, Norway, Singapore, Sweden, Switzerland, Syria, Turkey and Ukraine. Moreover, in states struggling from high rates of criminality, such as those of Central America, Colombia, Brazil and South Africa, the social experience is very different to those that are particularly peaceful, such as Norway.

This book is supported by carefully chosen illustrations. They capture the extent to which the world is experienced primarily through sight, and the record of this is better now than ever before. Not only are more photographs taken and other illustrations produced, but they are also preserved in far greater quantities than ever before, and in colour. As a result, the photographs here should be seen not simply as illustrations but also as interacting with the text, each illuminating the other. To that end, the captions are also significant.

This is history with a purpose. Every age is one that affects individuals differently, but this age, from 1950 onwards, represents the trust between the generations. It binds us together with our parents in the previous generation and with our children. There is often difference, if not division, in concerns, wishes, opinions and interests between the generations. That is part of history. It is also important that we try to understand the experiences of others, not least of the previous generation, as we would hope to be understood ourselves.

1 The Environment

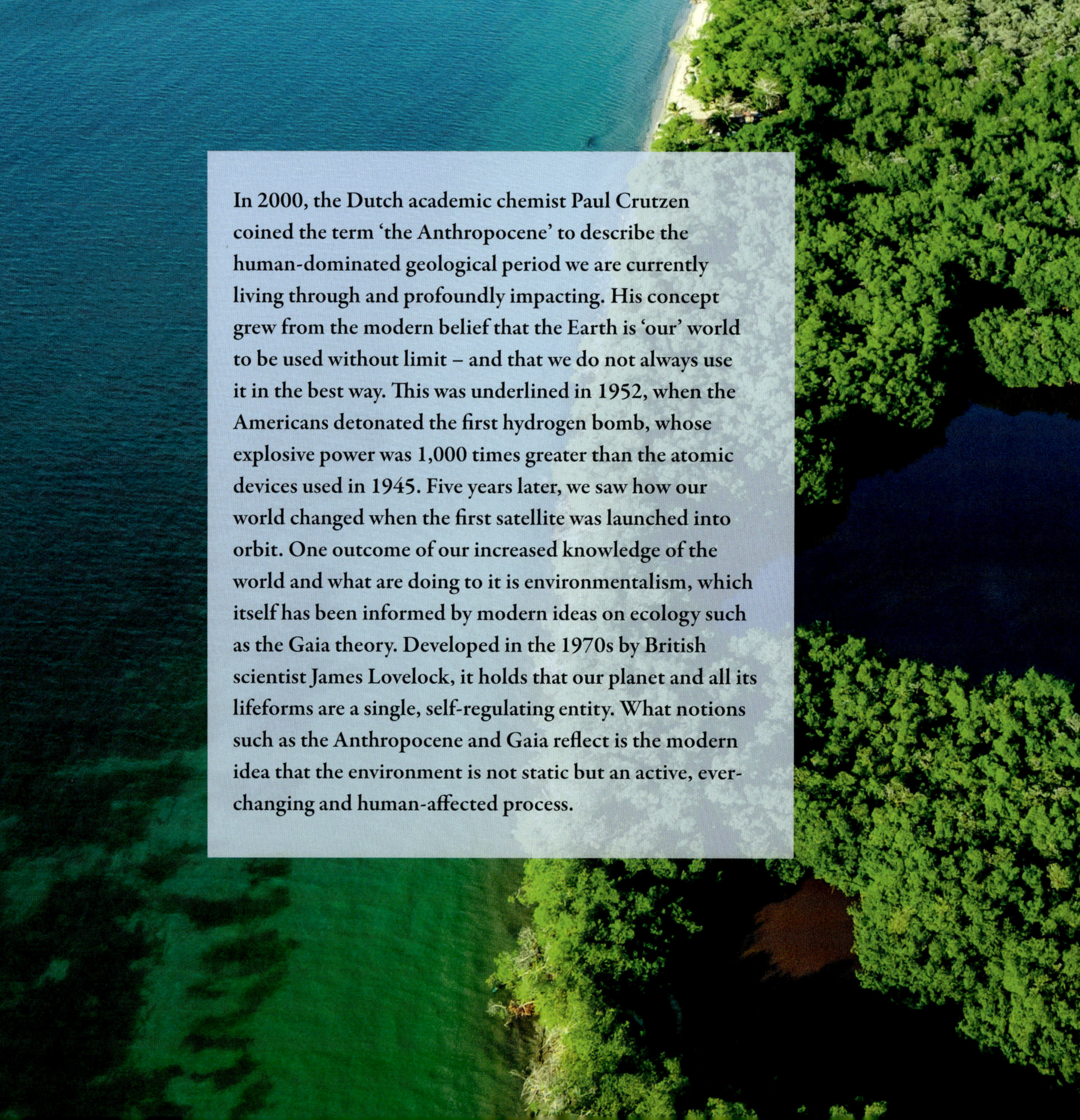

In 2000, the Dutch academic chemist Paul Crutzen coined the term 'the Anthropocene' to describe the human-dominated geological period we are currently living through and profoundly impacting. His concept grew from the modern belief that the Earth is 'our' world to be used without limit – and that we do not always use it in the best way. This was underlined in 1952, when the Americans detonated the first hydrogen bomb, whose explosive power was 1,000 times greater than the atomic devices used in 1945. Five years later, we saw how our world changed when the first satellite was launched into orbit. One outcome of our increased knowledge of the world and what are doing to it is environmentalism, which itself has been informed by modern ideas on ecology such as the Gaia theory. Developed in the 1970s by British scientist James Lovelock, it holds that our planet and all its lifeforms are a single, self-regulating entity. What notions such as the Anthropocene and Gaia reflect is the modern idea that the environment is not static but an active, ever-changing and human-affected process.

KNOWING THE WORLD

The understanding of the world is a matter of power, offering a linkage to chapter 7. This power was and is that of the major states over the remainder of the world, whether or not the latter were colonies.

Aerial photography began in the very early 1900s, soon after the first manned flights. It was only from the 1950s, however, that great advances were made, as the expertise developed during wartime was employed to map large areas, a method which was particularly valuable in inaccessible terrain. This was a key instance of the degree to which human presence in the air could bring change. It was also a reflection of the importance of implementation when discussing technological impact (see chapter 4). Last, but not least, it was an expression of political power (see chapter 7), with only the wealthiest and strongest states able to build the advanced flying machines and install the most sophisticated image-capturing devices in them.

Aircraft were not the only means by which we expanded our knowledge of the world.

RIGHT: *TIROS-1*, the first weather satellite, was launched on 1 April 1960.

Launched by NASA (the National Aeronautics and Space Administration) in 1960, *Tiros-1* (Television and Infra-Red Observation Satellite) was the first weather satellite. It was designed to provide systematic images of cloud cover and was an early instance of how the rapid change in environmental knowledge had been brought by technology (see chapter 4). From that moment on, orbiting satellites would be able to provide fresh images of the Earth and of the climate.

ABOVE: A *Landsat* image of the Amazon River.

In 1972, the Earth Resources Technology Satellite (later renamed *Landsat 1*) was launched by the US. Unlike *Tiros-1*, which used television cameras, *Landsat 1* was fitted with a telescope and a spinning mirror that scanned the Earth's surface to build up a digital image. The pictures it sent back to NASA were turned into maps created through a technique known as remote sensing, in which images are generated from electromagnetic radiations outside the normal visual range.

Using different wavelengths, it proved possible to focus on specific aspects of the planet's surface. Infrared, for example, was especially valuable for vegetation surveys and for detecting the water resources crucial to land use. By the 1980s, satellite information was offering key intelligence on a developing environmental crisis when it was used to supplement as well as correct information acquired by ground surveys regarding the faster than expected rate of forest clearance in the tropics. Satellite information was also used to map closed canopy rainforests for *The Conservation Atlas of Tropical Forests: Africa*, published by the International Union for Conservation of Nature (IUCN) in 1992. Particular attention has since focused on rainforests worldwide, especially in Amazonia and Indonesia. There, satellite imagery has shown a marked increase since 2019 in the incidence of fires set deliberately – and not always legally – to clear large areas of rainforest for soya cultivation and to raise cattle. As well as the large loss of environmentally friendly, carbon dioxide-absorbing trees, these fires also produce much environmentally harmful pollution.

Satellite mapping was also used to investigate the 'hole' in the ozone layer over Antarctica, a situation first reported in 1985. Ozone in the atmosphere offers protection from solar radiation, so any reduction of it – and the rate of reduction and where it is taking place – should be mapped. Without such mapping, the Anthropocene would be hypothesis only. The 'hole' itself is a product of groups of human-made halogenated hydrocarbons, ozone-

BELOW: Ozone hole recovery projection.

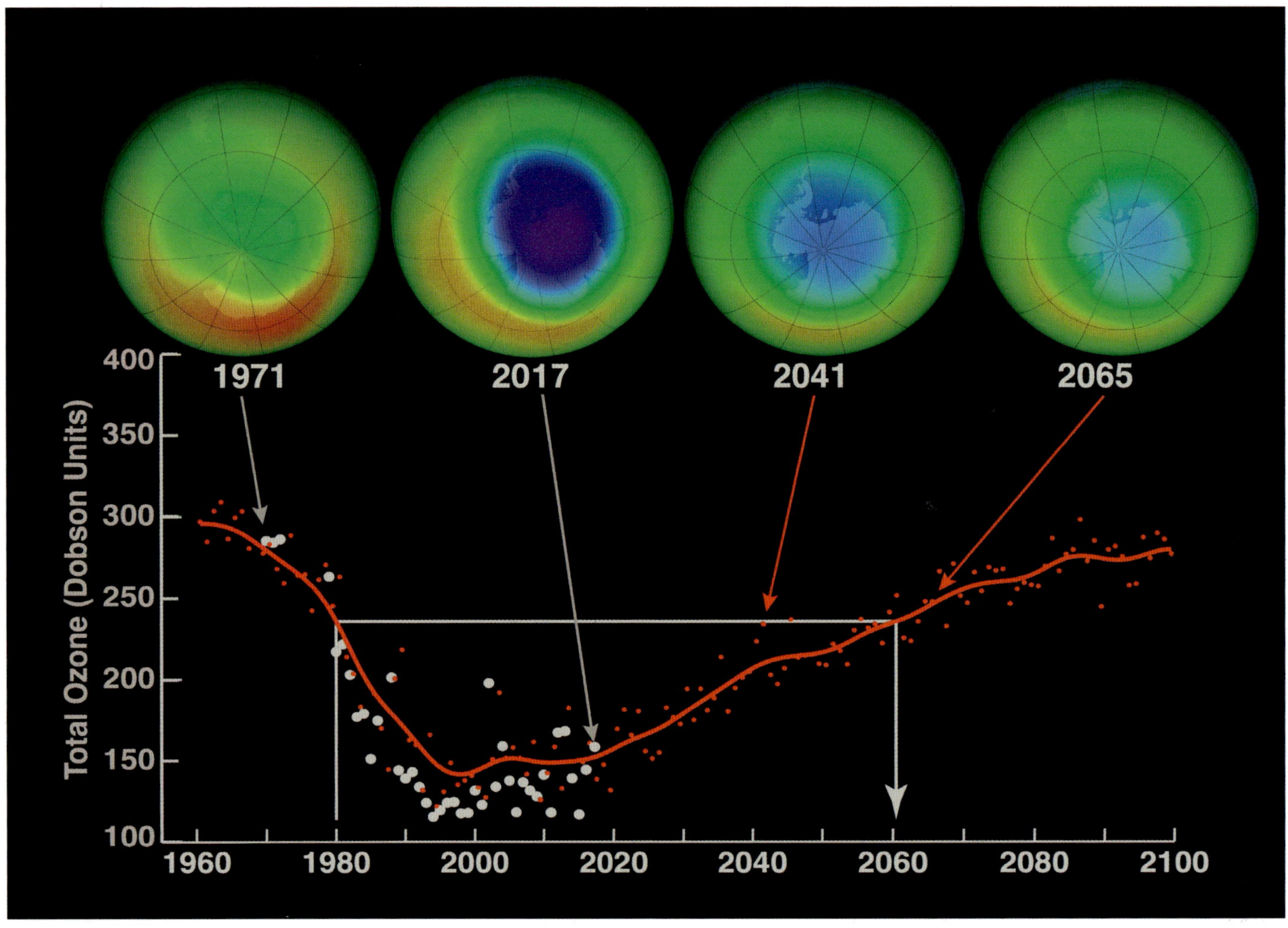

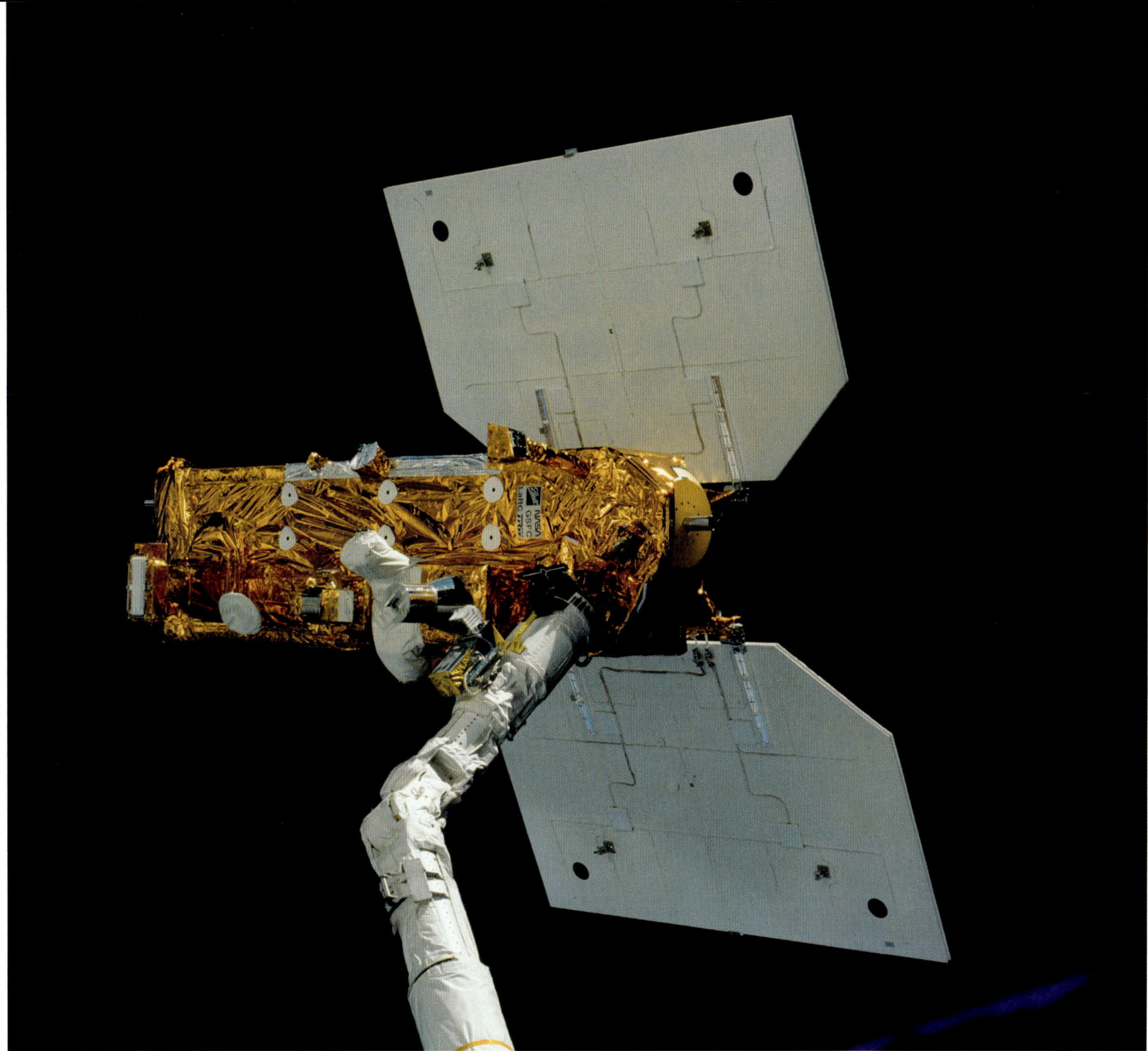

ABOVE: The Earth Radiation Budget Satellite was launched in 1984 to collect data on the climate and ozone depletion in the atmosphere.

depleting substances used for example in fridges and plastic foam manufacture. The discovery that Earth's protective shield of ozone was under threat led to the Montreal Protocol of 1987 (implemented in 1989), which initially saw 46 nations agree to phase out ozone-depleting substances (ODS). To date, 198 nations have ratified this agreement.

Looking to the future, satellite scrutiny of the world will become more detailed and insistent, with more states and companies operating satellites relevant to their needs and using the material accordingly. There is a political dimension. Surveillance, notably of and through the internet, will ensure that the human world is better understood and under scrutiny, and this will be matched by the very different surveillance of the natural world. As an instance of scrutiny, there has been a considerable increase in the deployment of facial recognition technology since the early 2000s, notably in China.

EL NIÑO EVENTS

Greater human understanding provides a sounder grasp of the interactions that affect climate and climate change. If the Pacific trade winds are weak an *El Niño* event occurs, with warm waters spreading east from the western Pacific, limiting the movement of cold deepwater northwards along the Pacific sea coast of South America and triggering broader changes in global weather.

HUMANS CONTROL THE OCEANS

The Anthropocene saw a determined drive to accumulate information on the world's oceans. This was information was not acquired merely for knowledge's own sake, but for practical purposes. Nowhere was this quest for information more visible than in the discovery of the growing environmental crisis, which was mapped out in ever greater detail.

Yet learning more about the world's oceans went beyond environmental concerns. Instead, as we will see in later chapters, it was part of the drive for military superiority, notably between the US and the Soviet Union in the Cold War that followed World War II and which lasted until 1989. The determination to know the oceans was linked in particular to submarine and anti-submarine capabilities, an important factor at a time when the Soviet Union was developing a major submarine force and both sides were deploying submarine-launched missiles with nuclear warheads.

In 1950, the Soviets published the *Morskoi Atlas* (*Marine Atlas*), which brought together all the new information on the oceans for the first time. Knowledge rapidly increased thereafter, and from a variety of sources, notably by surface ships using sonar, from submersibles, by

BELOW: A painting map of the ocean floor, based on the model created by Marie Tharp and Bruce Heezen in 1957.

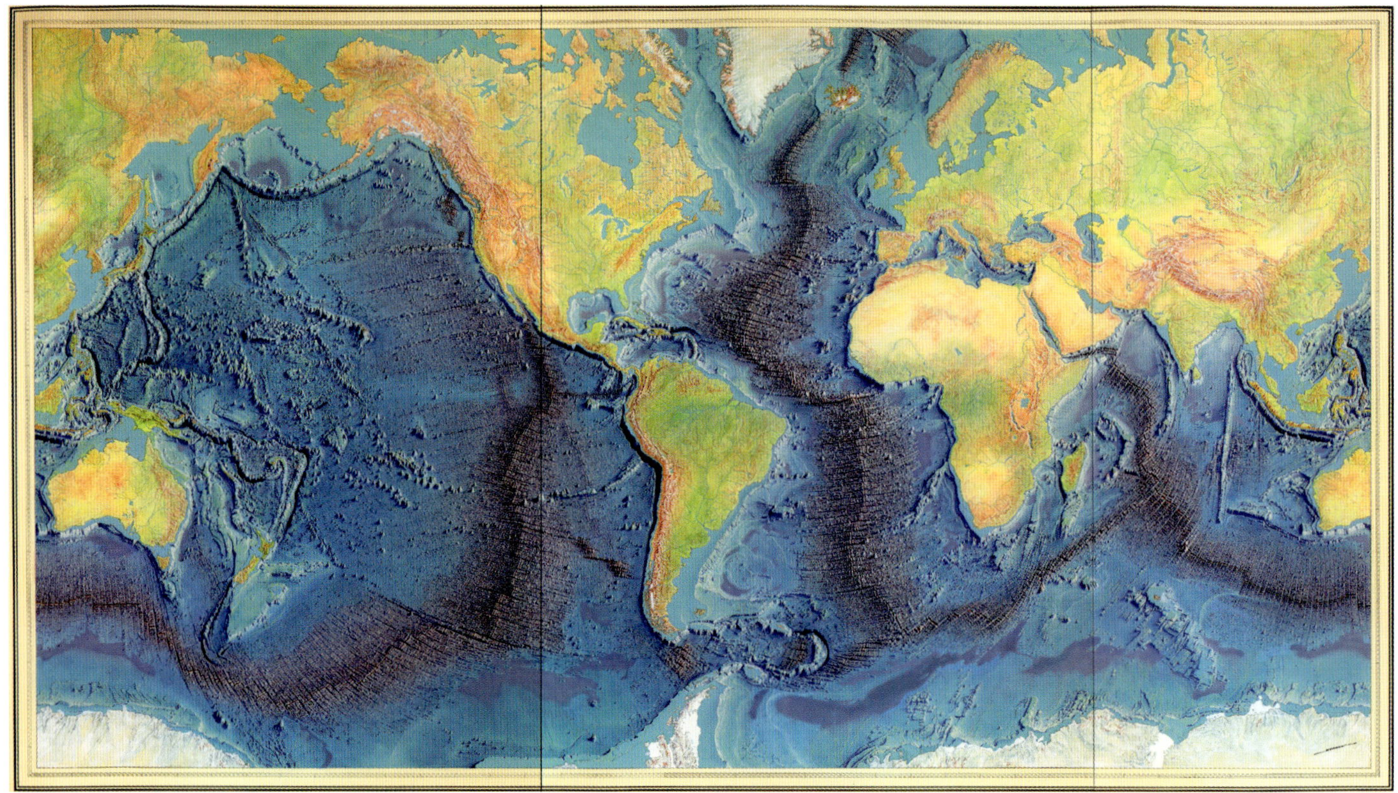

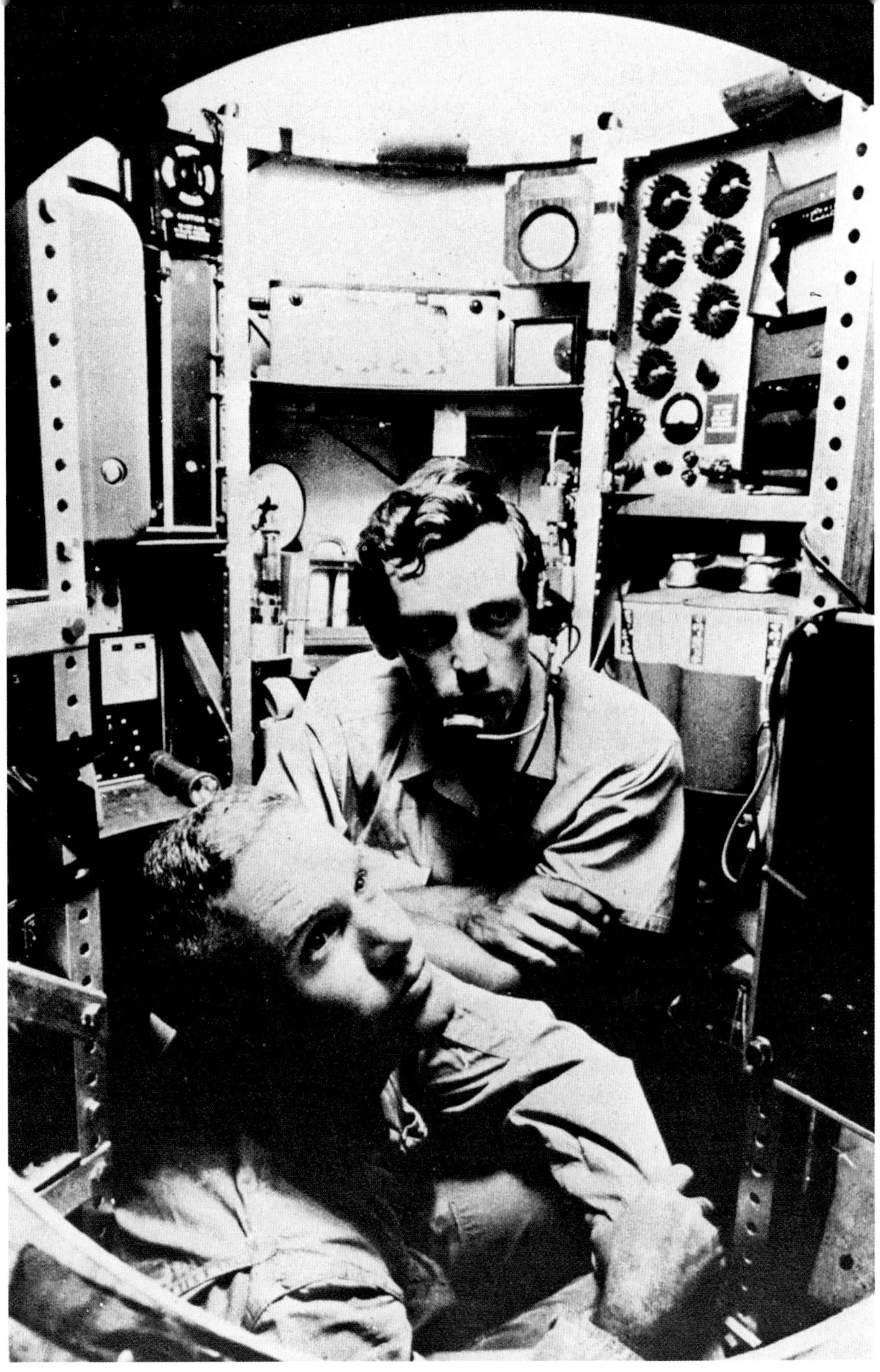

LEFT: Jacques Piccard and Don Walsh in the bathyscaphe *Trieste*.

boring into the ocean floor, and from aircraft and satellites. Ship- and airborne-towed magnetometers and deep ocean borehole core sequences gathered data about magnetic anomalies. Submersibles were built that were able to resist extreme undersea pressures and took explorers to the depths of the ocean; in 1960, Jacques Piccard in the bathyscaphe *Trieste* explored the Mariana Trench near the Philippines, the deepest feature in the oceans. Unmanned submersibles with remote-controlled equipment furthered underwater exploration and mapping, for example of 'hot spots' caused by vents on the ocean floor.

Thanks to such information, mapping the ocean floors became more ambitious. Radar images taken from aircraft and satellites were able to show how the contours and terrain of the ocean floor affect the surface of the water above. By the end of the century, thanks to *Seasat* imagery produced from 1978, a full map of the ocean floor was possible.

Such information gathering was linked to the growing interest in exploiting resources from the ocean bed. At first this was largely a matter of oil and gas from shallow waters, such as the Gulf of Mexico, but in time deeper waters were searched, for example the North Sea. Furthermore, interest in mining for minerals on and beneath the oceans developed, with, from the 1970s, metals on the ocean floors being mapped. China, Japan, South Korea, Belgium, Germany, France and Britain are among those involved in deep-sea mining projects in the Pacific. It is unclear how fast this will lead to large-scale extraction, but it is certainly in prospect.

More widely, a form of exploitation that became more prominent from the 2010s was factory fishing. In part, this reflected the existing over-exploitation of waters close to the borders of the major fishing powers, notably China, South Korea and Japan, leading them to fish further away. There was also the more specific issue of China's fishing fleet, which grew to more than 12,000 vessels, many of them fishing beyond the country's waters by 2018. This helped lead to industrial-scale overfishing that depleted stocks. Illegality

BELOW: The deepwater drilling vessel *Hidden Gem* has been equipped with tools to extract polymetallic nodules from the ocean floor.

ABOVE: Chinese fishing fleet, Zhoushan, 1 August 2024.

was part of the process. Boats took more fish than they were permitted, misreported the species caught, and used illegal drift nets. The environmental damage caused by this activity was immediate. Thus, in 2020, almost 300 Chinese vessels, including refuelling and fish processing ships, were stationed off the Galápagos, dropping plastic waste overboard and contributing to a 'city at sea' of debris off the coast of Peru that was last seen heading towards Easter Island. In 2021, a Chinese fishing fleet of about 200 boats off the Spratley Islands in the South China Sea produced human waste that caused an increase in bacteria and serious problems for coral in a major instance of environmental degradation.

Factory fishing is a form of modern imperialism, in particular hitting local fishing communities that use traditional means and/or have less access to the economies of scale. Thus, in Africa, the fishermen of Somalia and Namibia find their traditional fishing grounds denuded by factory fishing by distant states. Although not usually described as

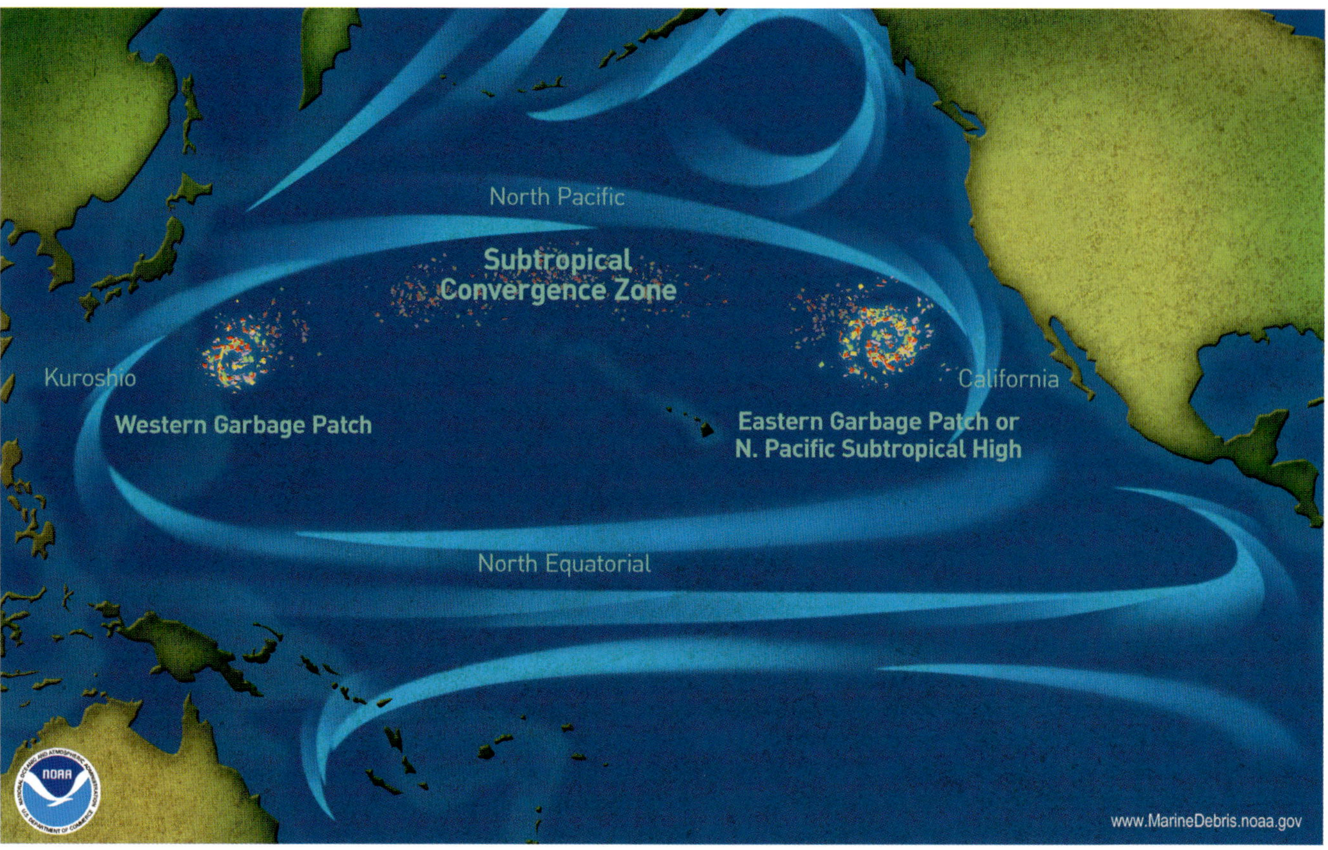

ABOVE: The Great Pacific Garbage Patch.

such, this in practice is a new version of the extractive imperialism of the 19th century (see chapter 7).

Another form of damage from fishing comes from nets that are lost or cast adrift, leading to the death of marine creatures, for example the dugong and turtle in the Torres Strait between Australia and New Guinea. In the Atlantic, the growing presence of plastic particles in the deep ocean is but one instance of the increasing extent to which what was once thought to be the mighty ocean is affected by human detritus. In 2020, scientists at the British National Oceanography Centre collected samples at ten Atlantic locations from Britain to the Falkland Islands. In a disturbing instance of human impact, the average cubic metre of seawater was found to contain about 1,000 particles of polyethylene, polypropylene and polystyrene litter. This study indicated that the Atlantic contained more than ten times as much plastic entering the ocean as the 8 million tonnes per annum estimated in a 2014 study; and with about 200 million tonnes of plastic in the Atlantic as a whole. There are no comparable figures for 1950, so it cannot be measured as a major development in our period, but it is a significant change. This crisis is particularly present in the North Atlantic Garbage Patch that was first documented in 1972 and which is now hundreds of kilometres across. When measured in 2020, the Eastern Garbage Patch between California and Hawaii contained nearly 90,000 tonnes of rubbish covering an area more than twice the size of Texas. The prolonged, sub-lethal exposure to plastics in the oceans hits ecosystems hard, with marine life much affected. Thus, the Great Pacific Garbage Patch greatly damages juvenile sea turtles who ingest its debris. More generally, carbon dioxide absorbed by the oceans makes them more acidic. This causes coral skeletons to corrode, which affects the fish that spawn on deep-ocean reefs.

CLIMATE WARMING

Geography is history, and history geography. Traditionally, the two were separated in much British analysis, but were regarded as inseparable by thinkers from other countries, notably France and Germany, for example the French scholar Fernand Braudel (1902–85), the leading historian of the last century and a key figure in intellectual culture.

In the British case, in contrast, geography was generally treated by historians as a long-term constant, and history as the product and record of human actions. Climate change has altered this equation, which in any case was always deeply flawed.

The history of climate warming is that of human action interacting with natural phenomena, and both require discussion. Concerns in the 1970s about climate cooling and the fear of a coming Little Ice Age proved short-lived. Instead, the focus soon – and correctly – moved to warming. Climate change led to a growing awareness of, and concern about, pollution, notably CO2 (carbon dioxide) emissions, accompanied by the widespread pressure to change energy consumption to produce cuts in emissions.

Climate accords, notably those of Kyoto (1997) and Paris (2015), sought to change the situation and to give force to the United Nations Framework Convention on Climate Change signed by 154 states at the Earth Summit held in Rio de Janeiro in 1992 and

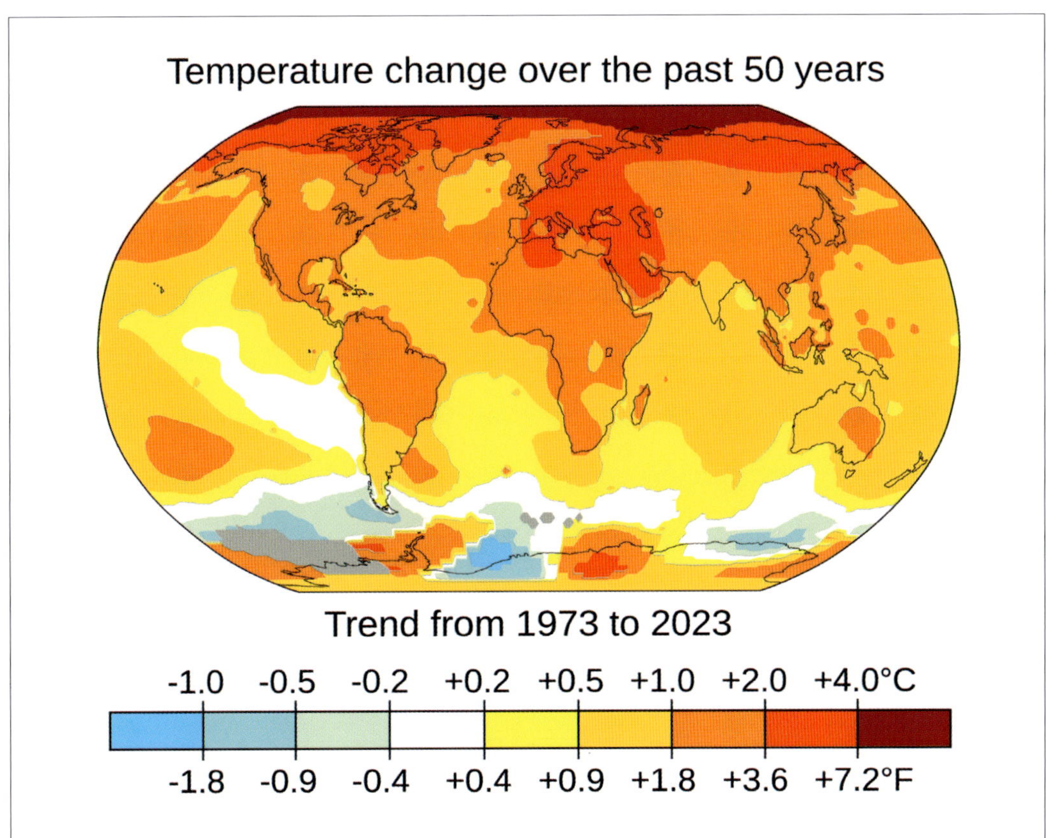

LEFT: Change in average global surface temperature, 1973–2003.

ABOVE: The UNFCC meeting at Kyoto in 1997.

implemented in 1994. It had agreed to the stabilization of greenhouse gas concentrations at a level preventing dangerous interference with the climate. In turn, there were attempts to establish guidelines. The Kyoto Protocol, which finally entered into force in 2005, was based on the principle that developed economies bore prime responsibility for tackling emissions. A decade later, the 2015 United Nations Climate Change Conference adopted the Paris Agreement, which sought to restrict the rise in global surface temperature to well below 2°C (3.6°F) above pre-industrial levels, and, to that end, to cut emissions. The agreement entered into force in 2016.

The variation between carbon emissions in different parts of the world was a major factor in negotiations, with strong demands for the early-industrializers in the West and the fastest-growing industrializers elsewhere (particularly China) to bear most of the burden. This is based on them producing proportionately more emissions. In 2023, for example, the US produced about six times the carbon dioxide of sub-Saharan Africa, which has a larger population. The US and China at that time produced about 40 per cent of the world's carbon emissions. However, the growing difficulties the two powers experienced in their political relationship made meaningful attempts to respond to global change less likely, while also making any response they did offer into an aspect of the competition in 'soft power' between the two nations.

At the same time, there was a degree of confusion created by the overlapping of climate science, climate communication, climate policy and climate activism. Arguably, too much of the warming, some of which may be due to natural temperature variability, was uncritically attributed to Anthropocene-era warming via greenhouse gases – warming, that is, due to human action. Indeed, climate change became almost a shorthand for environmental pressures as a whole. Yet, as measured in and through climate change, history has certainly speeded up in recent decades and that puts an emphasis on human action. Recently, the post-Ice Age raising of sea levels has rapidly accelerated, largely stemming from the essentially human generated build-up of greenhouse gases raising global temperatures and its impact on the ice caps. As a result, natural history becomes an immediate aspect of human history, possibly its most significant factor. It is a formulation that registers how this book is different from any others that would have been written in 1950, or even 2000.

This is particularly seen at the Poles where, each year, as a natural process, there is a melting of the ice caps during the summer and a freezing during the winter. But in the Arctic, however, there has been a net loss of ice every year since 1997, due to the warmer summers and winters. As a result, the 'equilibrium line', where winter snow freeze and summer melt balance each other, is moving towards the North Pole. The amount of ice lost varies each year due to temperature changes: in 2017, a warm year, 109 billion tonnes of ice were lost in Greenland; in 2018, when the Arctic was very cold, only 19 billion tonnes were lost from Greenland; but in 2019, a much warmer year, Greenland suffered a record loss of ice: 532 billion tonnes, with 12.5 billion tonnes lost on 1 August alone. In 2020, there was less ice in the Arctic (3.6 million square km/1.4 million square miles) than at any point besides the summer of 2012, when it had been 3.34 million square km (1.3 million square miles). This is

BELOW: Ice caps melting in the Arctic.

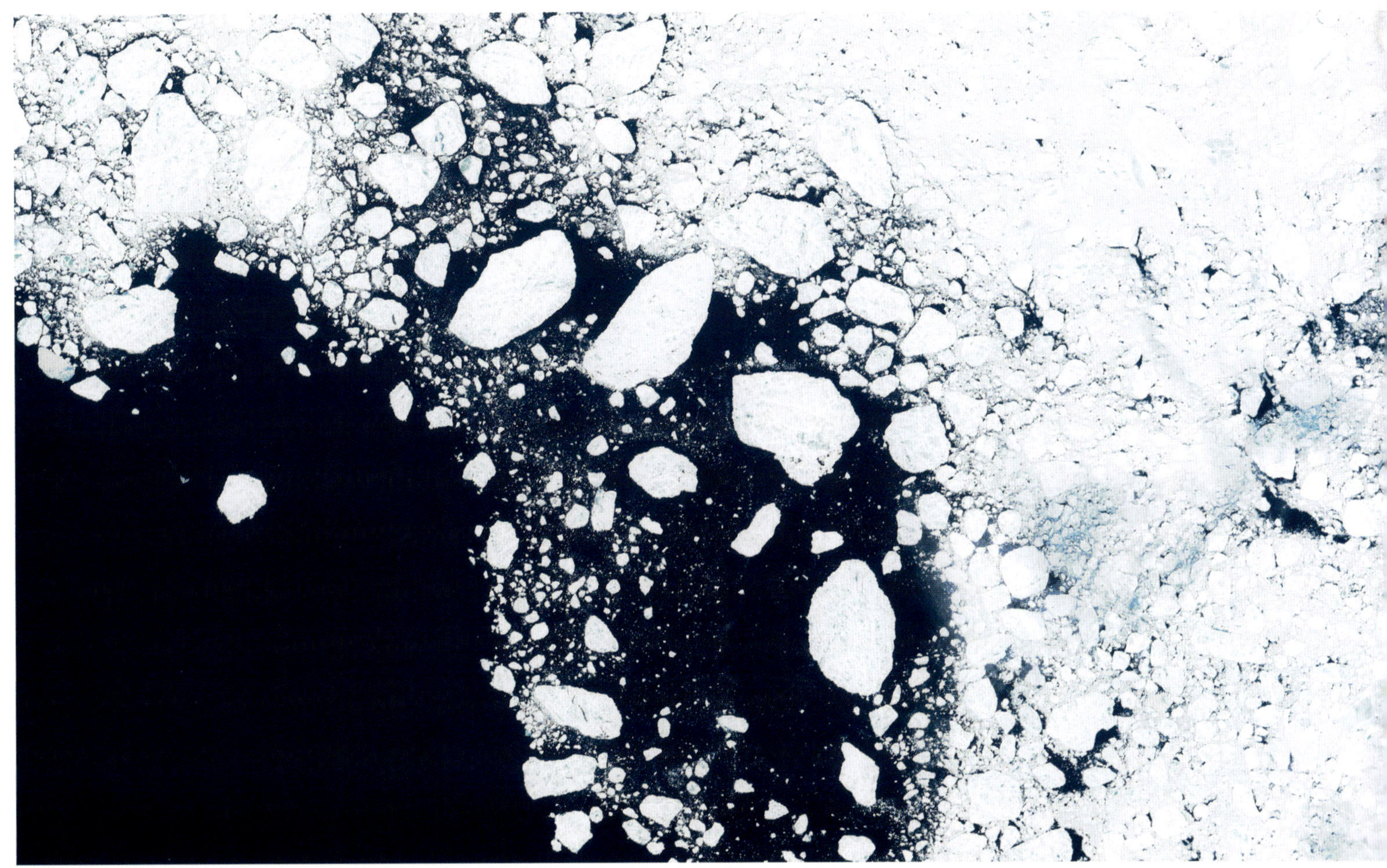

ABOVE: Palau has suffered greatly from climate change.

CLIMATE CHANGE HITS HARD

'Palau has lost at least one third of its coral reefs due to climate change related weather patterns. We also lost most of our agricultural production due to drought and extreme high tides. These are not theoretical scientific losses.... For island states, time is not running out. It has run out. And our path may very well be the window to your own future and the future of our planet.'

Tommy Remengesau, president of the Western Pacific archipelago state of Palau, 2001–9, 2013–21, interviewed in 2008.

a clear trend. In addition, in 2011, a large hole in the ozone layer in the atmosphere opened over the Arctic for the first time, probably a response to the release of chlorine-rich chemicals into the atmosphere.

Greenland is highly significant to the Atlantic as its ice sheet is more than 1.6 km (1 mile) thick and holds eight per cent of the world's fresh water, enough to raise sea levels by 6 m (19ft 7in). Crevasses and ice quakes on Greenland indicate that the ice sheet is not only melting but also moving towards the sea, with the meltwater helping to lubricate the ice sheet's bedrock and thus making such movement easier. This melting has led to projections of a rise in the Atlantic's water level, and to the realization that cities directly on the ocean, such as Dakar, New York and Rio de Janeiro, or, indirectly, because they are on estuaries or close to the ocean, such as London, will need to confront a much more difficult future. The Thames Barrier downstream of London, opened in 1984 and designed to prevent flood surges, has been used much more frequently than was ever intended.

Oceans absorb most of the world's excess heat and much of its carbon dioxide. Climate warming makes it more difficult for cold and warm layers of water to mix and, therefore, the supply of oxygen and nutrients is greatly diminished. More acidic waters are a problem for marine life, for example coral. More extreme climatic variations within this deteriorating pattern, whatever their specific cause, have become more frequent. Acute heat in Pacific North America in 2021 was linked to the death of hundreds of millions of marine creatures.

The rising seas due to climate warming threaten low-lying islands, such as the Maldives in the Indian Ocean and the Marshall Islands, Tuvalu and Kiribati in the Pacific. For their inhabitants, climate change is the major concern of recent history. Their governments press particularly hard on the issue. Already, as on Kiribati from 2008, rising seawater levels has affected fresh water sources.

The warming also causes greater evaporation on land and at sea, which reduces water availability (and therefore agriculture and hydroelectric power) and affects the climate. More generally, at present, the trend is clearly towards more stormy winters and higher summer temperatures, notably in Asia (as well as higher winter temperatures, as in South America in 2024), with more violent wind and rain conditions episodically across the year. Each of these factors creates issues for the sustainability of particular communities and practices. Thus, in 2024, Vietnam's coffee crop was hit by drought, while Indonesia faced a surge in dengue fever, which has also been a problem lately in Japan and France.

In the US, the climate has played a major role in dystopian events in recent years. This is particularly the case in terms of drought and fire. Both have been especially prominent in the most environmentally marginal area, the Southwest. In particular, rainfall was repeatedly poor from 2000, ensuring that groundwater levels fell, as did those in major reservoirs such as Lake Mead in Nevada and Arizona. Material on the bottom of reservoirs was revealed. Across the US, average snowpack continued its long term decline, river temperatures have risen, quarrels between states over water rights became more harsh, notably over water from the Colorado River, and wildfires became more common, especially in California and Colorado, which were hit by record numbers of them in 2020. Between 1895 and 2018, Santa Clara County, California, saw its temperature rise by 2°C (3.6°F), twice the

BELOW: Wildfires near Los Angeles in 2020. Extreme weather events have become more common in recent years, including the fires in Los Angeles in 2025.

global average. Meanwhile, between 2011 and 2019, drought in California killed nearly 150 million trees, and in 2020 the temperature in the appropriately named Death Valley rose to 54.4°C (130°F). There are fears that the southeastern part of the Midwest will become too dry to plant cereal grains in the near future. In the period 1900 to 2016, two-thirds of the counties in Minnesota saw the average midwinter temperatures rise by over 2°C. Nearly half of Americans were in areas subject to extreme heat alerts in July 2021. In 2023, based on paleoclimatology – tree-ring chronologies – the northern hemisphere had the hottest summer in 2,000 years.

Looking ahead, it is likely that climate change will continue, and that its impact will be felt more strongly as benchmark temperatures are breached. The responses are likely to include greater pressure on water and energy resources, as well as increased migration from countries where human life is becoming less bearable, such as those of the Sahel, the region to the south of the Sahara Desert. The relationship between human-caused climate change and that from other factors will remain contentious, but, at least in the short term, the former is likely to be to the fore.

The consequences of climate change will be acute – even if there is no further increase in global warming. This is because the changes that have already been made are 'locked

BELOW: A farming village in Chad. Farming will become more difficult and living conditions worse in the Sahel as climate change accelerates.

CLIMATE CHANGE AND ECONOMIC IMPACT

In May 2024, the temperature in Delhi reached 52.9°C (126°F), a marked increase on previous records. This hit people, with hospitals affected by cases of heatstroke, work rates reduced, notably in construction, and electricity supplies in crisis as the grid was overwhelmed. Looking to the future, this, plus signs of a growing weakness in the monsoon which is crucial to Indian agriculture, will have a seriously detrimental impact on the Indian economy, thus underlining the relationship between climate change and economic performance.

ABOVE: A boy pours water over himself during the Delhi heatwave when temperatures reached 52.9°C (126°F) on 29 May 2024.

in' and of great consequence. In any case, a steady state situation is extremely unlikely. Whatever the natural factors at play, the human ones are continuing and unlikely to alter greatly in their impact, even if the rate of impact changes.

As a result, there will be climate emergencies. These are likely to take three forms: an increase in storms and other severe climate episodes; excessively high peak temperatures; and periods of higher temperature. The timing of these is obviously uncertain, as will be the frequency and combination of crises. Nevertheless, climate change will become more serious, and more chronic as a symptom of poor health, social pain and anxiety. As climate and weather differ greatly over the world, it is also probable that the experience of and response to both will vary considerably. This will produce a new instance of the major contrasts of the mid-century world. As a human response, it is unclear how far it will be possible to apply solar geoengineering techniques, where sunlight and solar radiation are reflected out into space. More mundanely, it is likely that there will be many attempts to plant large quantities of trees.

HUMANS AND OTHER SPECIES

Across the continuum of human history, animals have been seen as a threat, as prey and as a tool. Little sentiment has traditionally been involved in any of these conceptions. Animals were cared for only in so far as it allowed them to fulfil their assigned roles, or were hunted or farmed in increasingly efficient ways. This was the case in 1950 and was a situation that went back to the end of the Ice Age, after which megafauna such as mammoths were hunted to extinction.

This attitude towards animals has changed over the last century, notably so in the West where it is in part linked to the movement of people off the land and away from agriculture. Animal charities have boomed, pets are more common and environmentalism is often focused on the fate of animals. Yet, while the basic historical narrative is one of increased concern, it is subject to human geography. There is far less concern about animals in Asia and Africa than in Western Europe and North America.

The lack of interest by the majority of the world's population in other species fits alongside the major change of the period: the marked decline of animal and plant

BELOW: Cod is unloaded at Reykjavik harbour with two Icelandic gunboats in the background, 1972. The 'Cod Wars' between Britain and Iceland lasted from 1958 to 1976.

ABOVE: Tristan da Cunha marine protection zone.

biodiversity. Linked closely to other changes, including global warming and deforestation, is the human impact on other species, a topic that has engaged greater public concern over the last half-century than ever before. First used in 1916, the term 'biological diversity' was later popularized by Raymond Dasmann and Thomas Lovejoy in books of 1968 and 1980 respectively. By 1988, the word 'biodiversity' entered common usage. This concern is the case both on land and at sea, and research has clarified the extent to which many animals are under threat or have been affected. Repeated surveys have suggested significant reductions in the number of species, with, following the 1992 UN Earth Summit in Rio de Janeiro, the 1993 UN Convention on Biological Diversity a focus for governmental action.

Fishing has been a key area of concern, not least because human activity within it can be quantified. Overfishing has hit major catches, such as the anchoveta (a species of anchovy) in the 1970s and the chub mackerel in the 1980s, both in the Pacific. In the Atlantic, rivalry over cod fishing led to the 'Cod Wars' between Britain and Iceland from 1958 to 1976. This caused a major fall in cod availability and led consumers to turn to other fish, notably squid, which saw a massive expansion in catch numbers from the 1980s. This affected seals and whales, whose diet includes squid.

Climate change is an issue for most species. The seas are warming at an accelerating rate, and the longer, more frequent and hotter marine heatwaves this causes means that Pacific sea turtles have to swim further north to catch prey, using extra energy that, in turn, leads them to lay fewer eggs on beaches, contributing to the decline of some other species such as those that feed on them. Also in the Pacific, grey whales, walruses and eider ducks moved into the

RIGHT: DDT spraying in Oregon, 1974.

northern Bering Sea as it warmed up, while the snow crab population in the Bering Sea fell from around 8 billion in 2018 to 1 billion in 2021.

Where to put the emphasis? Take the white whale. It has been dying out in the eastern North Atlantic, while numbers in the western North Atlantic have been hit by entanglement in fishing gear and ship strikes. But in the South Atlantic, numbers have risen in recent years, helped by the designation of marine wildlife sanctuaries around British overseas territories such as Tristan da Cunha, where fishing is banned.

On land, the human impact on other species is increasingly to the fore, but in very different ways. For example, wildlife can flourish under solar panels, not least because pesticides are generally not used there. The goldfish and tadpoles humans put in garden ponds become targets for herons, seagulls and other birds. Human rubbish is attractive to a range of animals and has led to them altering their lifestyles. Fast-food debris is particularly appealing to foxes and seagulls, both of which have moved into areas of human habitation, as have bears, for example in the US and Japan. Rats, a long-standing problem in urban areas, became more so, for example in New York. In Paris, the rat population in 2023 was estimated at 6.5 million – which is around three rats for every human resident.

In contrast, animals are also affected by development pressures, with wetlands drained, agriculture more intensive, and land covered by housing. The chemical warfare used in agriculture poses major problems. The use of DDT, notably against mosquitoes, affected fish and other species. For example, the use of DDT in Soviet cotton cultivation affected the fish in the Caspian Sea and then their predators, notably seals and humans. DDT has been linked to serious neurological damage that was found emerging often decades later. This is a classic instance of the convergence of environmental risks with health concerns. Although DDT was banned in 1972 in the US, it was only outlawed globally in 2004.

As another instance of land use pressure, deforestation affects animal habitats. Thus, illegal logging in Indonesia's national parks by commercial firms seeking hardwood for export has impacted greatly on the orangutan, Asia's only great ape, whose numbers halved in the 1990s. Woodland, farmland and migrant perching birds prefer areas where there is lower population density.

BELOW: The orangutan population was decimated in the 1990s as deforestation accelerated.

Alongside climate change, the spread of species also created issues. This could be unwanted and at every scale, including bacteria in water systems, as happened in Detroit in 2022. Asian hornets, first officially seen in Britain in 2016 and already established in France, swiftly became a predator of Britain's already declining honeybees. *Tapinoma magnum*, a species of highly aggressive ant from North Africa, has spread northwards in Europe from 1999, and the sheer size of their colonies has seen off human efforts to counter them, with serious damage caused to cables, power distribution boxes and road services.

In addition, the deliberate introduction of species can cause problems. The introduction of the predatory Nile perch in Lake Victoria in the 1960s led to the extinction there of many species of cichlid fish.

In many countries, notably in Western Europe, hunting became less acceptable in our period, with animals given protected status. This caused controversy in the early 2020s over the threat to farm animals from reintroduced wolves in Continental Europe. There were other hazards. In Italy, in 2024, the challenge to domestic pigs came from disease spread from wild boar, the numbers of which have been growing considerably. Similarly, there was evidence in 2024 that the Avian influenza (H5M1 'bird flu') that led to the culling of tens of millions of European poultry in 2022, and to the large-scale deaths of wild birds, had crossed into cattle in the US. This represented a threat to other mammals, notably humans: about half of those who contract the flu die. As a result of this spread, unpasteurized milk became dangerous.

BELOW: *Tapinoma magnum*, a species of ant from North Africa that has spread through Europe, causing significant disruption.

ABOVE: A poultry farm in West Bengal, India, 2023. Avian flu represents a significant risk to other animals – and to humans, too.

Moves against hunting can lead to an uncontrolled growth of the animal population, notably as carnivorous predators other than humans become less common. In the US, where hunting by humans has continued but other predators are absent or few, this led to a significant increase in the number of deer which, it has been suggested, are now as plentiful as they were in the 17th century, when European settlement began.

Looking into the near future, the human interaction with other species will in part be culturally specific and in part a matter of a more consistent rivalry. Examples of cultural specificity include the very different attitudes towards pets (dogs and cats are frequent in Western societies, but not those of Islam), as well as conventions on eating meat which affect particular attitudes to cattle (not eaten by Hindus) and pigs (not eaten by Jews and Muslims). Separately, it is likely for ethical and environmental reasons that hostility to meat-eating will increase in the West; but not elsewhere, or, at least, not to the same extent.

As far as rivalry is concerned, the traditional competition over food sources, for example wolves attacking sheep, and rats and mice raiding grain stores, will be matched by a much greater sensitivity to the vectors of disease. These will owe much to climate warming and the resulting spread of disease, although air travel is more central for human vectors. Insects will be the particular subject of concern, although other animals can also be involved, notably birds. As the debates over a series of pandemics from AIDS to Covid-19 showed, the practice of diseases bridging between humans and animals will become a matter of acute worry at the time of pandemics, with HIV, the virus that causes AIDS, jumping from chimpanzees to humans, and bats possibly playing a similar role in the case of Covid.

OVERCOMING NATURE

The attempt to manage nature is as old as human history. Adaptation was a key theme, but overcoming nature was to the fore from the extensive clearing of forests in the first millennium BCE to facilitate agriculture. There was no abrupt break in the mid-20th century, but, instead, an accentuation of existing themes. In part, this reflected more activist governments and interventionist ideologies and societies, notably Soviet and Chinese Communism and American Progressivism. In part, the resources, finance and borrowing capacity created by the 'Long Boom', the sustained economic growth from 1945 to 1973, provided resources that could be used to try to manage nature, with this management seen as a way to secure further growth. The context was one of international competition and concerns about domestic stability. Key elements included building infrastructure in areas it was difficult to do so, creating technologies to overcome the constraints of climate, and, as a linked feature, reshaping the landscape for agriculture. Thus, the Soviet Union sought to cultivate the Steppe.

The wish to meet the demands created by population growth, to raise living standards and to support national strength have all led to a determination to overcome nature. This was seen with Brazil under Jair Bolsonaro, president from 2019 until 2022. He backed *Ferrogrão*, a 1,000 km (621 mile) railway into Amazonia, as part of his controversial plan to develop the rainforest region, including making it less expensive to move soybeans and other grains for use and export to the Atlantic coast. As with his other policies, Bolsonaro's plan had scant concern for the environment or indigenous people, but reflected his strong links to agribusiness. So also in Southeast Asia with the clearing of forests for palm oil production. Conversely, the focus in Western agriculture on more productive farms has led to an increase in forest cover in Europe and North America, as small farms have been abandoned, for example in New England.

Communications links saw the repeated determination to overcome nature, often dramatically so, with waterways to be bridged, as with the Kerch Strait in Crimea (2016–19), or tunnelled under, as with the English Channel (1988–94) and the Bosporus (2011–16). A bridge-tunnel route was opened between Copenhagen in Denmark and Malmo in Sweden in 2000.

In part, terrain imposed distorting and/or insuperable costs, and many of the successes of bold plans in the period 1950–2020 were a consequence of economic growth, oil revenues or readily available cheap credit frequently provided by governments or guaranteed by them. Cheap credit became far less easy to obtain in the early 2020s, so the fiscal background for particularly optimistic building projects, such as a bridge across the Strait of Messina from the Italian mainland to Sicily, declined. So also with political instability. Plans for an ambitious transcontinental railway stretching 4,000 km (2,485

RAIL ON THE ROOF OF THE WORLD

In 2006, the Chinese railway system reached Lhasa in Tibet, a formidable achievement across very difficult terrain. At 5,068 m (16,627 ft), Tanggula in Tibet is the world's highest station. Much of the line is laid on permafrost and it also includes long tunnels and 675 bridges. The train carriages that run on the line have enriched-oxygen and UV-protection systems, and it is frequently mentioned on television as a great Chinese achievement.

By the end of 2021, there were 150,000 km (93,206 miles) of railway in China. In 2022, a line 825 km (513 miles) long between Hotan and Ruoqiang was put into operation, which represented the final circling of the Taklimakan, China's largest desert, the shifting sands and sandstorms of which posed construction, maintenance and operational challenges. To try to reduce this, reed fences were installed as short-term windbreaks and sand-stabilizing grids, as a preparation for the growth of the nearly 13 million trees that have been planted. Viaducts were built to allow sandstorms to pass beneath the tracks. Accounts of such lines were part of the heroic vision of rail beloved of the government. The overcoming of nature in this form is very much part of the Chinese public narrative. Such lines were also important in providing a capability to move troops, as in 2022, when China deployed forces against India using the new Tibetan rail system.

ABOVE: Tanggula station, Tibet – the highest railway station in the world.

miles) across Africa from Senegal to Sudan have long been on hold due to instability in the Sahel.

There were also the problems posed by physical geography. The issues of frost-thaw, and the resulting shifting of the soil, makes it difficult to build in sub-Arctic areas and affects rail lines across Siberia. Desertification is another problem, as in northern China. So also with the general impact of climate change in making areas either uninhabitable for expanding populations, or uninhabitable for lifestyles now judged appropriate. Thus, in East Asia and Southeast Asia, really high temperatures in May 2024, of up to 48.2°C (118.8°F), put great pressure on the power supply as a result of increased use of air conditioning, for example in the Philippines. More generally, air conditioning has become very necessary to life in the tropics and even in temperate areas. It is fundamental

BELOW: The bridge over the Kerch Strait in Crimea.

to rapidly expanding cities such as Phoenix and Houston in the US. Air conditioning is part of a built environment in which windows do not open, natural ventilation is ignored and energy needs are high, including for lifts. All are characteristic of modern building techniques across the world, especially for office buildings. That buildings often had a planned life of only about 20 years was also a huge problem. Building itself, and especially with cement, is also increasing carbon dioxide levels.

ABOVE: Peasants working on a farm during the Great Leap Forward in China, *c.*1958.

Looking ahead, the idea of conquering nature will be present in some contexts, for example political and cultural, and with reference to specific challenges. Authoritarian systems are more likely to talk of overcoming nature, as was done by Mao Zedong in China. Rejecting the traditional Chinese notion of 'Harmony between the Heavens and Humankind', instead declaring that 'Man Must Conquer Nature', Mao expressed both the Marxist idea that progress entails nature serving humanity, as well as a messianic and brutal authoritarianism. In 1958, when he launched his 'Great Leap Forward', Mao declared, 'Make the high mountain bow its head, make the river yield the way'.

In practice, such talk has proved most acceptable when it is a question of fighting pandemics and supporting living standards, and least so in wealthy countries and when major animal species and habitats are involved; and this contrast is unlikely to change. The 'Great Leap Forward', with its focus on enforced industrialization, helped cause a famine in which millions died.

ENERGY USE

Car culture for long meant the use of the oil derivative gasoline, and the politics of oil availability was of great consequence as a result. It was driven by demand. For example, in the US, annual per capita oil consumption rose from four barrels in 1920 to 26 in 1970, and that at a time of rapidly rising population.

The US, the world's leading consumer and strongest power, had moved from being a leading oil exporter to an importer in mid-century. This dependency reached 47 per cent in 1989 and peaked at 60 per cent of consumption in 2006. This was more than matched in Japan and Western Europe, and helped lead to acute sensitivity about political developments in oil-producing countries, notably when an Arab oil embargo in 1973 quadrupled the price of oil. US protectionism, banning crude-oil exports in 1975 in order to ensure supplies and restrain prices in America, made the situation more difficult elsewhere, notably in Europe, encouraging a reliance there on Middle Eastern and Soviet exports. There was another major hike in oil prices in 1979, due to the Iranian Revolution.

OPEC

Founded in 1960, the Organization of the Petroleum Exporting Countries drew together the major Middle Eastern oil producers, as well as Indonesia, Nigeria and Venezuela. OPEC pursued a foreign policy of its own in 1973, when it banned all oil exports to the US, the UK, the Netherlands and several other countries in protest at their support for Israel.

Thanks to its concern about the Middle East, which in 2003 held about two-thirds of the world's oil reserves, the US made a number of interventions in the region. In 1953, it supported a royalist coup in Iran, and soon after was rewarded by a foreign consortium being given effective control over the country's oil. Later involvements by the US included settling Israeli–Egyptian differences with the Camp David Accords of 1978, sending warships into the Persian Gulf to protect oil shipments during the Iran–Iraq War of 1980–8, sending troops to the protection of Saudi Arabia in 1990, and driving the Iraqis from Kuwait in 1991.

Despite the significantly rising fuel efficiency of cars, the world use of oil continued to rise, not only in the late 20th century but also in the early 21st, in part driven by increasing demand in China and India.

There was related talk of the decline, indeed redundancy, of coal in the later part of our period, due to the ascendancy of oil and thanks to the possibilities created by civil nuclear power, and also as a result of environmental concerns. In so far as this account was challenged in the early 21st century, it was from the perspective of the potential of renewables, notably wind and solar power.

Somewhat differently, fracking from oil shale became a major source of energy in the 2010s, notably in the US. The generation of civil nuclear power remained relatively limited, and in some countries, especially Germany, there was a move away from nuclear energy. Yet, from 2022, the Russian invasion of Ukraine, and the resulting international crisis, led to a major increase in worries about energy availability, security and costs, with Europe, notably Germany, rapidly seeking to reduce its dependence on Russian natural gas.

Issues about energy provision, for example from nuclear power, wind farms and fracking, all of which faced opposition, underlie the divisiveness of politics, notably between local and national, and between environmental sensitivity and energy needs. The

BELOW: The Iranian coup of 1953 saw the overthrow of Prime Minister Mohammad Mossadegh and the strengthening instead of the American- and British-backed Shah Mohammad Reza Pahlavi. He promptly granted the country's oil rights to a foreign consortium.

ABOVE: Fracking in the USA.

difficulties of facing up to realities in the shape of energy needs in a democracy, and of confronting the political, social and fiscal consequences, have become more apparent.

In many countries, there are issues with the cost of energy, which became a rising topic of concern in the early 1970s and, again, the early 2020s, but its very availability is also frequently an issue, with power cuts often a key problem, for example in the 2010s and 2020s in Albania, Antigua, Bangladesh, India, Pakistan, Papua New Guinea, Sri Lanka and the US. This problem is likely to become more serious as population pressure rises, and as energy usage increases.

Energy prices also affect food production as energy is necessary to make nitrogen fertilizers as well as to transport food. In these and other respects, the availability of energy is important, but so also is its cost. The partial decoupling of the world economy in the 2020s because of geopolitical rivalry between America and China complicated the problem.

At the same time, serious environmental issues emerge from energy production. Thus, an explosion in 1986 in the Chernobyl nuclear power station in the Soviet Union led to serious air-spread radioactive contamination. As a result, excessive levels of caesium entered the human food chain. A tsunami caused a catastrophe at the Fukushima nuclear plant in Japan in 2011, leading to the melting down of three reactors. Used to cool the aftermath,

170 tonnes of water were contaminated daily, and the disposal of that contaminated water into the Pacific, once treated, caused controversy – not least as the water still contains traces of the radioactive isotope tritium. So also with oil leaks into the oceans, notably from offshore and coastal oilfields, especially in the Gulf of Mexico and in Nigeria's Niger delta, but also from shipping.

Oil reserves continue to cause rivalry between states, as with Venezuelan territorial claims on Guyana in 2024 which led to the threat of war and to military moves to deter Venezuela, notably by Brazil. This factor will continue, for, even if oil provides a diminishing percentage of world energy, it will still be important.

The wish to move to a global clean energy system of 'de-carbonization' will become more expensive due to the emphasis on fossil fuels, oil and liquefied natural gas during the international crisis of the early 2020s. In China, while there is discussion of environmentalism, alongside a very strong interest in solar and wind power, there is also an unprecedented construction of coal-fired power stations. So also with India. In 2003–23, there was a 48 per cent increase in global coal consumption, two-thirds of which was due to China, as was three-quarters of the 34 per cent increase in carbon dioxide emissions.

BELOW: The ruins of the Chernobyl nuclear power plant on 29 April 1986, three days after the catastrophic accident.

ABOVE: The use of solar power increased significantly in the 21st century.

The international political crises of the 2020s and their impact on energy movements encouraged self-reliance and, linked to them, efforts to use renewable energy, rather than oil, natural gas and coal imports. Solar power was increasingly utilized, notably from the 1990s, and there was a rapid increase in its percentage of global electricity generation, from 1 per cent in 2015 to 5 per cent in 2023, by which time solar was the key form of new generation installation, in part due to the more costly nature of wind power capacity. The role taken by solar energy is currently rising rapidly, and it is far more efficient than burning fossil fuels as a producer of electricity. This was accompanied by a fall in the cost of solar energy. The flexibility of the method is impressive and contrasts with the dominant centralized provision of electricity in 1950.

By 2022 about 36 per cent of British electricity was produced from wind power, and its cost had fallen. China overtook British production in 2021, becoming the largest wind power producer in the world. The main costs with solar and wind electricity will be those of getting a distribution system in place. This may well happen in large parts of the world by the early 2040s.

Fusion energy looks deliverable on the same sort of timescale. It is likely that by 2050 there will be a broader pattern of energy provision, including of hydrogen as a fuel. Plasma fusion for energy production is about 40 years away, though it is currently the subject of much private investment and that date may well come sooner.

ENVIRONMENTALISM: FROM AGITATION TO STATE POLICIES

Environmental concern has been a growing theme of recent decades, one that has linked science and publications to politics and culture. The last saw dystopian thought increasingly focus not on religious or even political themes, but, rather, on environmental counterparts, as in the James Bond film ***Quantum of Solace*** (2008), where the supply of water to a Bolivia under great pressure is a key plot device. By the 2000s, indeed, environmental crisis as a topic was firmly established in the popular mainstream, as in apocalyptic fiction such as Kim Robinson's ***Forty Signs of Rain*** (2004) and ***Fifty Degrees Below*** (2005) in which Washington DC faces flooding from melting ice caps.

Such works drew on a variety of strands, not least hostility to industrialization and big business, and widespread concern about technological change. The environmental movement had developed from the 1960s, notably, but not only, in the US. Works, such as the book *Silent Spring* (1962) by the American marine biologist and ecologist Rachel Carson highlighted environmental threats, while Paul Ehrlich's *The Population Bomb* (1968), which had sold 2 million copies by 1974, encouraged support for contraception. In David Mamet's play *The Water Engine: An American Fable* (1977), big business was presented as corrupt and dangerous, seeking to suppress an engine that runs on water. At the end of the play the engine's inventor is killed. In cinema, *The China Syndrome* (1979) was a thriller about safety cover-ups at a fictional nuclear plant, which seemed prescient

ABOVE: Rachel Carson.

NUCLEAR TESTING

The testing of nuclear weaponry became a major issue in environmentalism and international diplomacy. There was particular sensitivity about US, British and, particularly (because it continued for longest), French testing in the Pacific, with hostility focusing on the fact that entire islands – and the living organisms on them and the fish in the seas around them – were seen as disposable. It is probable that the lives, livelihoods and the health of more than 100,000 people in the French Pacific were affected by fallout from at least 175 French underground and atmospheric nuclear tests from 1966 to 1996, when testing stopped after riots in Tahiti.

ABOVE: The Castle Bravo American thermonuclear test in Bikini Atoll, 1954.

when the Three Mile Island reactor went into meltdown in Pennsylvania a week after the film was released. Meanwhile, the film *Silkwood* (1983) focused on the true-life suspicious death in 1974 of a union organizer who exposed serious safety breaches at the nuclear power plant where she worked.

In turn, Green politics became significant, although not in the US or India. Established in 1980, the West German Greens took 1.5 per cent of the vote that year, 5.6 per cent in 1983, 8.3 per cent in 1987, and 8.6 per cent in the German election of 2002, which was followed by the re-election of their governing coalition with the Social Democrats established in 1998. The abandonment of nuclear power in Germany reflected Green priorities. In 2017, the Greens took 8.9 per cent of the vote, making them Germany's sixth-largest political party.

The Greens were less prominent in other countries, for example France, but Green attitudes and policies became widespread. Many millennials (people born between 1981 and 1996) and members of Generation Z (people born from 1997) have been especially scathing about the irresponsible policies of their elders regarding the environment.

At the same time, there were significant variations between countries over Green issues, not least over a willingness to pay increased taxes to help limit climate cost. There has also been strong criticism of higher fuel and heating prices, some of which have been linked to Green policies. There is particular opposition on the political Right to such policies, notably in the US, but not only there.

Institutionalization was important to protection for the environment. Thus, in France, although the word *environment* only came into common usage in the 1980s, the Ministry for the Protection of Nature and the Environment was established in 1971, while national parks had been opened earlier. In response to pollution affecting people's health, particularly mercury poisoning in the late 1950s, Japan eventually introduced legislation to limit it. Legislation in the US included the National Air Quality Control Act of 1971. Air pollutant concentrations in the country subsequently fell, very rapidly in the case of lead, but also with carbon monoxide and sulphur dioxide, while more slowly with nitrogen dioxide.

Although it may not always be painted as such, China is a key player in environmentalism and invested very heavily in solar power in the 2020s. In Africa and the Islamic world, however, environmentalists have often had a difficult time, as in Kenya where the Green Belt Movement often met serious police harassment. In poor countries, there are often no funds available for clean air, clean water and other environmental policies, although there generally seems to be sufficient money for armaments and corruption, a point also pertinent for India.

BELOW: A Green Party rally in Berlin, 2009. From the 1980s, the Greens became a more influential force in national politics across many countries in Europe.

DILEMMAS FOR THE PLANET

The long-term environmental challenge posed by a rapidly rising global population, a key theme in the 1960s, appears to have been superseded by climate warming, at least as far as public attention is concerned. In part, this reflects the political difficulties involved in tackling population numbers, and in part the extent to which climate change can be used in terms of anti-capitalist rhetoric, and therefore readily fits into established narratives. There is also a reluctance in many states, for example India, to adopt demographic measures that may be seen as limiting choice and religious commitment; as well as a widespread sense that population is an index of national strength. Indeed, many states seek to encourage birth rates, a policy seen in recent years in France, Italy and South Korea.

However, in practice, the growth in population (see chapter 2) poses enormous problems for the planet. This is obviously true in terms of land use, notably in the provision of housing, but can also be seen with reference to climate change, as the material needs of growing populations puts great pressure on the climate, most notably in energy usage but also that of water and food. Alongside resource consumption, there is waste production and carbon emissions. Each has serious environmental implications.

Earthquakes and volcanoes, like the impact of sunspots, put in context the human impact on the environment. The first two are most common where tectonic plates meet, as around the Pacific, for example at Rabaul, and on the Mid-Atlantic Ridge – where there was a volcanic eruption on the island of Heimaey off Iceland in 1973 – and in the Caribbean. A submarine earthquake in 2011 moved the main island of Japan 2.4 m (7 ft 9 in) to the east and caused a tsunami that led to a catastrophe at the Fukushima nuclear plant. A major earthquake is in prospect for California, courtesy of the San Andreas Fault that runs along much of the western edge of the state. Alongside the possibility of islands lost due to the rise of the oceans linked to global warming has come the extrusion of magma due to volcanic action both under oceans and above them, for example the island of Surtsey, which formed off Iceland as a result of a series of eruptions between 1963–7. Volcanic activity on Iceland became a major challenge to North Atlantic air travel in 2010, with over 100,000 flights cancelled.

Other environmental developments can interact with climate change, which raises questions about the respective roles of human and natural processes. Future dilemmas are most probably going to be the same (or similar) as at present, but possibly in a different combination and with contrasting severity. The long-term dilemmas of the destruction of the planet as the result of events in the solar system, notably an expansion of the sun in its red giant phase increasing its gravitational pull, or of the collapse of the solar system itself, will be beyond human experience. The extinction of all life on Earth in about four billion years has been predicted, offering a very different timetable to those of religious apocalypses.

However, there will be earlier dilemmas as a consequence of the interaction of humans and national environments. These dilemmas, notably the pressures of development and the consequences of war, will affect the environment, although less so than changes within the Earth in causing the movement of tectonic plates. The drama of volcanoes, earthquakes and tsunamis, indeed, are apt demonstrations that it is not only humanity that is an active agent, but also the physical environment. At the individual level, humans can be extremely vulnerable; and this vulnerability can extend to communities and countries. As far as human action is concerned, climate change is a major issue but so also is the possibility of large-scale nuclear conflict. Both are pressing, but the latter appears a more immediate threat in periods of international crisis such as the 2020s.

BELOW: The Surtsey eruption, 1963.

2 Humanity

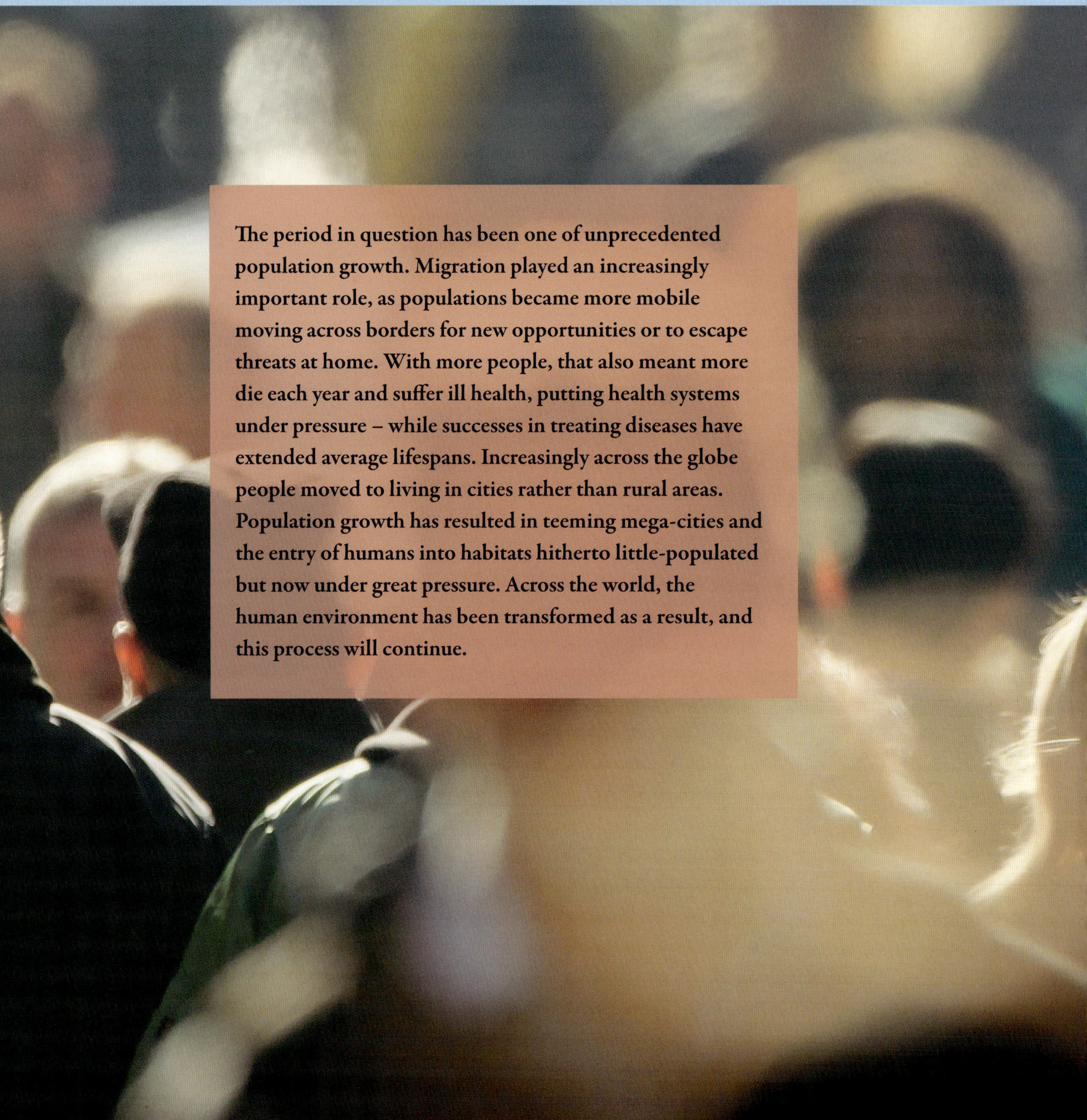

The period in question has been one of unprecedented population growth. Migration played an increasingly important role, as populations became more mobile moving across borders for new opportunities or to escape threats at home. With more people, that also meant more die each year and suffer ill health, putting health systems under pressure – while successes in treating diseases have extended average lifespans. Increasingly across the globe people moved to living in cities rather than rural areas. Population growth has resulted in teeming mega-cities and the entry of humans into habitats hitherto little-populated but now under great pressure. Across the world, the human environment has been transformed as a result, and this process will continue.

DEMOGRAPHICS

From 1950 on, the growth of the world's population has been astonishing. In 1950, when we begin our study, there were 2.5 billion people alive. By 2025, that figure had reached 8.2 billion. Such an increase had never been seen before in world history – and it came with important consequences.

WORLD POPULATION IN BILLIONS

1950: 2.5	1980: 4.4	2010: 7.0
1960: 3.0	1990: 5.3	2020: 7.9
1970: 3.7	2000: 6.1	2030 (projected): 8.5

Even the Covid pandemic of 2019–22 could not slow population growth. Many died, some in terrible discomfort. There was a dystopian character to the entire episode, talk of 'culling' by disease, and fear of a significant fall in the world's population. And yet, at the same time, this population continued its apparently inexorable rise. Indeed, it passed 8 billion in 2023.

BELOW: British children in an overcrowded school dining hall, 1952. The population increased rapidly in the wake of World War II, creating a 'baby boom' in the early 1950s.

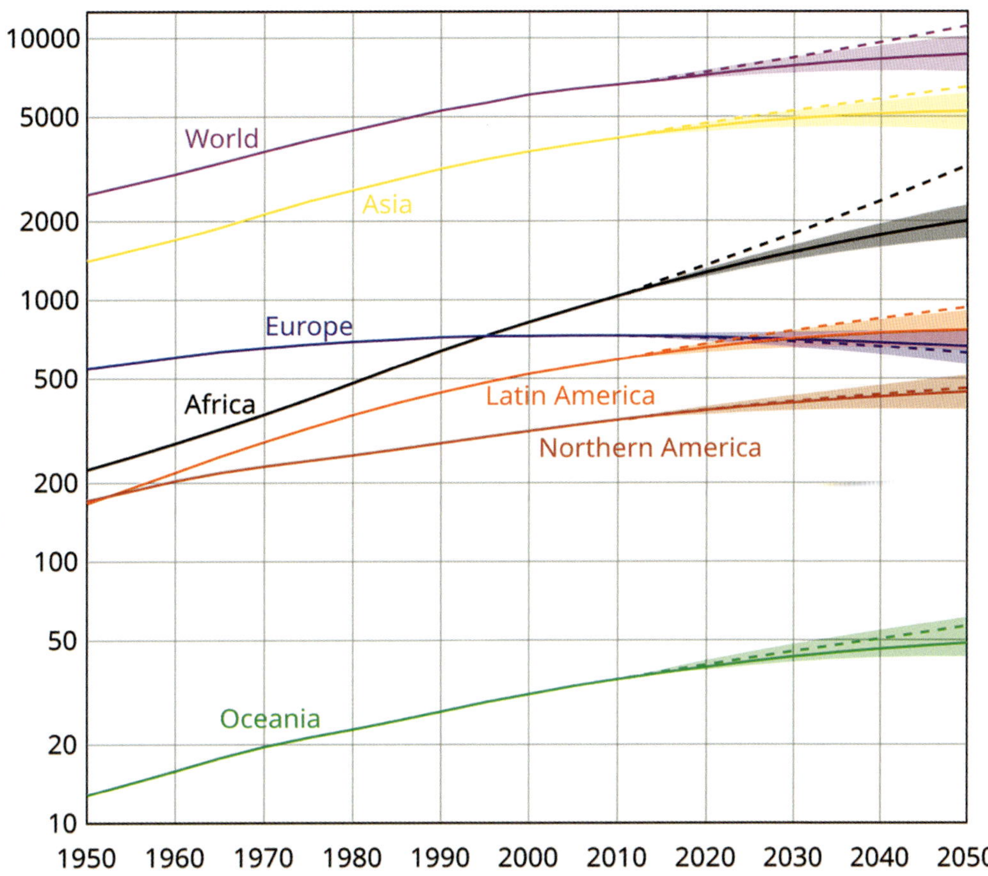

LEFT: World population growth based on UN estimates. The dotted lines show the projected population figures assuming fertility rates remain constant, while the solid line indicates the most likely projection.

In contrast it had been 3 billion 60 years earlier. The baby boom that followed World War II, with an annual population increase of over 2 per cent in 1955–8 and 1963–7, was an expression of recovery from war, and of economic growth and consumerism. It was followed, however, by smaller percentage increases. Never again above 2 per cent, they dropped below 1.8 per cent from 1989, 1.7 per cent from 1991, 1.6 per cent from 1993, 1.4 per cent from 1998, 1.2 per cent from 2015, and 1 per cent from 2020. The UN estimate of live births per woman was 4.86 in 1950, but only 2.32 in 2021, with a consistent fall from the late 1960s, especially in the 1970s and 1980s and continuing thereafter. Yet, the size of the underlying number of people, combined with lower infant mortality and greater longevity, still ensured that total population growth remained substantial, and this will continue to be the case.

There was confidence that there was some self-righting process that would cut this growth. It was until recently thought that greater education for women in particular would produce more modest figures, and that the likely global population would in part as a result of this top out at about 9.5 or even only 8.9 billion by 2050. It was also believed that the impact of AIDS could lead to an even lower figure. That currently seems very unlikely. There are now projections for a maximum population figure of 10.5–10.75 billion at 2100. Whatever the figure will be when that time comes, the current trend is upwards, with, at present, a population increase of one billion every 11 years.

ABOVE: A crowded street in Cairo, Egypt.

The rate of increase varies worldwide. UN data from 2020 indicated that African countries were disproportionately represented among those with high population growth rates, including Niger, Gabon, Sierra Leone, Togo, Burkina Faso, Tanzania and Ethiopia. Nigeria, the most populous country in Africa, is predicted to replace the US as the third-most populous country in the world. By 2018, Egypt's population was close to 100 million and was rising annually by 2.5 million. Even if numbers were to go on to a downward trend, there are now many young people – which will lead to more births in the future, even if the fertility rate falls. In 2021, the median age in Papua New Guinea was only 22 and it still had the world's highest population growth rate, at 2.31 per cent.

In contrast, there is a self-fulfilling process of decline for countries with ageing populations. This reflects a lack of children. The global fertility rate fell to an average of 2.3 children per woman in 2020, but in 2022, in the European Union, 49 per cent of families with children had only one. By 2019, only 16 per cent of German families had three children or more.

As a result, at the same time as a general global increase, there was a decline of population in particular areas, notably much of Europe. The lowest population growth rates in Europe were in Moldova and Ukraine. Other European countries facing decline included Lithuania, Romania, Estonia, and Italy. In 2023, the fertility rate in the European Union was about 1.5 births per woman, compared to the 2.1 rate required to sustain the population. That of Italy has fallen to about 1.2, with only 379,000 births in 2023, an all-time low in a decline that began in 2009; children were outnumbered by the elderly by five to one. In May 2024, Pope Francis claimed that an ageing population was making Europe 'old, tired and resigned. Homes are filled with objects and emptied of children, becoming very sad places... Without children and young people, a country loses its desire for the future.' That was an analysis applied in particular to Italy. As far back as 2006 it, like Germany, already had a median age of 42, with 26 per cent of the population (also like Germany) over 60. The lack of domestic population growth also directed attention to the rate of immigration.

This was also a serious issue in East Asia. In Taiwan, the fertility rate in 2024 fell to 1.1 children per woman and in South Korea to 1.12, the lowest figures in the world. Indeed, in South Korea deaths exceeded births in 2020–3, with only about 230,000 people born in South Korea in 2023 to a population of 52 million. This led that year to the creation of a Ministry of Low Birth Rate Counter Planning. Affected by a very low birth rate, Japan's population is declining about 0.5 per cent a year, and its age structure poses additional problems.

In contrast to Europe, the US continued to see significant growth (leaving aside immigration), while, in 2023, India overtook China as the most populous country in the world, at 1.43 billion. At the same time, its growing economy benefited from the West's attempt to lessen its supply-chain dependency on China. In 1998, when China claimed a population of 1.25 billion, the government argued that another 300 million would have been born but for the country's one-child policy. Despite the switch from a one- to a two-child policy in 2015, and permitting three in 2021, the Chinese population fell from 2023 and the

BELOW: Elderly people in Italy. The birth rate has greatly fallen in Italy, making it a much older country on average.

ABOVE: A mural promoting the one-child policy in Chengdu, China, 1985.

share of the population that was elderly continued to rise, putting pressure on the working-age population. Moreover, selective abortion and other practices ensured that there were more boys than girls, creating social problems for poor young males. In very cruel processes, women are imported from rural areas to the city and from nearby countries.

At both global and national levels, a lack of consistency across time and a related moderation in population growth was a key element, as a birth boost in one period, for example Japan in the 1950s, translated into an ageing population down the line, which could be exacerbated if there was a fall in births in that period. The problem of an Asian birth boost in the late 20th century was particularly acute in societies that did not achieve comparable economic growth, such as Thailand, Vietnam and rural China. These suffered a decline in the working-age population without the resources or borrowing capacity that provided social capital. In contrast, in the US, Europe and Japan, earlier growing populations had seen high annual growth rates building on an already strong economic base. Nevertheless, ageing populations created problems for government finances in the early 21st century. Moreover, at the individual, family, community and national levels, fertility will become an increasing problem, and concern about birth rates will encourage a large industry in IVF. A very different aspect of labour shortages might be an encouragement of the technological processes by which machines become properly conscious. They may acquire legal rights.

MIGRATION

Aside from growth of the existing population, the movement of people became a major issue, not least of Africans into Europe and of Latin Americans into the US. Economic growth after World War II had encouraged immigration as well as the rising birth rate that produced the 'Baby Boomers'. Thus, by 1973, the foreign workforce in France was 11 per cent, many from the former empire, notably Algeria, but others from Spain and Portugal. However, the end of the 'Long Boom' of 1945–73, and economic problems, notably rising unemployment, greatly increased opposition to immigration and helped ensure that it became a political issue. So also with sensitivity to the movement of dependents as opposed to simply workers, with dependents widely perceived as a pressure on social welfare, whereas the money earned by immigrants tended to be underplayed. There was also concern about the aggregate size of migrant numbers.

Migration became highly contentious politically, as well as leading to debate among economists about its respective benefits and costs. While migration by skilled workers was clearly beneficial, and, indeed, could be actively encouraged, this was far less the case for unskilled workers, let alone their dependents. Unskilled workers could depress pay-rates to the detriment of the existing workforce, while dependents could lead to acute pressure on social welfare. Yet, unskilled workers were also necessary.

LEFT: A group of Jamaican immigrants arrive in Newhaven, UK, in 1958.

There were particular migration links, many from former imperial colonies, as with Pakistanis to Britain, Senegalese to France, and Somalis to Italy. In other cases, there was no such link. While Puerto Rico, a US territory, was the source of a large-scale movement into America, the majority source, Latin America, had no such link. On a smaller scale, there have been movements of American Pacific islanders, for example from Guam to Hawaii and to continental America, and of Samoans to New Zealand. Providing cheap factory labour, the Samoans mostly live in poor-quality housing in overcrowded Auckland suburbs. The massive migration to New Zealand from Polynesian islands saw larger indigenous populations living there than in their own islands, for example the Cooks, Niue, Tokelau and Pukapuka.

Germany drew heavily first on Italians, then Spaniards, then Yugoslavs, later focusing on Turks. The country had no colonial links with any of these peoples. Some immigration was far less welcome, notably that of Syrians and Albanians to Greece, and of North Africans to Italy. Hostility, socially and in the workplace, to immigrants can extend to their descendants, and, indeed, to minorities in general, as with that toward the Roma in Europe; in Bulgaria, there was rioting against the Roma in 2011. There can also be a fear of being overwhelmed, as in the hostile response of many Mongolians to Chinese workers.

Although most of the debate was over migration into the West, there was also acute tension over migration elsewhere. This could be seen as unwelcome in affluent countries with a strong cultural dislike of large-scale immigration, such as Japan, which had relatively few; but also in poorer countries where the theme was more one of competition for resources. Thus, in Pakistan there was opposition to the scale of Afghan immigration, and in Bangladesh to that from Myanmar. In South Africa, there is opposition to immigrants seeking work from elsewhere in Africa, for example Somalia.

RIGHT: An anti-immigration protest in Frankfurt, 2015.

ABOVE: Children at school in London's Chinatown, 1951. Some countries saw major demographic changes in the second half of the 20th century as immigration reshaped the composition of the population.

There was scant migration into China or India, the world's most populous countries, but significant emigration from them, notably in pursuit of economic opportunity in the US, but not only there. Chinese money and immigrants, notably from Hong Kong, transformed central Vancouver.

Migration between countries was matched by that within them, with the percentage of the world's population living in cities increasing. It is projected to rise to three-quarters by 2050. In India, the 2011 census recorded 450 million internal migrants. In China, economic opportunity encouraged movement to cities on or near the coast, such as Shanghai. Rates vary greatly, Americans being more willing (and able) to move than most Western Europeans. California gained 1.1 million residents between 1955 and 1960 and was the most populous state in the country by the 1960s, as jobs and the climate attracted new residents, ensuring that its representation in the House of Representatives rose by 22 seats between 1950 and 1990. In turn, higher taxes and the tarnishing of the earlier Californian dream helped lead to a significant outflow from California from the mid-1990s to other states, notably Colorado, Wyoming and Arizona.

The enforced movement of people within states, for example mass deportations within the Soviet Union, became far less common after the death of Stalin in 1953. Yet, there was still encouraged movement within states, for example to areas deemed less populated, such as Borneo in Indonesia, or in order to anchor control, for example the movement of Han Chinese to Xinjiang to offset the influence of Uighur Muslims there.

URBANIZATION

As more people came to live in cities, so direct experience of the countryside became relatively less common. Whereas in 1950 large urban areas were concentrated in Europe and North America, elsewhere the shift occurred later, in Latin America from the last half of the 20th century and in China and Africa from the last quarter. Far from being reversed, this trend has continued. Although agricultural mechanization and bad harvests provided specific incentives or 'push' factors for this migration, more generally it was the grinding poverty of rural life and its inability to provide employment for the young that was crucial in encouraging the flight from the countryside.

In contrast, the availability of jobs in towns encouraged migration, and life there had its appeal, with excitement, consumption and apparent social mobility. Thus, the proportion of Nigerians living in an urban area rose from a fifth in 1963 to more than a third in 1991. The largest Nigerian city, Lagos, was by 2012 adding half a million people yearly and possibly heading towards a mid-century population of 40 million. This dynamic city reflected the tensions of urban growth: many more people, terrible congestion, corruption, a poor power supply, and a lawlessness that led to vigilante groups keeping the peace for payment. At the same time, improvements in tax collection in the 2000s made it possible for Lagos to access capital and long-term debt markets, and to issue bonds, permitting investment in infrastructure, including the construction of light railways. Such a process was very difficult in 'failed states' where credit was largely absent, for example Haiti and Afghanistan.

RIGHT: A crowded market in Lagos, Nigeria. Estimates placed the population of Lagos as high as 21 million in 2022, although official figures for 2025 suggest 17 million.

ABOVE: São Paulo, Brazil, the largest city in South America.

Around the world, the size of cities, both leading ones and middle-size ones, rose. São Paulo, the largest city in South America, saw its population rise from about 2.2 million in 1950 to 22.8 million in 2024. The population of Rio de Janeiro in the same period increased 2.4 million to 13.8 million. This process could be very difficult, due to the problems of providing adequate housing, social capital (such as schools and hospitals), employment, transport and law and order. Crime rates could be particular problems, for example in Johannesburg, Karachi, Lagos and Rio de Janeiro. In the state of São Paulo, the rate of murders per 100,000 fell considerably, to 8.4 in 2022, which represented 3,044 murders.

'Push' factors have included environmental ones, with drought encouraging movement into the city, as in Mauritania in the 1980s, where nomadic herding was hit hard and many moved to the capital, Nouakchott. Conflict has also led many to flee, notably to other countries, as from Syria in the 2010s, principally to Jordan, Lebanon and Turkey. Conflict in the Sahel, the region south of the Sahara, in the 2010s and 2020s similarly encouraged large numbers to leave. Conflict also led many to flee within countries to cities, including to shanty towns and refugee camps, as in Sudan in the early 2020s, with the focus there on Khartoum.

State support such as food and fuel subsidies was greatest in major cities, notably capitals, which were the most politically sensitive. However, urban infrastructure proved particularly deficient on a number of counts, including water supply, public health, housing and transport. The percentage of the population in the developing world with access to safe drinking water and sanitation was greater in urban than rural areas, but, even so, many urban areas lacked clean water, which led to disease. Many major cities have inadequate water supplies and poor water infrastructure, and neither are adequately prepared for the rapidly rising population. This is seen in Mexico City and Havana, in which water trucks supplement the system, while rainwater is collected from rooftop tanks. The extraction of water from underground aquifers leads to the land surface, and with it buildings, sinking, as in Mexico City.

The 20 biggest cities in 2015, in terms of urban agglomerations (a criterion that leads to variations in the data based on differing definitions), were: Tokyo-Yokohama, Jakarta, Delhi, Manila, Seoul-Incheon, Shanghai, Karachi, Beijing, New York, Guangzhou-Foshan, São Paulo, Mexico City, Mumbai, Oaka-Kobe-Kyoto, Moscow, Dhaka, Cairo, Los Angeles, Bangkok and Kolkata. In practice, Istanbul, Lagos, Kinshasa and Johannesburg are also very important, and many marginal residential districts, notably squatter camps, tend to be under-reported in population figures. At any rate, by 2015 the world had 34 megacities (cities with a population of more than 10 million). Of the 1,000 largest urban areas, 56 per cent were in Asia.

BELOW: Smoke rises over Khartoum in 2023, in the midst of a devastating civil war.

HEALTH AND DISEASE

Healthcare is one of the leading forms of private consumption and state expenditure, although the results are arguably less significant in public health than developments in other spheres, such as the provision of clean water. In particular, there was the greater production of food in Asia associated with the 'Green Revolution', and the more general growth of the world economy in this period. At the global scale, there has been a marked reduction in infant mortality and a major increase in life expectancy, for both men and women. Global life expectancy at birth rose from 46 in 1950 to 73 in 2023.

Greater life expectancy has helped change the pattern of disease, as has the increase in the diseases of affluence. In the first case, dementia and other illnesses more frequent among the over-70s have risen in frequency, while in the second there has been an increase in diseases linked to obesity, including Type 2 diabetes and cancer. Pollution has also affected health, being linked to male sperm counts dropping from the 1970s, most notably, as in Italy, in urban areas, and least in remote rural ones.

'THE PENICILLIN FOR CHOLESTEROL'

Akira Endo (1933–2024), a Japanese research chemist from a poor farming background, played a key role in the 1970s in the discovery of statins, cultivating fungal samples from 1971 and testing their ability to inhibit an enzyme important to cholesterol production and therefore to the risk of heart attacks and strokes. He discovered a compound known as mevastatin and between 1978 and 1980 carried out clinical trials that encouraged research by the American company Merck, which patented Simvastatin in 1980. Lovastatin was approved by the American Food and Drug Administration (FDA) in 1987 and was the first statin to be thus authorized for sale. In 2003, atorvastatin became the best-selling pharmaceutical in history. Statins cut the risk of heart attacks and strokes.

ABOVE: Akira Endo.

Differing levels of prosperity and tobacco consumption between countries have interacted with contrasting age structures to produce very differing health profiles. In Russia, even before the Ukraine war started in 2022, male life expectancy was falling significantly, in part due to excessive alcohol intake. Indeed, alcoholism, smoking and suicides helped to cause a major decline there in male life expectancy from the mid-1960s to the present.

So also with public provision for health. This varies greatly – although, whatever the system, the wealthy, well-connected and articulate do best, and poor countries far less well, notably in Africa. In 1950, life expectancy was 72 in Norway and 69 in Britain; in Mali it was 26. Female life expectancy is higher in part due to the improved care of mothers as well as babies in childcare.

ABOVE: President Lyndon Johnson signs the Medicare bill, 30 July 1965.

The US is not generally seen as a country with much public healthcare, where it is a politically contentious subject. President Harry Truman, in office from 1945–53, was unable to bring his hope for healthcare for all to fruition; Bill Clinton, president between 1993 and 2001, failed in 1994 to provide the universal health insurance programme he sought to promote. This failure demonstrated the strong conservatism of the US political system, the role of vested interests and the hostility to measures that might benefit others. Clinton was accused of trying to socialize US medicine, a prime instance of health as political rhetoric; while racism came into play in the indifference towards the uninsured poor who were disproportionately Black, although many poor whites were also uninsured. Nevertheless, the Medicare Prescription Drug Improvement and Modernization Act of 2003, which came into effect in 2006, represented a massive expansion in entitlement. However, in accordance with Republican preferences, the benefit was administered through competing health plans managed by insurance companies. The state did not play a significant role other than as the funder. Despite rising life expectancy, US public health has been hit hard by drug use, alcoholism, suicide and diseases linked to obesity, notably coronary heart conditions.

In practical terms, immunization programmes as well as measures to provide clean water were more significant in public health, both in the US and more generally, than medical care.

This level of public health provision, however, was threatened most by war and instability, as in Congo in the 1990s and Sudan in the 2020s. These factors could be accentuated, as in Afghanistan in the 1990s, if there were religious and social constraints on aspects of public health, notably the use of female medical personnel or direct care for women.

Wealth distribution is also significant in public health. Thus, China, which has more public provision, has proved more successful than India in health outcomes and raising life expectancy, just as it has in tackling illiteracy.

Thanks to scientific work and its application, notably the use of genomics, it is probable that the ageing process will be slowed down, with cancer targeted by personal medication with mRNA technology (mRNA, or messenger ribonucleic acid, being a molecule that acts in a similar way to DNA and which plays in role in how all of the body's biological functions work). Less positively, increased resistance to antimicrobials, including antibiotics, is making it harder to treat common infections, putting many of the gains of modern medicine at risk and driving up healthcare costs.

LEFT: Life expectancy changed dramatically in China, rising from about 35–40 in 1950 to 77.6 in 2024.

CHANGING LIFE EXPECTANCY IN CHINA

The dramatic change in China came after 1950. In 1850, life expectancy was about 32 and in 1950 about 35–40. By 2024, the figure was 77.6. The growth between 1950 and 1980 was particularly dramatic and most of it was due to major falls in infant and under-five mortality. There was a major fall in 1959–61, due to the famine accompanying the failure of the 'Great Leap Forward' economic programme, but from 1963 to 1980 life expectancy rose again, from 61.2 to 67.7.

DISEASES AND PANDEMICS

Disease did not grab headlines as war did, but, for the world's population in general disease was a more obvious daily threat. In countries affected by war, disease was always a grim accompaniment, for example in Congo in the 1990s. There were national and international campaigns to eradicate diseases. In addition to the successful elimination of smallpox, there were concerted – though not quite as successful – efforts to rid the world of polio and other diseases, including malaria and sleeping sickness. The responses varied, with pharmacological research and immunization policies both significant. There were also attacks on the vectors of disease, such as the spraying of waters in which malaria- and yellow fever-spreading mosquitoes bred, followed by selective breeding programmes to reduce transmission from mosquitoes.

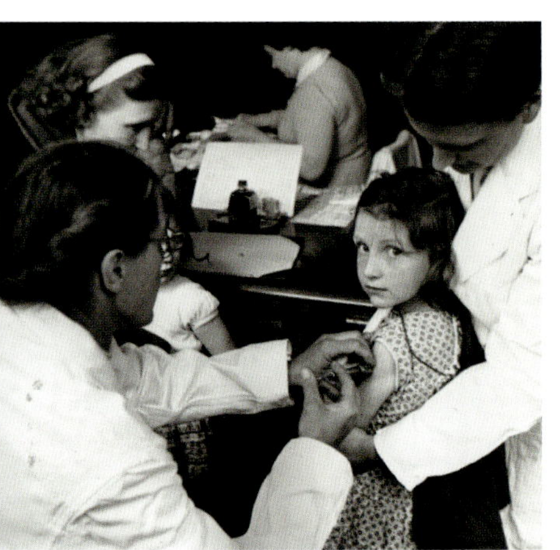

ABOVE: Vaccination against polio, 1956, UK.

The idea of eradicating disease was important to the progressivism of the late 20th century and was an aspect of the international cooperation developed under the auspices of the United Nations. At the same time, there was concern about some of the environmental consequences of the intervention linked to eradication programmes, in particular spraying with DDT.

Alongside the challenge from established diseases came epidemics of new or newly recognized diseases, such as Lassa fever, the Ebola and Marburg viruses, Legionnaires' disease, AIDS (Acquired Immune Deficiency Syndrome) and SARS (Severe Acute Respiratory Syndrome).

First recognized as an infection in 1981, AIDS spread rapidly across the world and affected large numbers, notably in Africa, including, by 2010, 11 per cent of adults in

SMALLPOX ERADICATION DAY

The World Health Assembly declared Earth free of smallpox on 8 May 1980. The last known natural case was in Somalia in 1977. The end of smallpox vaccination means that immunity is currently low. This is the only human infectious disease to have been wiped out. In 1958, around two million people died each year from smallpox.

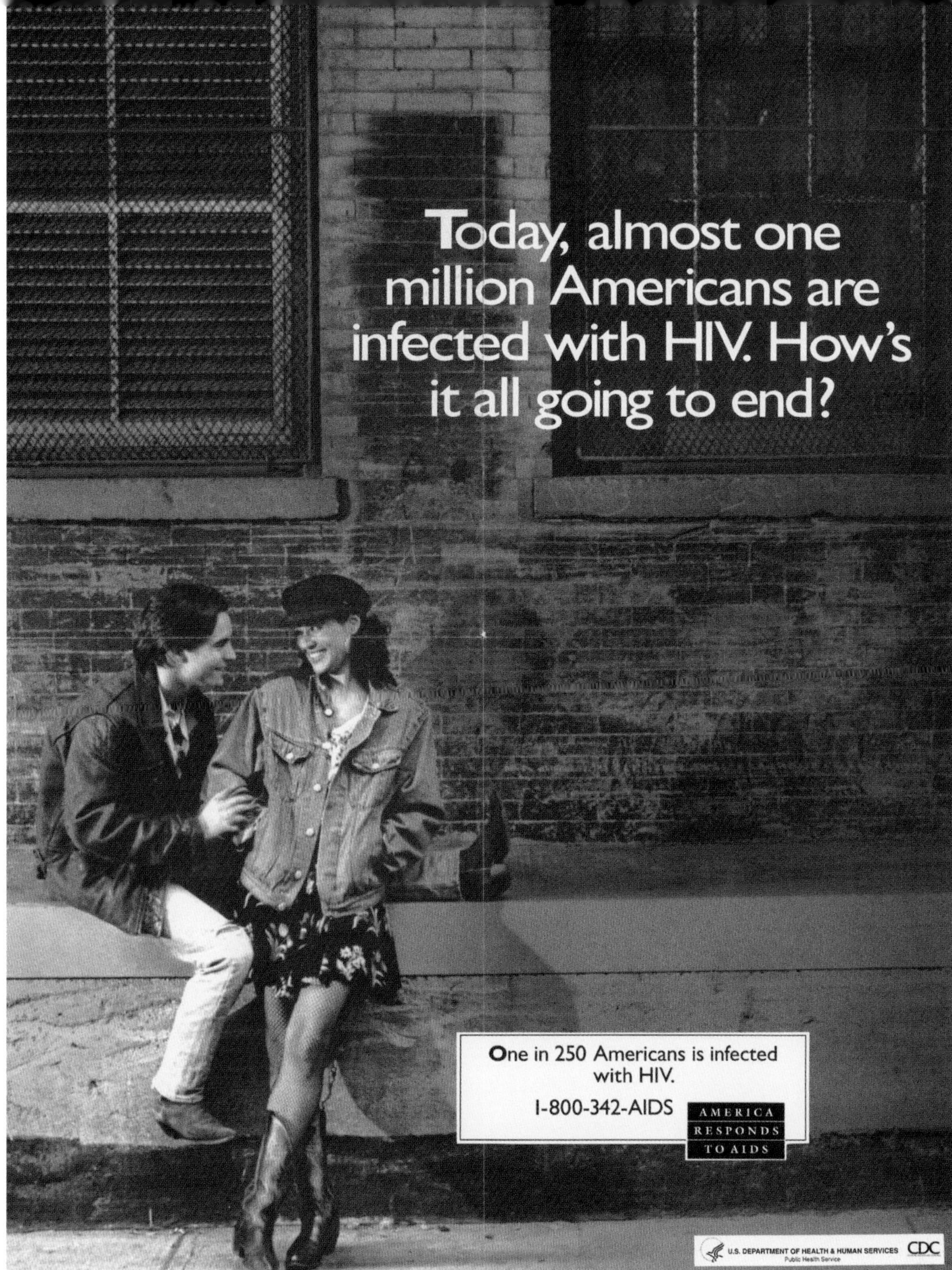

LEFT: A poster warning about AIDS issued by the US Center for Disease Control from the 1990s.

Malawi. SARS, a form of coronavirus, infected more than 8,000 people from 30 countries across the world, causing 774 known deaths. This again indicated the speed with which diseases could spread, but also provided little indication of potential death rates. The origin of AIDS was a matter of considerable controversy and has served as a lightning rod for ethnic, religious and sexual prejudices, notably against homosexuals. In fact, AIDS derived from the consumption of diseased chimpanzees, so that their viruses spread to humans. Subsequent transmission among humans was related to social practices, such as sexual behaviour, contraceptive use and sharing needles.

The Covid-19 pandemic of 2019–23 directed attention to human vulnerability in response to rapidly spreading diseases, in this case one that originated in China, possibly in a poorly supervised laboratory, and spread swiftly around the world. In the early stages, in the face of this spread and a lack of knowledge about the disease, as well as how best to counter it, there was much alarmism. This included talk of a new Black Death, a reference to a pandemic of the mid-14th century that led to death rates in Eurasia of a third to a half. Governments tended to respond in 2020–2 with 'lockdowns' designed to reduce transmission and ease pressure on hospitals, and with stopping movement between countries.

In practice, while Covid itself mutated, the disease was swiftly analyzed and vaccines invented, manufactured, distributed and applied. By 2023, the crisis was essentially over (with 7.05 million reported deaths by May 2024), and it seemed arguable that the response had been unduly histrionic. Covid overwhelmingly killed the very elderly; the world's population had actually gone up every day during the pandemic and, indeed, crossed eight billion in 2023. The 'lockdowns' badly hit not only economies (and therefore the ability to generate resources to pay for public health), but also socializing, as well as many health indicators, including exercise. Nevertheless, although most people did not experience serious symptoms, every death was a shock. There were also unpleasant after-effects in the shape of Long Covid.

The Covid fatality rate was 1.02 per cent by 10 March 2023, which opened the question of what would have happened had there been a higher rate. In practice, there is

BELOW: Empty roads in Penang, Malaysia in March 2020, a few days after lockdown was imposed.

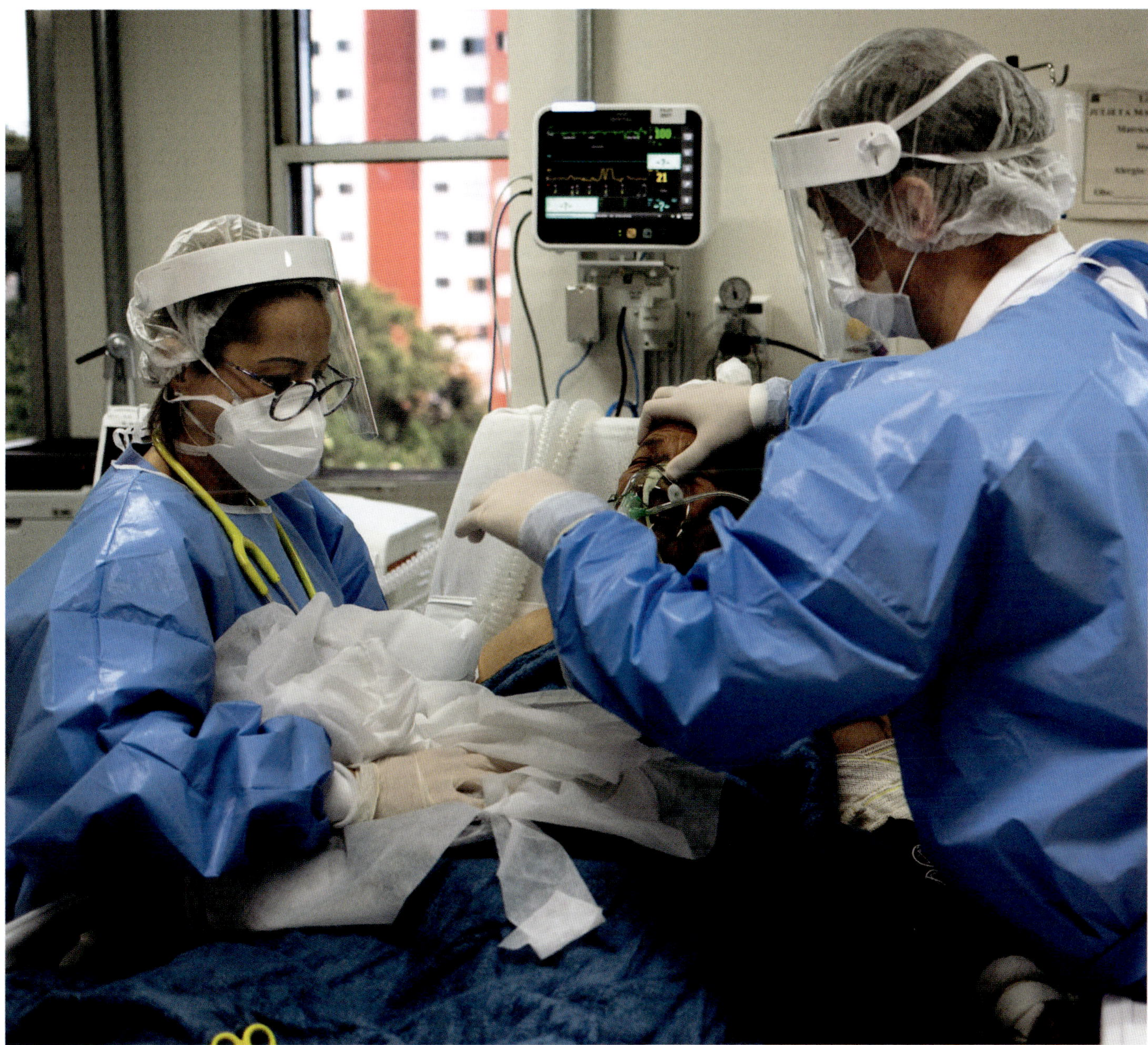

ABOVE: Medics treating a Covid patient in Brazil, May 2020.

more risk at present of high casualties and global devastation through the use of nuclear, thermonuclear, chemical and bacteriological weaponry in conflict. Indeed, bacteriological weaponry might be the source of the greatest number of deaths through a pandemic.

At the same time, antimicrobial resistance – the resilience of disease to drugs, notably antibiotics – is a rising problem, leading to 'superbugs' which currently kill more than a million annually. There are predictions it could rise to ten million by 2050. The situation has been exacerbated by a shortage of new antibiotics since the 1980s.

To counter pandemics, and in particular engineered pandemics and bioterrorism, the fast detection of viruses and bacteria to screen passengers and goods in transit will become common. Separately, there will be concern about 'diseases' affecting both the genetic modification of humans and robotic systems.

3 Society

Poverty was a seemingly immovable fact of life for people in 1950. While still a major problem, a large percentage of the world's population has been lifted out of poverty due to economic growth. This may be the most unremarked feature of our period.

The very meaning of society has changed greatly from 1950, when class was perhaps the overriding consideration. Left-wing thought was the dominant mode of looking at the world, in part because Marxist Communism was the official ideology of large areas of Eastern Europe, Asia, South America, and parts of Africa. 'Softer' forms of Socialism also enjoyed periods of power and influence. Capitalism, meanwhile, flourished elsewhere, most spectacularly in the US. As with Communism, it was concerned with socio-economic differences of wealth – but these were seen in terms of opportunity, not exploitation.

Fascism persisted in Spain and Portugal, while right-wing authoritarian regimes held power at different times across Latin America and in Pakistan, Thailand and Turkey.

The major change in our period has been the rise of other identities as social markers, notably those of gender, sexuality and ethnicity. At the same time, socio-economic criteria remain relevant.

USB

GENDER

Women's rights and women's position in society changed considerably, albeit very unevenly, from the beginning of the 20th century, with this process becoming more prominent from its second half, and playing a greater role in public policy and social debate from the 1960s. It was only in 1950 that the equal right to vote was extended to women in Canada; in Switzerland not until 1971. More generally, the electoral norm of the secret ballot lessened the potential influence of fathers and husbands.

Male attitudes were scarcely conducive to women. In the US, the monthly circulation of *Playboy*, a fashionable magazine for male voyeurs, rose from 1 million by 1959 to 7 million in the early 1970s. Alongside social and cultural attitudes, the dominance of politics in the treatment of women was seen in very differing legal, government and social contexts for their position in society; linked to this was the extent to which laws giving women rights were actually enforced. Thus, the illegal but all-too-common 'honour killings' of women, the forced marriage of brides against their will and sometimes the views of their families, and the 'dowry killings' of brides who did not bring with them sufficient wealth in cultures including those of Pakistan and India. The failure to prosecute these crimes reflected not only the weakness of governance but also the strength of misogyny, especially when directed against

RIGHT: A protest campaigning for women's suffrage in Switzerland, 1969.

independent-minded women. This has been a consistent element throughout the period. The constitutions of newly independent states, many issued from 1947 to 1975, provided for women's rights, but enforcement was very patchy.

ABOVE: A protest against honour killings of women in Pakistan in 2008.

In contrast, Communist, Socialist, and Liberal cultures allowed for an equality before the law that they sought to enforce, although this was carried forward differently in terms of legislative and fiscal support. Thus, in the period from the 1950s to the late 1980s, in Communist East Germany, where all the population was under state surveillance and denied liberty, the legal position of women was nevertheless better than in West Germany, where the Catholic Church encouraged more conservative norms: East German women were integrated into the workforce and received support during pregnancy and the first year of motherhood, subsequently being guaranteed re-entry into the workforce with kindergarten places for children. In turn, some East German women benefited from the political changes and prosperity offered by the unification of West Germany and East Germany after the fall of the Berlin Wall in 1989, a unification very much on West German terms. Other East German women suffered from the new weaknesses in family, work and neighbourhood support systems. These owed much to the disruption brought by large-scale migration to the former West Germany and to a different attitude to women on the part of post-Communist employers. Moreover, the industrial decline of the former East Germany hit the economic prospects of many women who did not migrate to West Germany, with numerous factories closing due to widespread deindustrialization.

This range of experience and response is true of changes not only in this section, and indeed chapter, but also across the book. Repeatedly, it is necessary to put aside the idea

ABOVE: Women at work in a factory in East Germany, 1962.

that 'history' is unidirectional, that change is the same as progress, and that society always responds in a given way, or could do so, or should do so were its members to be well-informed. That approach is misleading.

The major expansion in employment in the service sector across the world (see chapter 5) provided women with many opportunities. This was particularly seen in jobs in social care, notably health. In contrast, jobs traditionally done by men, particularly those involving manual labour in farming, forestry, mining, fishing, heavy industry and the military, suffered an absolute decline in numbers and significance, and, frequently, in relative pay. Moreover, in many jobs where women had traditionally been held in low esteem and kept in junior roles, for example the police and the prison service, they came to have access to the senior ranks, more responsibility and more pay.

German unification dramatized what was more generally the case, the relationships between gender opportunities and, on the one hand, political changes and, on the other, economic prosperity. German women benefited from the country's economic growth. As individuals and as members of collectives, from families to nations, women were affected by the interplays of the individual, the structural and the contingent. This was in a context made dynamic not only by developments specific to women, notably access to contraception, which became easier with the availability from the early 1960s of the pill, but also ones general to all, such as conflict, environmental changes and economic growth.

The categorization in terms of men and women that came to the fore from the 1990s, as class declined from prominence, notably in the West, as a social indicator, has been eroded by more recent emphases on ethnicity and sexuality, and by contention over gender change, especially from the 2010s in the West. Nevertheless, gender remains a key indicator of conditions and opportunities. This is particularly so in countries where social, cultural and governmental attitudes to women are discriminatory, and often hostile to female self-assertion. This is the case with some Islamic societies, such as Iran and Pakistan, but can also be found more generally. Indeed, the place of women outside the West deserves more attention.

At the same time as discussing the issue of gender, it is important to note that, aside from the customary differences on social, religious, ethnic, ideological and political lines, there were also specific divisions between women, for example, married or unmarried, mothers or childless, older or younger, housewives or employed, feminists or non-feminists, and heterosexuals or lesbians. These differences are important and it can be seriously misleading to think of a female monolith.

The same is also true for men. Indeed, the extent to which discussion of gender in books of this type focuses on women is a reflection of the degree to which they overcame the constraints of a male-dominated society. In addition, it is also a product of an often serious failure to assess issues of male society and masculinity other than in stereotypical terms or with reference primarily to homosexual assertiveness as if, alongside feminism, this was the sole narrative worthy of consideration. As with women, there are a range of differences, not only along social, religious, ethnic, ideological and political lines, including, in particular, in terms of married or unmarried, fathers or childless, and older or younger. The principal change in the period has been the relative decline in the authority of older males over younger and, as a central point, fathers over children. There are social variations, but this has been the key development.

BELOW: A march organized by the Women's Liberation movement in the US, 1970.

It is repeatedly unclear, and for gender and other topics, whether the emphasis should be on variations across time, between countries or within groups. Possibly the leading change has been the breakdown of a central narrative. From the mid-20th century, there was such a narrative, with rights for women an increasingly prominent part of human rights, and with both narrative and rights adopted by societies across the political spectrum from the US to the Soviet Union. This process became even more marked from the 1990s, as the American model became more prominent. However, from the 2010s, the resurgence of the authoritarian Right and, separately, of fundamentalist Islam, were linked to explicit criticism of women's freedoms as part of a more general assault on the concept of Human Rights. This was seen most explicitly in Iran, with major assaults on women dressing in a way that was even a slight variation to officially endorsed cover-up norms. Religious fundamentalism frequently involves the control of women.

BELOW: Women dressed in the hijab in Iran.

THE SEXUAL REVOLUTION

'Sexual intercourse began
In nineteenth sixty three...'

The British poet Philip Larkin was being sarcastic in his poem 'Annus Mirabilis' (1967), but he captured the sense that there was a major transformation in the 1960s. Separating childbirth from sex was central to the sexual revolution. They had never been identical, not least due to issues of infertility, age, contraception and infanticide. Nevertheless, there had been a close relationship between childbirth and sex, and this relationship had encouraged restrictive social and sexual practices, notably so for women.

The situation changed from the 1940s. In part this was due to the relaxation or fragmentation of established social and cultural mores as a consequence of political developments. These were principally as a result of World War II, but were due to postwar changes, notably the Communist takeover of China, most of Eastern Europe and a number of other states. The Communists attacked the role and influence of religious bodies and norms.

Technological change was also crucial, in the shape of the contraceptive pill as well as regulations and pricing policies that made it readily available. Approved in America

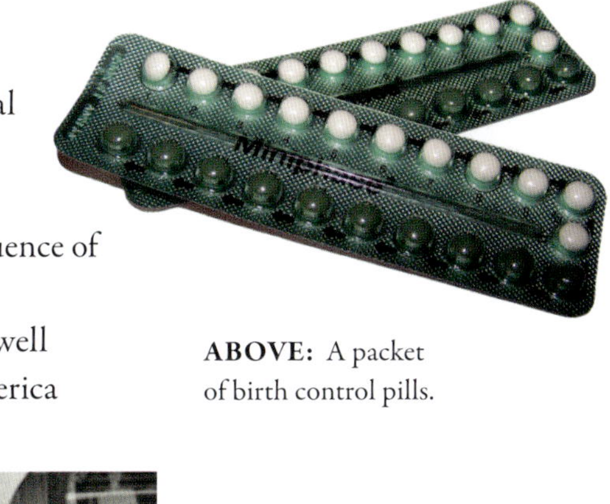

ABOVE: A packet of birth control pills.

LEFT: The no bra protest, San Francisco, 1969.

RIGHT: Betty Friedan.

in 1960, 'the pill', the term itself overshadowing all other pills, such as aspirin (which was already in widespread use), paracetamol (developed 1956) and ibuprofen (developed 1962), gave women far more control over decisions about having children. Indeed, birth rates fell. This latter change was followed by a rapid increase in the number of young women expecting to be employed at 35, so that, by 1979, the percentage of 20- and 21-year-olds doing that was 80 per cent.

Contraception as an issue was followed by abortion, with 'choice' by the woman the key demand. The feminist Betty Friedan claimed in 1969, in a speech at a conference on the liberalization of the restrictions on abortion: 'As the Negro was the invisible man, so women are the invisible people in America today... The real sexual revolution is the emergence of women from passivity.'

In 1968, censorship barriers seemed to collapse at once in print and films in both Europe and North America. Already in 1967 there were hippies, but taking the pill was still rare in 1966, branded as 'indecent', and women feared pregnancy. This changed rapidly in 1967–8.

By 2024, many societies that had previously criminalized abortion, generally due to the influence of religion, notably Catholicism, had ended these restrictions. Thus, in Portugal, after a referendum (the country's first) of 1998 had rejected legalization, a second in 2007 accepted it; while, in Ireland, a referendum of 2018 provided 66.4 per cent support for the 2019 law allowing access to abortion. Mexico followed in 2021.

Yet, about 40 per cent of women still live in states with major restrictions. In Islamic countries, only Tunisia and Turkey allow abortion. Moreover, there have been more restrictions of late in a number of countries including the US, El Salvador and Poland. In 2024, the re-criminalization of abortion was an important issue in the US election.

Separate to abortion, there was a marked drop in the birth rate in many Catholic countries, such as Portugal. This change was an aspect of a broader pattern of social change. Thus, in Portugal, over half of babies are born to parents who are not married, even if most live together. Divorce, which was legalized in 2001, now claims the majority of marriages there.

SLAVERY

Slavery took two major forms, private and public. The former is the type more commonly considered and concerns slavery to individuals or companies.

Public slavery, meanwhile, receives insufficient attention. It can be defined as control by a state, particularly over those who are imprisoned, but, in general, over the entire population. This type of enslavement was particularly present in the second half of the 20th century, with the imposition of Communist power, notably in Eastern Europe, China, North Korea, Vietnam, Laos, Cambodia and Cuba. Those imprisoned were used as forced labour, for example in canal construction in Romania, and with high death rates. This form of slavery became less common when authoritarian rule ended, but remains the case in North Korea, or, in the form of very long military conscription, Eritrea. Moreover, the use of prisoners as soldiers by Russia in Ukraine from 2022 was a deadly form of slave labour. Separately, there are still forms of private slavery.

The sight of Africans and others – for example, Sri Lankans – in open boats being intercepted by the Spanish, Italian, Australian and other navies in recent decades in an attempt to keep them from the European and Australian economies invites attention to the varied reasons, across time and national boundaries, why people are motivated by economic difficulties and political problems to move from one country to another. The current situation also underlines the continuing complexity of the relationship between Africa and the forces that drive the world economy.

The same point is pertinent for labour flows elsewhere not involving Africa – for example, from Latin America to the US – although, as from Africa, many of those who

RIGHT: A rare photograph of prisoners at work in a North Korean labour camp.

ABOVE: Cambodian police rescue women who have been trafficked.

travel are refugees as well as work-seekers. Some of those who travel north, into both Europe and the US, are seriously exploited, both as they travel and once they have arrived. The exploiters include those who transport the would-be migrants, the traffickers, and those for whom they subsequently work. The same is true of the movement from the Balkans, and elsewhere, into the European Union. People from outside the latter are frequently trafficked in, becoming illegal immigrants. Many are then used for work in which they are treated harshly and paid very little, if anything.

Prostitution is a major element of this trade. Although some women travel voluntarily, others are frequently brutalized as part of the trafficking. This is a reminder of the violence, degradation and misery that is part of the slave trade. Moreover, there is a specific sexual dimension, with modern sex slavery being a continuation of the sexual victimization of enslaved people in previous ages. A related form of exploitation is provided by the extent to which those vulnerable to slavery disproportionately include orphaned children. Technology enters the issue with the spread from the 2010s of 'virtual trafficking', where predators exploit children in video-chat rooms.

Aside from international trafficking, there is also trafficking within countries. Thus, in the US and Britain, as elsewhere, the homeless are trafficked for work on exploitative terms, in what is seen as a new form of 'rip-off work' slavery. The homeless come forward to seek work, but they are definitely exploited and thereby kept in poverty.

The exploitation seen in the West can also be found elsewhere. North Koreans who have fled into China are frequently trafficked: women are used as sex workers and shackled when not working so that they cannot escape. In 2014, there were revelations about the use of slave labour to farm and process prawns in Thailand.

ABOVE: Construction workers in Qatar. The *kafala* system gives employers a huge range of powers over the people who work for them.

Slavery today is a brutal part of an often wider range of harsh labour conditions. For the Gulf states, the key source of labour is no longer enslaved people from East Africa but nominally free workers from South Asia, who are subject to harsh controls. For example, several hundred thousand Nepalese construction workers, brought into Qatar in the 2010s to build its facilities and infrastructure for the 2022 FIFA World Cup, experienced not only 12-hour shifts, sweltering heat and often hazardous environments, resulting in high death rates, but also labour controls, frequently in the shape of the confiscation of migrant workers' passports. Pay is often withheld for months. Conditions for many workers in the Gulf region represents a form of indentured servitude or, indeed, slavery that scarcely matches free labour conditions. Similar points can be made about the women brought into the area to act as servants. Some have been mistreated. Qatar's 1.39 million migrant workers formed 94 per cent of the workforce in 2013. The sponsorship system, *kafala*, gives employers great control; they have to approve exit permits, for example. Moreover, the ultimate sanction for breach of contract is criminal detention. According to a 2014 report by N.A. Piper, a law firm commissioned by Qatar's government, this detention 'lends weight to the allegation that the *kafala* system constitutes forced labour'. Singapore's economy works in part as a result of cheap labour from India and Indonesia.

A very different form of labour that may in future be discussed in terms of slavery relates to the enhancement of robots and the addition to them of human characteristics. Herbert Simon, a pioneer in Artificial Intelligence (AI), claimed in 1964 that machines would be capable within 20 years of doing any work a human could do. These high hopes proved mistaken, as often happens with technological futurology, but the work that could be done by machines greatly expanded. Claims that machine-work might lead to a new form of slavery, however, were misplaced, as machines are not human. Instead, the comparison is more clear in regard to the use of animals to provide labour.

The extent to which the situation might change if cloning extended to humans invites speculation. A sense that modernity brought unwelcome power was captured in the arts, notably the modernization of the horror genre with a concern about zombies, the living dead, as in George A. Romero's films – for example, *Night of the Living Dead* (1968). Moreover, the idea of clones raised underground to provide perfect body parts for their donors was the theme of the movie *The Island* (2005). Such stories captured the long-standing idea that a new technology would enable humans to develop a brutalized subhuman world, and also the anxiety that such a world might be the fate of the species itself. In short, a new, more insistent slavery was outlined in the world of fiction. Linked to this were concerns about the nature of the society that might be responsible for such an outcome, concerns that refracted anxieties about changes and possible future developments in the world.

BELOW: An advertisement for George Romero's film *Night of the Living Dead*.

SOCIAL STRUCTURES

The pyramidical social structures of three classes – wealthy, middle class and working class, with the third by far the most numerous – that were dominant at the outset of our period were brought under great pressure. The working class had been divided into skilled and unskilled, but both were greatly hit by technological and economic transformations and the competitiveness born of globalization which gathered pace due to the spread of free trade from the late 1940s. The working class encompassed the poor and destitute, and it is necessary to understand the savage consequences of social structures. In the very cold winter of 1954, the French Catholic priest and founder of the charity Emmaus, Abbé Pierre appealed for help on Radio Luxembourg. 'A woman froze to death tonight at 3 am on the pavement of Sebastopol Boulevard,' he said, referring to a road in the centre of Paris. In 2018, when the populist Andrés Obrador easily won the Mexican presidency, about half of his country's population lived in poverty.

Meanwhile, the middle classes greatly expanded around the world, with the boom in office work, the expansion of state bureaucracies and employment, and the rising number of female workers – and female workers with good salaries – which ensured dual-income couples. However, the middle classes found it difficult to sustain their ambitions, as divisions opened within them, in part due to technological and economic transformations and the competitiveness born of globalization.

ABOVE: Havana, Cuba. The infrastructure in the centre of the city gradually crumbled as wealthy élites fled to the suburbs.

Both capital and income were generally distributed in very inegalitarian ways, as were pension payments and housing, the last leading to social differentiation. Thus, in many Latin American cities, the wealthy moved to newbuild suburbs with running water, while there could be a crumbling of buildings and infrastructure in increasingly poor centres, as in Havana. There, and elsewhere, the wealthy can respond to climate warming by the use of air-conditioned houses, offices and cars, but the poor have no such remedy. Indeed, the tin roofs widely used by the poor lead to greater exposure to the heat.

In part to ensure that the working class did not turn to political extremes, governments sought to counter these differences by social welfare, economic protection and redistributive taxation. These policies provided a basis for political alignments such as Christian Democracy in Western Europe and Socialism. However, the results of both policies and politics helped ensure differences in social attitudes and conditions between countries.

RIGHT: Fulgencio Batista.

The state of economies was crucial not only to providing the necessary domestic demand to sustain activity, investment and productivity, but also to ensuring a significant middle class hopefully able to encourage consensual politics. In many countries, however, both elements were missing, and, often against a background of corruption and/or criminality, politics was in tension between populists, who did not understand economics, and élites only mindful of their own interests. At the same time, governmental mechanisms themselves were employed for 'state capture' by private interest groups, such as businesses, who bought influence in government and co-opted public officials for their own personal benefits – most notably in the case of South Africa, where the Gupta family exercised an astonishing degree of influence over government policy until 2018. In turn, governments used their bureaucracies to provide jobs that secured support for the system, as in India or Spain.

ABOVE: Batista's golden telephone, a symbol of corruption.

As an aspect of these equations, the nature of government can vary greatly, with criminality to the fore in some countries, notably as a particularly malign form of 'state capture'. Thus, there can be linkages, as with Guinea–Bissau, to the money made by the drug trade. Fulgencio Batista, who ran Cuba in 1952–9 after a coup, co-operated with US Mafia gangsters, taking a cut from the casinos they built and ran in Havana. He was overthrown by Fidel Castro in 1959.

LEFT: Ripped jeans – a new fashion of the 2010s.

As part of this greater variety of circumstances, different social trends co-existed. Thus, at the same time as division between social groups, there was an increased casualization of society across most of the world. The decline of formality in all respects was a major feature of the West, notably in dress. The visual identifiers of class, position and status all became much less common, for example men and women wearing hats and gloves, and men wearing hats, stiff collars, and, later, ties. For men, dark clothes were replaced by lighter colours, while shoes became more casual.

In place of clothes and shoes that were mended, the norm in the 1950s, came 'disposable fashion'. This change came most rapidly in the West, especially among the young from the 1960s, but was readily apparent in urban China by the 2010s. The fashion among young

Western women (and, less commonly, men) in the 2010s for trousers with holes in them, and increasingly large holes, was a clear instance of a non-utilitarian choice that appeared almost wilfully negligent at the individual level, a rejection of staying warm and not wasting resources. These holes were deliberately produced.

Means of address, both verbally and in correspondence, also changed. There was an increased use of first names; and distinguishing signifiers were lost, for example for unmarried and married women and for widows. More generally, writing conventions altered greatly. Furthermore, gender stereotypes were rapidly affected, at least in the West, from the 2010s by increased discussion of changing gender.

At the same time, change varied between societies, and politics played a role. Thus, in China, the Communists who gained power in 1949 particularly pushed changes in appearance and address as aspects of modernization, and this was taken even further during the 'Cultural Revolution' of the late 1960s, which was a classic instance of modernization as repression. In Japan, in contrast, there was a much greater continual deference to age, which also tended to be the pattern in Islamic societies.

Looking to the future, robotic manufacturing and AI systems will transform the world of work, thus affecting the respective appeal of types of job. In so far as employment patterns affect social structures, this will contribute to a sense of instability.

BELOW: Red Guards during the Cultural Revolution in China, 1966.

SOCIAL MODELS: THE US

US, Chinese and European social models were the most influential. From 1945 to 1973, there was what would subsequently be termed the 'Long Boom', a rapid economic development, quantitative and qualitative, in scale and sophistication, in which the US was dominant. This created a society of mass affluence, positive images of which were spread by advertising, news magazines, television and films, in all of which the US dominated the West. Companies such as Coca-Cola, Ford and Hoover were brands across the West and their names would become synonymous with the products they made.

ABOVE: President Lyndon Johnson signs the Civil Rights Act on 2 July 1964. Martin Luther King can be seen immediately behind him.

In the 1950s and 1960s, 83 per cent of US population growth took place in the suburbs, and a consumerism that centred on the car flourished. The detective novelist Raymond Chandler, in his novel *The Little Sister* (1949), referred to Dad 'in the fancy suburbs thinking he is high class because he has a three-car garage'. Prosperity for working class and middle class alike was seen as central to US stability. The poor were left in what became the 'inner cities', a term associated with poverty, crime and decay.

In turn, there was an attempt in the US to encompass all in the new benefit, with the Supreme Court's 1954 unanimous decision that segregation in public schools must be ended. This was followed by the Civil Rights Act of 1964, passed with President Lyndon Johnson's eager support and, thanks to Republican Congressional backing, prohibiting employment discrimination on the basis of gender, race and religion.

Education was funded to help ensure social mobility. This was a highpoint of American progressivism, yet also in line with the policies of the Republican Eisenhower presidency of 1953–61 which did not dismantle the earlier Democrat-created New Deal but, instead, expanded social security. This was a liberal conservatism.

The progressive image of society, however, was hit hard from the late 1960s by political contention, economic difficulties and a social fissiparousness which saw at the same time the rise of drug culture, a key element of the counterculture, and, conversely, a new strength for Protestant Evangelicalism. The bitterly contested presidential election of 1968 was a product of this division. It was won by the Republican, Richard Nixon. In turn, Ronald Reagan, who won the 1980 election, was an open opponent of government as a solution, and very much supported a low-tax economy.

Most Americans were far from extreme, and, alongside the political froth, there was a degree of agreed social progressivism, as with measures to extend rights for women, notably the Lilly Ledbetter Pay Act of 2009. Despite predictions about social collapse, for example because of pre-marital sex and divorce, there was a general desire for stable relationships, and, as elsewhere, divorces very commonly led to remarriages. Society was reshaped, with a differing mix of conformism and individualism to that in the 1950s.

However, alongside the boom of the 1990s, economic globalization hit much traditional manufacturing. This created a new pool of workers and former workers who were angry and worried, helping Donald Trump to victory in the US presidential election of 2016, although he gained the minority of the votes: 63 million (46 per cent of the vote), compared to 66 million (49 per cent) for Hillary Clinton. Trump won 'Rust

BELOW: Donald Trump campaigning in the 2016 election.

WALLS

Walls to separate countries and social systems came to the fore with the Berlin Wall of 1961–89 intended to keep people in, and the comparable North Korean system. There was also pressure to keep immigrants out, notably the wall built by Donald Trump for the Mexican border and the defences of the Channel Tunnel near Calais. Governmental centres were frequently defended against possible domestic discontent, and, increasingly, against terrorism. There was also the defence against the fear of crime represented by gated communities, which became more frequent, notably in the US.

ABOVE: Soldiers at work constructing the Berlin Wall, August 1961.

Belt' swing states, notably Michigan, Ohio, Pennsylvania and Wisconsin, where the economic globalization that had gutted manufacturing was rejected. He did so again in 2024.

The inegalitarian nature of American society is abundantly shown in the response to calamities. Thus, in Hurricane Katrina in 2006, the poor, mostly Black population of east New Orleans found their homes flooded, lacked insurance, and many left. Again, in 2020–2, the Black population of Louisiana were particularly hit by Covid, in large part due to poverty, less access to healthcare and a higher rate of underlying health problems, notably diabetes, hypertension and heart disease. These and other issues of US poverty were widely discussed in the media.

ABOVE: A Black Lives Matter protest in New York, June 2020.

Race played a significant role in US society, but also, in some respects, a decreasing one, as in less discrimination in mortgage lending than in the past. As an instance of the linkage of themes in different chapters, in this case chapter 4, it was suggested in 2022 that this owed something to the automated processing of mortgage applications, as the machines had no innate capacity for racial bias.

At the same time as its problems, the US remained the prime destination for migrants, from the richest to the poorest, which was a consistent feature from the 1950s to the 2020s. Furthermore, alongside the brutal intolerance seen with the killing by a white policeman of the unarmed George Floyd in Minneapolis in 2020, which launched the 'Black Lives Matter' movement, that year more than 8 per cent of babies were mixed heritage and one in three couples meeting online were of different heritage. There was also a widely diffused patriotism that encompassed Blacks and whites.

SOCIAL MODELS: CHINA

China has been the great enigma in recent decades. Communist capitalism, referred to in China as a 'Socialist market economy', had an unclear meaning, and was subject to political changes. This was seen in different versions of policy under Mao Zedong, the country's leader from 1949 to 1976, and further variations between the periods of dominance by later leaders. Thus, there was a tightening of governmental control under President Xi Jinping, paramount leader from 2012 and president from 2013, as part of his attempt to use centralization as a means to direct and strengthen the state.

At the same time, there has been a basic consistency in the post-Mao period, notably with the overcoming of the radicals who tried to carry on his stance. Mao pressed for an egalitarian society, but the subsequent social practice has been one of greater differences in capital and income; a high rate of geographical mobility from countryside to cities; a continued bar on religious commitment, one seen in particular in opposition to what

LEFT: Mao Zedong.

RIGHT: Xi Jinping.

is regarded potentially as separatism in Xinjiang (Islam) and Tibet (Buddhism); and a continued embrace of an ideology of disciplined opportunity, notably for the poor and for women. There has been a major expansion of the middle class since Mao, but much of its wealth has been surreptitiously moved abroad due to concern about possible government expropriation. Moreover, with post-Maoist economic growth, China became a society of great inequality, not on the scale of India, but, nevertheless, an inequality that contrasted significantly with its public ideology. This helped fire up Xi's campaign against corruption, a campaign that also served to consolidate his political position.

China's demographic structure, notably an ageing population, alongside a heavy debt burden, encouraged scepticism in the early 2020s that it could sustain economic growth rates. Indeed, they fell while unemployment rose, notably among the young, especially in 2024, which further lessened the appeal of having children. The Chinese model at the same time, despite recent problems, is seen as very attractive to governments wary of

Western liberalism, human rights and economic and fiscal policies, including free trade. Most notably, these governments include authoritarian states allied with China. Yet, in addition, Chinese economic growth, to become the world's second largest economy, has also made aspects of its model appear attractive more widely.

Furthermore, China has deliberately set out to use trade, aid and propaganda to spread its model, both economic and political, as an alternative to that of the US. Its essential argument is that social cohesion and political harmony are key enablers of growth. In practice, they can be difficult to reproduce, as such cohesion and harmony are generally imposed, rather than organic, however much it is attractive to assume the alternative.

In the early 2020s, China's economy looked set to overtake that of the US in the foreseeable future; but, at the same time, that would have produced a very different social structure. In part, this is because aggregate (overall) economic strength was not the same as per capita (individual), and in the latter China greatly lags behind the US, with many Chinese poor and with social assistance limited. Separately, despite the very major disruptions of Communism and mass urbanization, the Chinese social model is also different to that of the US in that to a degree it takes forward traditional Chinese communal expectations.

BELOW: Yantian Port at Shenzhen – both a driver and a symbol of China's economic growth.

SOCIAL MODELS: EUROPE

To outsiders, there is a European social model, one of state support for social services funded by high taxation. The more conservative anti-statist right-wing parties in Europe were discredited by having been linked with the Hitlerian system, and, in their place, from the late 1940s, in Italy, West Germany, the Low Countries and France, Christian Democratic governments of one type or another provided tax-funded social care. They were able to do so due to the economic expansion of the 'Long Boom'. Scandinavian countries, which were more left-wing, were traditionally held to epitomize this welfarist approach in Western Europe, while Britain was regarded as being the most prone to a low taxation alternative, notably under and after Mrs Thatcher's Conservative administration of 1979–90. In both Western Europe and Britain, there was an Americanization of society and culture which was very much seen in a focus on consumerism.

There was also the obvious addition of the Eastern European Communist countries that offered cradle-to-grave care (and state control). In Spain and Portugal, until the 1970s, there were authoritarian right-wing governments which had a conservative Catholic authoritarian-communitarian approach, one similar in many respects to Ireland.

Christian Democratic and Socialist approaches were put under pressure in the 1970s as economic problems removed the fiscal underpinnings of social welfare systems. Even more dramatically, the fall of Eastern European Communism in 1989–91 was a major blow to

RIGHT: The Christian Democrats' conference, May 1976, Hannover, Germany.

ABOVE: A strike against pension reform in Orléans, France, October 2010.

established assumptions. Successive economic and fiscal crises ensured pressure to rein in expenditure, notably from the 1990s, while there were attempts in Eastern Europe and Scandinavia (especially Finland and Sweden) to lessen state provision.

In contrast, the state sector and state provision have remained very strong in some countries, for example France, where, in 2006, five million workers, about a quarter of the workforce, were in the public sector. Attempts there to lessen the very generous nature of pension provision led to angry responses, including debilitating strikes in 2007 and 2010.

Consumerism with security is the political goal for many, not least in the shape of generous pensions that cannot be afforded, as in Italy. The extent to which economic growth and/or fiscal loosening would provide for this illusion was extensively tested but led to very high debt-to-GDP ratios, as in Greece, Italy and Britain. The unwillingness to accept the fiscal weakness of social aspirations proved an important aspect of politics.

More seriously, there was a generational bias, with social provision most helpful to the elderly, notably in terms of pensions and health expenditure, and least so to the working young who are expected to pay, through higher taxation, for this provision. The sustainability of this intergenerational bargain was further lessened by the above-average cost of property for new entrants to the housing market, such that a high percentage of young workers still lived with their parents, as in Italy, while others found much of their income absorbed by rent, indeed a higher percentage than in the 1950s. The European social model, strong in the 1950s and 1960s, appears increasingly under pressure.

RELIGION

On the model of that at Rio de Janeiro built from 1922 to 1931, a large statue of Christ, finished in 1958 shortly before Fidel Castro seized power, continues to overlook Communist Havana. Misleadingly treated in the late 20th century as a somewhat redundant force, notably by progressives in Communist societies and the West, as well as in some 'non-aligned' countries, there has been a major re-evaluation of the significance of religion since the fall of Communism in Eastern Europe in 1989–91 revealed the strength of popular commitment there. There are many indications of such commitment. In 2020, the attempt in Nicaragua to ignore the Covid-19 epidemic was widely attributed to Rosario Murillo, the vice-president (and wife of Daniel Ortega, the president), a mystic who wore turquoise rings on every finger to ward off evil spirits.

ABOVE: The statue of Christ overlooking Havana, completed in 1958.

More centrally, the significance of Islam as a political force, a significance increasingly apparent from the Iranian Revolution of 1978–9, encouraged a focus on religion. So did President Putin's strong alliance with the Russian Orthodox Church, which is totally different to the situation under Soviet Communism, when state atheism was to the fore. Putin and the Orthodox Church strengthened their alliance, reminiscent of pre-Communist Russia, when he attacked Ukraine in 2022. In the US, Protestant Evangelicalism became more significant for the Republican Party as it pivoted from the 1980s increasingly to become a party that dominated the South and emphasized a moral conservatism. In turn, the Democrats were identified with a looser alignment with organized religion. At the same time, religion became more diverse and less denominational in the US. Helped greatly by Hispanic immigration, Catholics became more important.

Israel operated as a Jewish state, but with the Orthodox minority unwilling to accept aspects of citizenship, notably conscription. In 2024, the country's Supreme Court declared that government-subsidised religious seminaries must provide conscripts.

Catholicism itself became less centralized with popes finding their authority increasingly challenged. Pius XII, John XXIII and Paul VI had had different emphases, but their dominance, not least that of John XXIII as a reformer and Paul VI as a consolidator, was clearer than that of John Paul II, Benedict XVI and, in particular, Francis, who came to power in 2013. These last three, the first two conservative and the third more of a reformer, were not Italians, being Polish, German and Argentinian respectively. John Paul II played a major role in focusing attention on the problems of Communist control of Eastern Europe and was particularly

THE SECOND VATICAN COUNCIL, 1962–5

The most recent ecumenical (i.e., worldwide) Council of the Catholic Church, informally known as Vatican II, was designed to complete the First Council (held in 1869–70) and to address the needs of the contemporary world. Called by Pope John XXII, and continued by Paul VI, who felt the Church needed updating, the Council sought to encourage the participation of the laity by renewing the liturgy, notably by using native languages, a decision promulgated in 1963. Relations with other Christian denominations were approved, as were interfaith dialogues with other belief systems. Traditionalist Catholics were unhappy and some criticized Vatican II. Reformers subsequently argued that 'the spirit of Vatican II' needed to illuminate decisions.

ABOVE: The Second Vatican Council.

influential in Poland, where his visits in 1979, 1983 and 1987 represented a challenge to official ideology. But he was criticized by reformers for his conservatism and had to confront the increasingly fissiparous character of the Catholic Church. On his 1991 visit to Poland he strongly criticized abortion.

The discussion so far in this section is of different phenomena in contrasting political contexts. That does not allow for the importance of religious themes, formal or informal, in helping many individuals and communities find and renew faith, make sense of their lives and define their values. Yet, alongside this emphasis on faith, there are also wider

LEFT: Pope John Paul II in 1981.

CANONIZATION

A papal prerogative in the Catholic Church, the canonization of saints was pushed to a new level under John Paul II (r.1978–2005), who, having canonized 482 saints, was himself canonized in 2014. In comparison, Pius XII (r.1939–58) canonized 36, John XXIII (r.1958–63) ten, Paul VI (r.1963–78) 85, John Paul I (r.1978) none, and Benedict XVI (r.2005–13) 45.

RIGHT: Osama bin Laden holds an assault rifle in a recruitment video for the fundamentalist terrorist group al-Qaeda.

social implications. Thus, the extent to which the religious tend to have more children than the less or non-religious is highly significant, as is the degree to which Europe, where religious commitment is in decline, is seeing a fall in population. Migration helps ensure that it is often difficult to separate religion from ethnicity in themes of identity, assertion and discrimination. This is compounded when groups oppose intermarriage with those from other groups.

The idea of a 'clash between civilizations' was advanced in the 1990s, notably by the American political scientist Samuel P. Huntington, as a way to try to explain international relations after the Cold War ended with the fall of Soviet Communism. This idea was strengthened when in 2001 al-Qaeda, a fundamentalist Muslim group, launched deadly terrorist attacks on New York and Washington DC. The US response, a 'War on Terror', pitched the country and its allies and ideology against radical Islam. In doing so, it underplayed many other elements in international relations, including rivalries within the blocs supposedly present in the 'clash between civilizations'.

Within states, there were also clashes between religious groups; although that presentation minimized the degree to which one of the prime tensions was within such groups, and notably so between the fervent and the less committed. That is not the sole division in religiosity, but is the one that is most politically potent.

In France in 1984, cultural conservatism was marked in the form of major demonstrations, including one where a million people in Paris protested against the Socialist government's attempt to cut subsidies to private Catholic schools. This was correctly seen as motivated by a desire for secularization. The legislation was withdrawn. Such protests tend to be ignored in an account centred on progressive attitudes and radical politics.

There are also states where atheism is pursued, for example China and North Korea, with the former, in seeking to expunge religious practice, being particularly harsh on Islam from the 2010s, notably in the Xinjiang region. Many minarets and mosque domes have been demolished, and children discouraged from attending mosques.

In other states, notably Japan, South Korea, and those in Western Europe, Australasia and North America, religious practices are less prominent than in the 1950s, and both individualism and secularization far more common since the 1960s. Attendance at church has fallen, notably so among the young. Twenty per cent of German Catholics abandoned the Church between 2000 and 2020. Religious observance is episodic. The rate of infant baptisms in Britain fell from 67 per cent in the 1950s to 15.3 in the 2010s, while, by 2009, a majority described themselves as having no religion.

More generally, in most Western countries religion has been and is still being supplanted by growing 'scientism' and new-age metaphysics, as well as a general indifference to anything beyond individualistic materialism. Even in the US, while the percentage of white Protestants identifying as Evangelical rose from 53 in 2009 to 56 in 2019, that of white Evangelicals in the population as a whole fell from 20 to 16, and those who described themselves as Christians from 77 to 65. Black churches frequently had largely, or exclusively, Black congregations and particular types of religious practice, but there is a common Christian creed.

Looking forward, the recent overtaking of China by India as the world's most populous country will probably further ensure that religion remains crucial to the identity, mores and practices of many, even if strong religious commitment as a percentage of the world's population continues to be affected by the nature of life in multi-religious countries and by aspects of secularization. On the other hand, states with one established faith are more likely to remain centres of religious practice, and this will be especially true of Islam. Islamic states tend to have limited tolerance for other religions.

Latin America and sub-Saharan Africa will be key areas for understanding the future of religious practice, not least due to the high rate of population growth in the latter. Competition between Christianity and Islam is particularly intense in Nigeria and Sudan. In contrast, in Latin America the dominant Catholicism is under pressure, not least in Brazil, from Protestant sects.

More generally, the ratios of young and old will be important to the trajectories of religious practice around the world. Furthermore, despite new cults and sects, for example the South Korean cult of the Reverend Moon, there is no sign that the period will see the establishment of a major new religion.

RELIGION, RACE AND HOPE

Martin Luther King Jr., a Baptist minister and First President of the Southern Christian Leadership Conference, used religious language in 1963 in a powerful speech in front of the Memorial to President Abraham Lincoln in Washington DC, a speech made more influential by the publicity it received:

'the life of the Negro is still sadly crippled by the manacles of segregation and the chains of discrimination.... We cannot be satisfied as long as the Negro's basic mobility is from a smaller ghetto to a larger one.... I have a dream that one day even the state of Mississippi, a desert state sweltering with the heat of injustice and oppression, will be transformed into an oasis of freedom and justice.'

ETHNICITY

Ethnicity as a definition of identity became more pronounced when empires were replaced by nation-states, giving a new burst to nationalism. This was a major trend from the late 1940s to the early 1990s, with particular episodes of change in the late 1940s, 1960s, mid-1970s and early 1990s. Decolonization was therefore crucial to the presentation of ethnicity. There were states where national identities were consciously created in an attempt to supersede ethnic ones, as with Nigeria, Sudan, and in post-apartheid South Africa; and others where ethnic identification became stronger with independence, for example Poland after the end of Soviet control and, with it, of Communist ideology. As independent, however, the former category of state proved unable to sustain national identities, and Nigeria and Sudan succumbed to civil war, while South Africa found it difficult to overcome an ethnic basis for loyalty aside from the nation state, in particular with Zulus in Natal.

New states were generally opposed to the internationalisms they had overthrown, notably Western and Soviet imperialisms. This meant trouble for ethnic and religious minorities that had frequently enjoyed favour or at least safety from these imperialisms, such as Copts in Egypt, Jews in Arab countries, for example Algeria, and Russians in parts of the Soviet Union. From the outset, the degree to which the reality of new states matched

RIGHT: Hindu worshippers in the Ganges River, 2019.

ABOVE: Syrian refugees arrive at the island of Lesbos, Greece, in 2015.

the prohibition of ethnic and religious discrimination proclaimed in most of their constitutions varied greatly, and there was often active discrimination against minorities. This led Jews to flee Arab states.

Furthermore, subsequent concern about immigration and, separately, political changes, could lead to a sharpening of themes of ethnic and/or religious discrimination. Sometimes, these changes have been linked to the fall of the governing party that had won independence, as in India, in the shape of Hindu nationalism, with the end of government by the Congress Party linked to the rival BJP's endorsement of such nationalism.

There has been less of a sharpening of ethnic identity in the US, China or Japan, although in the US racial tension played a generally unspoken role in domestic politics. Immigration took a significant role in the 2024 presidential election campaign, with 'control over the border' an issue driven by the official estimate of illegal entries under the Biden presidency in 2021–4 as more than seven million, and with an increasing percentage of them coming not from Mexico and Central America (90 per cent in 2020, 50 per cent in 2023), and thus linking into existing American Hispanic communities, but, instead, from Africa, the Middle East and Asia.

ABOVE: South African workers on their way to work in a segregated township near Johannesburg, 1962.

APARTHEID (APARTNESS)

This policy was introduced by South Africa's Nationalist Party elected in 1948, which enforced racial segregation. The 1950 Immorality Act declared sexual relations between all races illegal. The 1950 Group Areas Act limited to particular areas the races classified by the 1950 Population Registration Act. Other legislation limited Black trade unions and segregated public places such as railway stations and public toilets. Education became highly discriminatory, and 'Bantu homelands' designed to keep Blacks in rural areas were established by the Promotion of Bantu Self Government Act of 1959.

Dissent was punished, notably by the Suppression of Communism Act of 1950. Protests and opposition, which became more of a factor from the 1960s, were repressed, not least under the state of emergency declared in 1960, the 1962 Sabotage Act, and the 1967 Terrorism Act.

In European countries, success in the integration of immigrants varies greatly, and is, conversely, related in part to the extent to which ethnic-religious attitudes to nationhood are to the fore, as in Hungary and Poland. Providing yet another link between sections, the international and civil warfare of the 2010s and 2020s (see pages 203–4) helped produce an increase in migration. Thus, the bitter civil war in Syria contributed directly to an immigration crisis in Europe in 2015, with border defences hastily erected, as by Hungary. Ironically, immigration had been far less of an issue during the Cold War, when borders had been militarized and movement more difficult.

In Latin America, there could be significant opposition to immigration, as in the Dominican Republic where there had been long-standing, and often violent, hostility to immigration from Haiti. This opposition returned to play a significant role in the 2024 election at a time of great political and economic difficulties in Haiti.

There is also the question of the attitude to the host society, its values and law, by immigrant groups. This can be easier in some states than others, and has caused particular issues in France and Sweden, while being far less of a problem in the US, where assimilation has proved less difficult. Lawlessness in Sweden, the Netherlands and more generally is blamed on immigrant groups, although most immigrants are far from lawless.

In the Pacific from the 1990s, as a result of many greater legal rights for indigenous citizens, many part-indigenous citizens, claiming, for example, one-eighth or one-sixteenth so-called 'native' ancestry, now associate themselves totally with a suddenly esteemed ethnic group, often for personal financial benefits. This is particularly evident among Māoris and Hawaiians, and it is unclear in this context what precisely 'ethnic identity' means. It is clearly related to opposition to colonialism.

IDENTITIES

The complexities and tensions focused on defining identities and then pursuing these identities were the cause of much division around the world. Gender, nationality, ethnicity, class, age and sexual orientation were all key means of identification; although what that could mean varied and was contested. Sexual orientation was an important issue to many in the West, but far less so in China and the Islamic world. In the West, class became less significant from the 1990s, as the traditional working-class agendas of left-wing parties and commentators changed considerably. With the current 'identity' issues dominated by the middle classes, in turn, many of the working class moved to support conservative movements, as in the US, Britain and France, and notably so if the movement was populist.

In particular countries, there were also more specific identities that could have considerable weight, for example what was bound up in the distinction between secular and religious Jews in Israel and, separately, between Mizrahim (Jews from Arab lands) and Ashkenazi (Jews from Europe). As so often, there were overlaps with other categories, the Mizrahim being poorer and having few links to the levers of power.

ABOVE: A rally of BJP supporters, 2021.

In India, the world's most populous country, an important identity was that of caste, a form of hereditary social stratification linked to racial purity, which to outsiders could appear to be a type of racism. The lower castes were the vast majority and were very deprived, living in different housing and streets, and separated by discriminatory and exclusionary practices, as in marriage arrangements. There was also a political dimension, with the opposition Congress Party supporters of the interests of the Dalits, formerly the Untouchables. This was a stance deplored by Prime Minister Modi, notably in 2024, as a way to divide Hindus to the benefit of Muslims, whom he presented as unloyal Indians (see pages 222–3). Census findings released in 2023 for the state of Bihar, show that of its 130 million inhabitants, only 15 per cent were from the 'forward' castes, 20 per cent were Dalits, and 63 per cent were from castes considered 'Other Backward Castes' or 'Extremely Backward Castes'. Because in theory Dalits are protected by law, the situation is different to the racial zoning seen in much of the US South into the second half of the 20th century to the detriment of that country's Blacks (see pages 106–9). However, the distinction might not have meant much to those involved. There has been much unpunished crime, including violent crime, by upper-caste Hindus at the expense of 'backward' castes.

CIVIL RIGHTS MOVEMENTS

Racism, the culture of claimed superiority by one racial group, and the politics of the exclusion and suppression of others, had been fundamental to the German and Japanese imperialisms defeated in World War II, and also central to the empires that ended over the subsequent three decades. Racism, moreover, was seen in domestic politics, most clearly in the apartheid system of white-run South Africa and in the comparable theme of separate development in the US South.

ABOVE: Nelson Mandela.

The nature of Civil Rights movements varied depending on domestic and international contexts, the latter that of foreign support or opposition for the government, the former in part the character of discrimination and the degree of force behind it. In South Africa, apartheid, a malign instance of 1960s' values, was developed to keep power from the majority Black community and to entrench a repressive white supremacism that was ready to use violence, as with the Sharpeville massacre of 1960 in which 69 people were killed by the police. Anti-apartheid activists such as Nelson Mandela (1918–2013) were harshly imprisoned, in his case from 1962 to 1990, or killed, as with Steve Biko (1946–77), a key figure in the Black Consciousness movement.

Apartheid was opposed from within South Africa, but a growing hostility in the international response, notably by the US, a former supporter of South Africa, once the Cold War was over, proved more important. Apartheid ended in 1994. There was no comparable

RIGHT: A protest against apartheid, 1961.

LEFT: Martin Luther King and Malcolm X, 1965.

international pressure to help human rights under Communist rule, or the position of indigenous populations in Australia and Canada.

In the US South, there was no external intervention, although there was concern in the 1950s and 1960s in government circles that the issue might become part of the Cold War, with the Soviet Union exploiting Black anger. Instead, desegregation in the South arose from Black direct action, with charismatic leaders, notably Martin Luther King (1929–68), and from political action in Washington DC.

There was considerable resistance to Civil Rights. Revisiting Alabama in 2005, Condoleezza Rice, the first Black Secretary of State, declared, 'I remember a place called Bombingham [sic for Birmingham], where I witnessed the denial of democracy in America and where Blacks were terrorized by rebel yells and nightriders.' In this, she was referencing a racist bombing of 1963 that killed four Black girls. The willingness of local and state bodies, such as the Birmingham police in 1963, violently to suppress attempts to protest about segregation, and to do so in the full view of the national media, now more immediate and

ABOVE: A Greyhound bus carrying Black and White Freedom Riders was attacked by a white mob outside Anniston, Alabama, in 1961.

potent due to television news, ensured pressure for federal intervention, which in fact was one of the main goals of anti-segregationist activism. Indeed, Federal Marshals were dispatched to the South, while National Guardsmen were federalized to end state control over them. Protests involving buses and facilities at bus terminals, mounted by 'freedom riders', were particularly effective in encouraging federal intervention as the regulation of interstate travel was a federal matter.

The range of discrimination and the determination for reform were such that success for reform in one sphere was followed by pressure in others. Demands for an end to methods used to prevent Blacks from voting led to demonstrations and a violent response, most clearly in Selma in 1965, and also to the passing that year of a Voting Rights Act that allowed many Blacks to register to vote, thus helping change the nature of the Democratic Party in the South. President Lyndon Johnson (r.1963–9) strongly backed desegregation.

Violent episodes in the South might suggest that the issue was a sectional one, but there was also to be significant opposition outside the South to school and workplace desegregation, for example in Boston to the busing of pupils to end school segregation there. Although the reasons varied, and more radical Black activism by leaders such as Malcolm X (1925–65) played a role, there were also large-scale riots in Black neighbourhoods in cities outside the South. This was particularly so in Los Angeles in 1965, Detroit and Newark in

1967, and Washington DC in 1968, but also in Atlanta, Chicago, Cleveland, Tampa and many other cities. The rioting was suppressed or just ran out of steam, but much damage was done. Most Blacks in the urban ghettos were stuck in poor housing, and their areas were generally short-changed in terms of metropolitan and state expenditure on infrastructure, as well as on new industrial and retail investment. Many of the riots reflected a particular sense that there was police oppression of Blacks, which was frequently the case.

More than federal action and Black activism were involved in the changing position of Blacks. The degree to which the South was integrating with the national economy, which was dominated by Northern markets, manufacturing and finance, was also important. It created a sense of opportunity, particularly in such 'New South' centres as Atlanta and Dallas. As with gay and lesbian rights in the early 21st century, national employers were far less prone to adopt segregationist practices than local or regional counterparts. The Black middle class expanded, in part thanks to public hires, but also due to changes in corporate America; although, proportionately, more Blacks than whites lived in poverty, and that remains the case.

More recent human rights movements have ranged widely in character and context. Some movements have faced repression, for example liberals in Iran, who were very brutally treated in 2009 when complaining about electoral fraud, and also democrats in Hong Kong. Others have attracted greater prominence, for example the 'Black Lives Matter' and 'Me Too' movements that spread from the US, but have not faced repression, instead being greatly supported by many institutions in the West. To a degree, the language of civil rights and human rights became so widely employed by the 2020s as to lose their particular value. So also with terms such as genocide.

LEFT: The March on Washington, 1963.

HOMOSEXUALITY

The criminalization of homosexuality was an important aspect of strong state control over sexuality at the beginning of our period. This criminalization brought together a number of concerns, religious, eugenicist, military (a key element given conscription) and social. It was increasingly challenged from the 1960s by a gay rights movement that had considerable traction in Europe and the US, but far less so in the Islamic world, Russia, sub-Saharan Africa and Latin America. Indeed, there was often active hostility in these countries, as well as legal discrimination, as in Uganda, although the end of apartheid in South Africa in 1994 led to a more tolerant attitude. Moreover, homosexual sex was decriminalized in Botswana in 2019 and Mauritius in 2023.

ABOVE: A gay rights demonstration in the USA, 1970s.

Presenting homosexuality as normal, and as deserving equal treatment with heterosexuality, the gay rights movement led to social and legal changes in the West. Change was often supported by the Left, notably in Catholic countries. Thus, in France, the Socialist government of François Mitterrand, which gained power in 1981, decriminalized homosexual acts, while the Socialist government of François Hollande legalized homosexual marriage in 2013. In West Germany, the right-wing and Catholic-leaning Christian Democratic Union opposed homosexual rights, but a Social Democratic Party government legalized it in 1969, and the age of consent was equalized with that for heterosexuals in unified Germany in 1994. In Italy, the Catholic Church was hostile to government support for homosexual civil partnerships. In Protestant Britain, the prohibition on adult homosexual sex was lifted in 1967, and the Marriage (Same Sex) Bill was passed by Parliament in 2013, with the first same-sex marriages following in 2014. In the US, Republicans are more opposed to homosexual marriage than Democrats. The acceptability of homosexuality was and is in part related to the current political narrative, being more open and accepted in many countries in the 1970s, less so in the 1980s, and again very much the case now.

Liberalization for homosexuals was followed by the same for lesbians, and by greater

ABOVE: Demonstrators in Minnesota in 2013 on same-sex marriage.

tolerance for bisexuality. In 2016, the *Oxford English Dictionary* added the words 'gender fluid' to describe a person who does not identify with a single fixed gender, a term first recorded in 1987. Language played a part in challenging norms and proposing new ones, just as pejorative language was employed by those opposed to liberalization.

In turn, although the issue was not identical, changing gender became both a practice and highly contentious. Again, there was a political dimension, with the Left tending, as in Britain, to be more supportive of 'trans' (transexual) issues, while conservatives were more cautious. The degree to which the process of 'gender reassignment' required medical approval was divisive. The process brought together, in an uneasy relationship, legal, medical, political and technological aspects.

This was rejected by the governments of many states, notably in the Islamic world and Africa, the latter causing tensions within Christian churches, particularly the Anglican communion. President Putin of Russia offered a particularly hostile characterization of the West in terms of its acceptance of sexual fluidity and gender reassignment. This response was a reminder of the absence of shared values in the world, including at the official level, but not only there.

In cultural terms, as well as their social counterparts, there was the issue of how far identity was a matter of self-identification and, in contrast, the degree to which there was an inherent reality, as in sex-linked chromosomes. There were also differing individual communal, political and national ideas of what tolerance and acceptability meant, and, over this particular issue, many feminists opposed the idea that being a woman was simply a matter of identification. There were also frequently contrasting assumptions by age-group. That the issue was largely a new one underlined the rate of social change, the complexities of social categorization, and the tensions within cultures.

4 Technologies

Technological developments since 1950 have delivered repeated surprises, most impressively perhaps when humans landed on the Moon in 1969.

This embodied the growing belief throughout the century in progress and indeed perfectibility, of technology as the enabler of the future. Rather than the *mechanization* of life, there was a machinization, with machines assuming an ever greater importance. This, though, brought problems, or at least anxieties about machines becoming too powerful and/or concerning the heartlessness of scientific solutions. Differing attitudes to nuclear power and, separately, abortion were symptomatic of the extent to which technology appeared increasingly powerful but also far from value-free. Environmentalism frequently focused on hostility to technological use.

One thing to bear in mind for our period is that science and technology did not all advance at the same pace and at the same rate. This chapter reflects that. It also recognizes that cutting-edge technologies, while important, should not be the primary focus and that there were technologies that were more effective, easily introduced and widespread, for example shipping containers or particular types of drugs. The most important technologies were those that led to the 'Green Revolution' in agriculture.

SCIENCE

The 'Green Revolution' reflected the applicability of science, in this case the selective breeding of plant strains able to handle the difficulties of particular growing conditions, for example temperature and rainfall rates, and to repel specific bugs, as well as the development of effective pesticides and herbicides. These were developments in what proved to be a particularly benign period for science, that of the 'Long Boom' from 1945 to 1973, when funding was plentiful, notably from governments, benefiting from rising tax revenues, but also from businesses profiting from economic growth, and before environmental concerns (see chapter 1) came to the fore.

ABOVE: Jonas Salk, inventor of the polio vaccine.

Science became both ideology and a means for progress. In the early 1950s, science was considered the new world saviour; from atomic power to Jonas Salk's wonder vaccine against polio. The hope in science was greater than the science itself. It was the utter belief in the imminence of a new world order, a grand phenomenon that had never occurred before. Science was seen by some as a necessary alternative to religion, both as an explanation of the universe, and of human purpose within it. Theories such as Relativity appeared to leave scant role for any deity, although that approach was countered, notably in the US, by arguing that the universe showed the existence of 'Intelligent Design' and, therefore, of a presiding creator. So also with the reconceptualization of time, which was presented as originating from an original Big Bang when the universe began, a theory first put forward in the first half of the 20th century but influential from the 1960s. The availability of more data, from both ground-based telescopes and satellite observation, and of far greater computational capability, have helped in the measurement of the phenomenon.

The process of investigation, analysis and explanation extended from infinity to the more precise analysis of the building blocks of life. The latter included the discovery and utilization of subatomic particles, an understanding of how light travels, the explanation in 1953 of the correct atomic structure of the genetic material DNA, and research on neurobiology and the workings of the brain. Research on the brain's cellular components uncovered an astonishing diversity of cell types and thus the complexity of the brain and the way it conveyed messages. Further light was thrown on differences between humans and apes, and thus on evolution. At the same time, the brain itself became the subject of virtual reality systems, prominently so by the 2020s.

Science as answer, however, experienced a degree of fading from the early 1960s and met a degree of hostility. In part, in a long-standing tension, this was on religious grounds, particularly by fundamentalists. There was also mistaken scepticism to medical advice, especially about vaccines and, notably from the late 1990s, in response to vaccines against first the MMR illnesses (measles, mumps and rubella) and then Covid-19. The MMR vaccine, licensed for use in America in 1971, was responsible for a major fall in deaths, for example of measles globally from 2.6 million annually to a few thousand.

DNA

Deoxyribonucleic acid, a polymer in the shape of a double helix, is responsible for genetic instructions for organisms. First isolated in 1869 and better understood from the 1920s, DNA's role in heredity was confirmed in the early 1950s, as was an understanding of the accurate structure of DNA. Molecular biology owed much to this work. The genome, the set of DNA instructions found in a cell, has been largely understood by genome sequencing work, first published in the early 2000s. This provides an opportunity for work in biomedical science and other aspects of science, including anthropology.

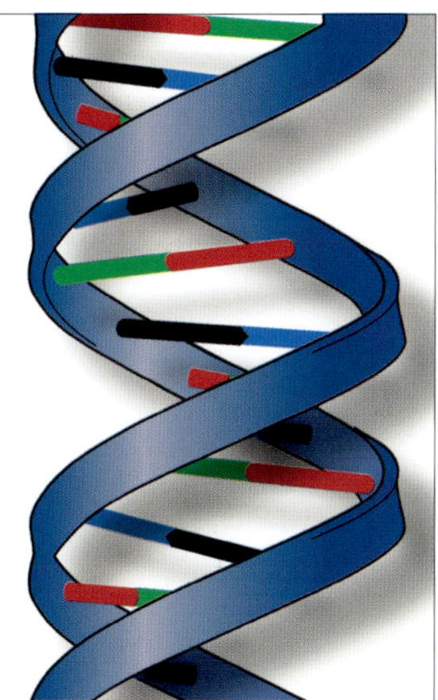

From a different direction, environmentalism and science sat in a difficult relationship. Furthermore, the surveillance possibilities of the modern state led to hostility from civil libertarians.

Science also served as a battlefield for rival powers, especially in weapons development. This encouraged both general funding for science and more specific investment, both during the original Cold War and also in the revived Cold War of the early 21st century. Chinese science was very much state-funded, although, in addition, dynamic Chinese companies, such as Huawei, sought to match their US counterparts.

The degree to which science could move beyond governmental funding controls is unclear, but, nevertheless, probable due to the fiscal problems facing many states. Science also offers many challenges in terms of securing the international cooperation that helps produce information and, sometimes, outcomes.

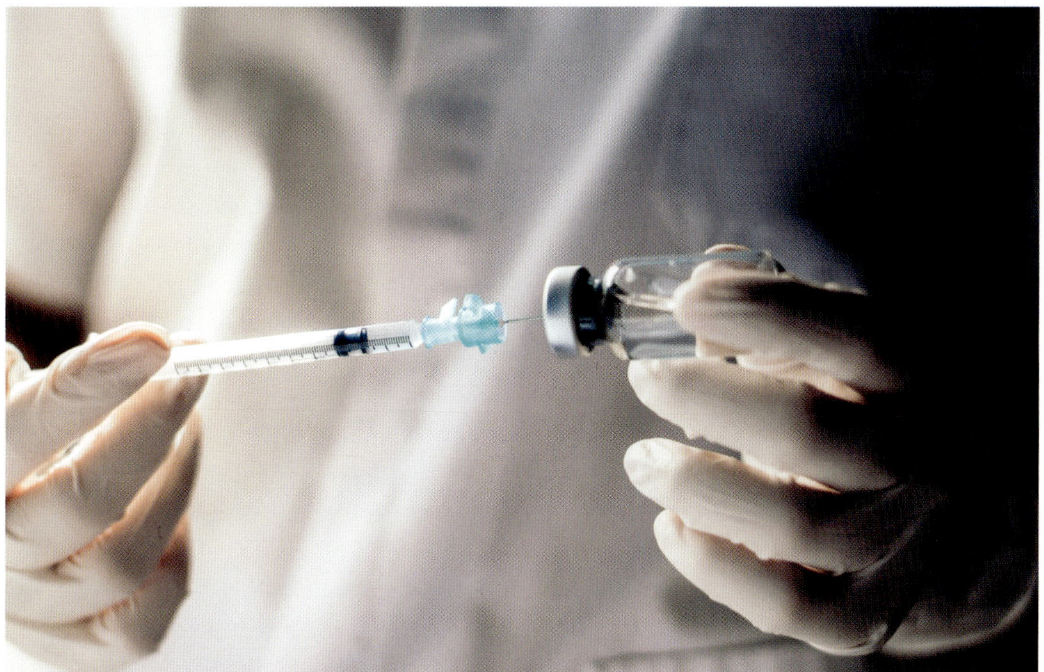

LEFT: Vaccines were responsible for major falls in death rates across the world, but also suffered from a backlash against science and faced intense scepticism from some quarters.

TECHNOLOGIES OF THE 1950s

In 1950, little technology was automated, and much was unmechanized. This was particularly true of agriculture. Alongside the spread of petrol- and oil-driven agricultural machinery, notably tractors and combine harvesters, most agricultural technology remained powered by humans or animals, as in harvesting by hand and picking crops, and the use of horse-drawn ploughs. This was notably the case for Asian, African and Eastern European agriculture; it reflected not only a lack of investment but also the availability of cheap labour, including household workers, namely women and young children. The method of rice cultivation in East and South Asia that fed much of the world had changed little for centuries.

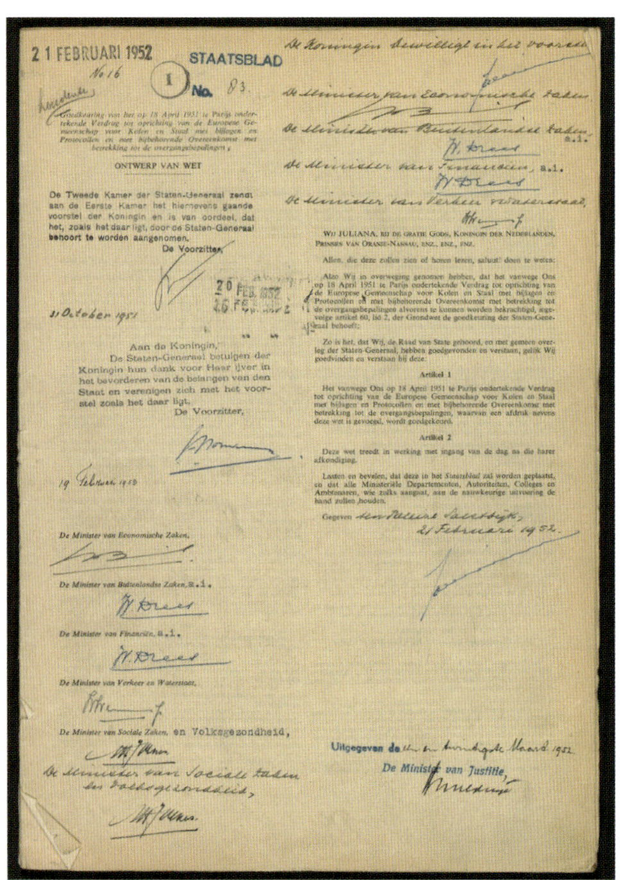

21 FEBRUARI 1952

STAATSBLAD

No. 83

Goedkeuring van het op 18 April 1951 te Parijs ondertekende Verdrag tot oprichting van de Europese Gemeenschap voor Kolen en Staal met bijlagen en Protocollen en met bijbehorende Overeenkomst met betrekking tot de overgangsbepalingen,

ONTWERP VAN WET

De Tweede Kamer der Staten-Generaal zendt aan de Eerste Kamer het hiernevens gaande voorstel der Koningin en is van oordeel, dat het, zoals het daar ligt, door de Staten-Generaal behoort te worden aangenomen.

De Voorzitter,

Aan de Koningin,
De Staten-Generaal betuigen der Koningin hun dank voor Haar ijver in het bevorderen van de belangen van den Staat en verenigen zich met het voorstel zoals het daar ligt.

De Voorzitter,

De Minister van Economische Zaken,

De Minister van Buitenlandse Zaken, a.i.

De Minister van Financiën, a.i.

De Minister van Verkeer en Waterstaat,

De Minister van Sociale Zaken en Volksgezondheid,

WIJ JULIANA, BIJ DE GRATIE GODS, KONINGIN DER NEDERLANDEN, PRINSES VAN ORANJE-NASSAU, ENZ., ENZ., ENZ.

Allen, die deze zullen zien of horen lezen, saluut! doen te weten:

Alzo Wij in overweging genomen hebben, dat het vanwege Ons op 18 April 1951 te Parijs ondertekende Verdrag tot oprichting van de Europese Gemeenschap voor Kolen en Staal met bijlagen en Protocollen en met bijbehorende Overeenkomst met betrekking tot de overgangsbepalingen alvorens te kunnen worden bekrachtigd, ingevolge artikel 60, lid 2, der Grondwet de goedkeuring der Staten-Generaal behoeft;

Zo is het, dat Wij, de Raad van State gehoord, en met gemeen overleg der Staten-Generaal, hebben goedgevonden en verstaan, gelijk Wij goedvinden en verstaan bij deze:

Artikel 1

Het vanwege Ons op 18 April 1951 te Parijs ondertekende Verdrag tot oprichting van de Europese Gemeenschap voor Kolen en Staal met bijlagen en Protocollen en met bijbehorende Overeenkomst met betrekking tot de overgangsbepalingen, waarvan een afdruk nevens deze wet is gevoegd, wordt goedgekeurd.

Artikel 2

Deze wet treedt in werking met ingang van de dag na die harer afkondiging.

Lasten en bevelen, dat deze in het *Staatsblad* zal worden geplaatst, en dat alle Ministeriële Departementen, Autoriteiten, Colleges en Ambtenaren, wie zulks aangaat, aan de nauwkeurige uitvoering de hand zullen houden.

Gegeven

Uitgegeven de

De Minister van Justitie,

ABOVE: The Dutch Act approving the formation of the European Coal and Steel Community.

In addition, industrial technology across much of the world continued to be of a craft character with machinery, if any, powered by relatively simple means, such as water-powered mills. In much of the world, the generation and the application of electricity were still limited.

Yet, electricity, the generation of which was particularly pursued in the West and the Soviet Union, was widely seen as a means and sign of modernity. It made it easier to transmit and use power, and to move from the physical centrality of coal, which was the previous technology of modernity. Electricity was seen as a clean fuel, although most of it was generated by burning fossil fuels.

Metal-bashing technologies were to the fore at the start of our century, and notably those that drew on the long-established coal/iron/steel nexus to produce metal goods such as cars and ships. As a result, the formation in 1951 of the European Coal and Steel Community was a major step in Europe, by aligning France and Germany, and looked towards its sequel, the European Economic Community established in 1958, which subsequently, in 1993, became the European Union. There was a dynamic element in manufacturing. Car production in particular linked the existing industrial infrastructure to consumerism, and the latter was seen as increasingly significant in satisfying the public and thus ensuring stability.

As with cars, new consumer demands were linked to mass production, from washing machines to nappies. Rather than new technologies, though the creation of the transistor in 1947 was

important, it was the implementation of existing ones in more efficient and therefore less costly ways that were more significant, as in 1960s Japan when ordinary families pursued 'the three Cs': car, cooler and colour TV, and weekend leisure driving became normal.

At the same time as the continued use of coal, there was also a growth in oil-based manufacturing, and petrochemicals became particularly important with oil refineries and the associated processing manufacturing plants key centres of industrial activity.

More generally, technology and mechanization were key themes, not least the dissemination of American best practice, especially in Japan and Western Europe. New technology was also labour-saving, helping lead to a move of workers from the land. Civil nuclear power developed, notably in Britain and the US, but also elsewhere. In 1964, France commissioned its first nuclear power station, at Avoine. The response to civil nuclear power was an aspect of the need for optimism in confronting the risk involved in accepting both change and particular new processes.

ABOVE: A Volkswagen factory in Wolfsburg, West Germany, 1956.

ABOVE: Construction of the Avoine nuclear power plant.

ECONOMIC COMPETITION

'The Americans got it. They understood that if ordinary people were to live the way the kings and merchants of old had lived, what would be required was a new kind of luxury, an ordinary luxury built up from goods turned out by the million so that everybody could have one.'

Nikita Khrushchev, Soviet leader from 1956–64, who in 1959 squared off with Richard Nixon, US vice-president (later president from 1969–74), in Moscow debating the virtues of the two systems, after Nixon boasted about US colour television.

SPACE

A presence in space was a military necessity in the arms race of the 1950s between the US and the Soviet Union. Seen as trumping air attack, missiles could go far faster and appeared invulnerable to interception at every stage in their flight. In 1957, the Soviets launched a missile that carried *Sputnik I*, the first satellite, into orbit where it circled the world at 29,000 kph (18,000 mph). The launch did not mean that the Soviets yet had intercontinental ballistic missiles able to carry atomic bombs, as was feared, but it meant that such missiles would soon be close. Many technologies came together in this process, such as the ablative heat shield, developed from composites in the 1950s, that protected a rocket from burning up in the atmosphere when it re-entered.

In part to discredit the previous Republican administration, but also related to the missile race between the two powers, President John F. Kennedy (r.1961–3) presented the US as falling behind the Soviet Union in a new Space Age, and in 1961 committed to sending a man to the Moon. On the Apollo 8 mission in December 1968, astronauts became the first humans to see the Earth rise over the Moon and photographed it accordingly. The task was completed on 20 July 1969, with the Apollo 11 mission, the landing on the Moon watched live on television by 600 million people. This was an iconic moment, but the image of US power was already tarnished by the Vietnam War, while internal cohesion and purpose were under threat. The Apollo missions cost about $100 billion, but the achievement no longer seemed so full of promise.

LANDING ON THE MOON

'The Eagle has landed. We are breathing again. Thanks a lot... [The Earth was] big, bright and beautiful.'
Neil Armstrong, Flight Commander, landing Apollo 11, on 20 July 1969, in the Sea of Tranquillity on the Moon.

'The scientific and operative development of man has arrived at a goal which seemed unreachable ... perhaps even to the point of folly.'
Pope Paul VI.

LEFT: The Moon Landing.

Moreover, travel further into space did not match the horizons that had been and were suggested in public discussion and in fiction. Bold talk of human bases on other planets have remained simply that. However, the constraints affecting manned travel, which only reached as far as the Moon, did not limit unmanned probes which travelled far farther across the solar system. It is possible that unmanned probes may eventually mine commercially useful quantities of rare metals, but this is currently unlikely.

It is also highly unlikely, certainly at present, that relations will be established with sentient creatures from another part of the universe. The scale of the universe makes this unlikely, even if, as is more plausible, among the multitude of other planets there are ones with potentially similar environments. The science and processes of discovery have not altered this equation, but the falling cost of satellite launches, now about $4 million, will encourage the large-scale exploration of space from the 2040s. Commercial mining in space may become closer with a collapse in the cost of getting into orbit, not least thanks to reusable rockets.

BELOW: The famous 'Earthrise' photo taken by Bill Anders on 24 December 1968 during the Apollo 8 Mission.

ABOVE: SpaceX's reuseable Starship in an October 2024 launch.

NEW TECHNOLOGIES OF THE LATE 20TH CENTURY

The metal-bashing industries were increasingly pushed into second place, in both the interest of investors and the concerns of government, by the rapid rise of electrical engineering. Indeed, this rise was to be important to US success over the Soviet Union in the 1980s (see chapter 7), as Soviet and Eastern European industry increasingly appeared obsolescent, and to Soviet leaders as well as foreign commentators. There was large-scale under-employment in the Communist bloc resulting from a failure to use new technology and related production methods, as well as an unwillingness and total inability to allocate resources in accordance with market mechanisms, including the productively costed use of resources. In the late 1970s, for example, Huta Stalowa Wola, the major Polish steel plant outside Warsaw, employed 20,000 workers when it only needed 8,000. However, running what appeared to be full employment was a major goal even if the resulting efficiency was low. Technological mismanagement was differently seen at the disastrous explosion at the Soviet Chernobyl nuclear plant in 1986, when a test was run with safety back-up measures disabled.

ABOVE: Robert Noyce with a diagram of the integrated circuit for which he was famous.

The US economy, in contrast, invested in the new and backed applied science. Thus, the first patent for an integrated circuit was filed in 1959. Electrical engineering in the shape of computers (which the Soviets did not produce well) attracted particular attention in the late 20th century, especially from the 1980s, and opened up a new world of, and for, communications. This was seen as a way to enhance consumer choice and, separately, greatly shifted the balance within the industrial world.

Nevertheless, 'legacy' manufacturing, for example metallurgy, remained important, notably in China. It indeed came to dominate steel production, whereas many US and Western European steel plants, for example Consett and Corby in Britain, were closed and became part of what in the US was known as the 'Rust Belt'. So also with shipbuilding, although in that case it was South Korea and Japan that benefited, whereas Western Europe and the US became less important, notably so with Britain. In 2024, the largest surviving shipyard in Germany, Meyer Werft at Papenburg on the River Ems, had to be rescued from bankruptcy by the government. Petrochemicals also continued to benefit from the extent to which oil had become important in industry.

COMPUTING

Superintelligent computers seized control from humans on the screen, as in *2001: A Space Odyssey* (1968) and *Colossus: The Forbin Project* (1970). While this was totally fictional, it was a precursor to modern anxieties about AI (Artificial Intelligence).

Computing methods were in use prior to World War II, but were taken forward greatly during the conflict, not least in codebreaking. After that war, the new confrontation of the Cold War led to fresh investment, especially in the US. In particular, the Semi-Automatic-Group Environment Air Defense System, launched by the US in 1958, enabled the prediction of the trajectory of aircraft and missiles, and the largest computers ever built were developed at the Massachusetts Institute of Technology for this system.

There was also a search, notably in the US and, less successfully, Britain, for commercial application with the development of integrated circuits offering considerable potential that drew on advances in solid-state physics and the advances of semiconductors. This required investment, with IBM (International Business Machines) the key player. Introduced in 1965, the IBM System/360 used integrated circuits, reframed what a computer was assumed to be and do, became the industry standard, and made substantial profits. This helped lead to investment in more accessible computing, IBM launching a PC (personal computer) in 1981. Both interfaces with other machines, and the miniaturization that

BELOW: The IBM System/360.

ABOVE: Three personal computers from 1977: the Commodore PET 2001, Apple II, TRS-80 Model 1.

permitted handheld computing, assisted greatly in the spread of computing as a widespread system. So also with the investment appeal produced by profits, as well as by the West's success in the Cold War which encouraged the shaping of technology in terms of consumerism rather than government needs.

The US continued to play a key role, being the major site for the new information technology. In 1998, based in Los Angeles, the Internet Corporation for Assigned Names and Numbers was established to manage the internet, assigning the unique indicators essential for the address system. Also in 1998, nearly half of the 130 million people in the world with internet access were Americans. By 1999 half of US households had a computer. By 2006, about 70 per cent of Americans had mobile phones. The US increasingly saw itself as an information society. Culture, economics and politics were presented as dynamic, with 'messaging' a major form of interaction, work and opinion-formation. Whereas, in 1970, it cost $150,000 to send a trillion bits of data between Boston and Los Angeles; the cost in 2000 was 12 cents. This was the most important development in transport, that of data.

A series of new companies, all American, made key initiatives, and lent their names to crucial machines and systems. In 2012, after a major rise in earnings that drew on the global popularity of the iPod (digital music player, 2001), touch-screen iPhone (2007) and iPad portable tablet (2010), Apple had the highest valuation on the American stock market, at over $630 billion – more than 1.2 per cent of the global equity market. Launched in 2004, Facebook had 900 million users by the spring of 2012, by which time Google's Android operating system ran on more than half the phones sold globally. The combination of government, company and consumer purposes, and sales, made IT (Information Technology) particularly profitable, with innovation to the fore as a way to realize market share.

ABOVE: A first-generation iPhone, released in 2007.

IT was adopted in many countries to leapfrog existing limitations, as with payment systems in sub-Saharan Africa, which thereby acted as a substitute for banks. There was also the use of IT for new roles, Estonia in 2007 becoming the first country to use internet voting in a national election.

The internet was powered by data centres, which contained masses of connected computer banks running nonstop and requiring power, not least for cooling the equipment. By 2024, these centres used up to 1.5 per cent of global electricity, but increased computer usage and the likely demands of AI will increase this.

NEW TECHNOLOGIES OF THE EARLY 21ST CENTURY

While machines cannot yet think like humans, they are able to draw on banks of online data and make calculations far faster. As a result, computer-aided design has become, and will continue to become, more prominent across a range of functions, including medical diagnostics, financial trading and weather prediction. All require sophisticated systems and, for the last two, formidable banks of computers. An instance of the capacity of AI was provided in 2024 with the use by Sarah de Lagarde, in London, of a prosthetic replacement arm that is powered by AI which, with familiarity, became better at predicting what she wished to do. In 2024, Nvidia, a company making the chips that run AI systems, became the wealthiest in the world by share value, a reflection of investor interest in the transformative potential of AI.

Concern over technology, however, took many forms. Thus, stem-cell research met serious ethical objections, notably in the US, in part due to religious objections. By the 2020s, with military conflict to the fore, confidence in the technological future was less clear-cut than in the 2010s when the emphasis, instead, in potential and opposition, had been on new computing capabilities and products. The idea that Covid-19 had been a man-made pandemic escaping from a Chinese research laboratory had been far from encouraging for much of the public. However, by 2024, the notion that AI might take charge from human inventors was more troubling, not least as it was linked to the prevalence of new technology in warfare, notably drones. Earlier anxieties about robots were given new force and direction.

In May 2024, when many new AI products were announced, the first International Scientific Report on Advanced AI Safety concluded that 'No currently known method provides strong assurances or guarantees against harm associated with general-purpose AI'. It was also claimed that developers building AI systems 'understand little about how their systems operate' and, in an instructive guide to the mismatch of science and technology, that scientific knowledge was 'very limited'. By then, there were no relevant federal regulations yet in the US, although the EU had passed the restrictive AI Act.

At this stage, AI was seen more immediately in terms of the likely impact on the need for workers, a long-standing concern about technological development; and also with reference to its possible use for disinformation, fraud and deepfakes. There was also opposition arising from the extent to which AI Generative systems using pattern recognition to mimic human-created material

ABOVE: Sarah de Lagarde. She possesses an AI-powered robotic prosthetic arm, an example of the new possibilities of technology in the modern world.

ABOVE: The AI safety summit held at Bletchley Park, UK in 2023.

were trained in part by ignoring the copyright of creatives and other individuals and companies. At the same time, the potential future capacity of autonomous systems aroused increasing anxiety. The possible merging of humans with robots, becoming 'transhumans' in the end, with a man-computer symbiosis is one possibility. So also with AI usurpation.

Technology was more directly the concern with the linkage of automatic surveillance CCTV cameras with the internet and identification software, notably through face-recognition. Such worry about autocratic possibilities was directed in particular at China, but also drew on a more widespread unease about futurism. China also blocks and hacks to help achieve the 'Great Firewall of China': words and phrases deemed sensitive were barred by internet censoring.

Thus, just as there was earlier adaptation to print by governments, other institutions, individuals and, indeed, the human brain, so the same will be true of the electronic age. For example, electronic purchasing helped ensure that the factors that influenced purchasing and consumption online, notably algorithms, but also the location of advertisements, were of great significance. So also with artistic and consumer criticism by 'influencers'. Electronic means provided opportunities for artistic and entrepreneurial innovation, digital enhancement becoming very important to cinema and popular music in the 2020s. Computerized graphic design, CGI (Computer-Generated Imagery) and de-ageing technology are playing a major role in films.

Very differently, there were the deadly technologies of drug addiction. In America, drug overdoses became the leading cause of accidental death from 2008, passing the (high) rate from road accidents, and more than 400,000 Americans died of opiate use by 2019, fentanyl

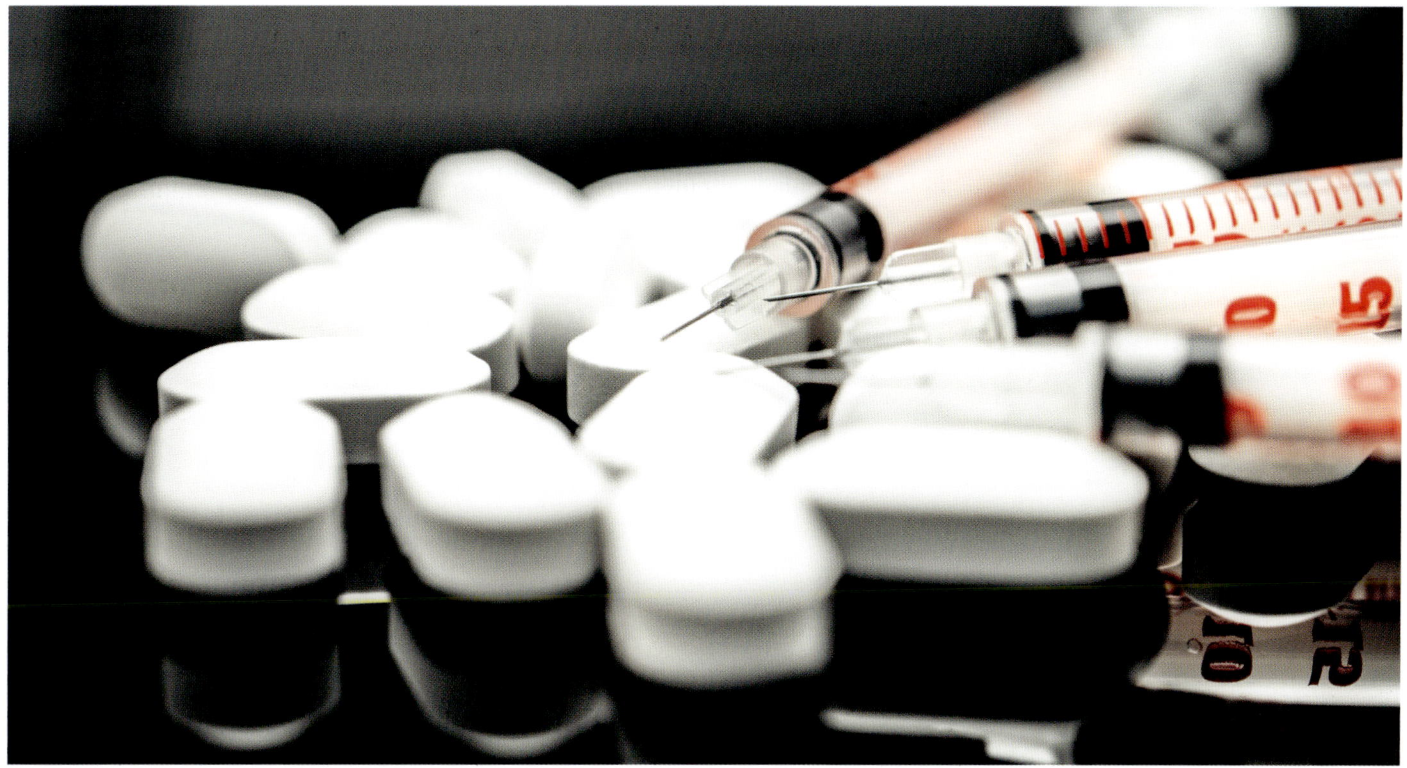

being the prime killer. It was responsible for 71,000 deaths in 2021. Separately, the strength of cannabis has been enhanced.

Turning to the positive side of the equation, technology, notably in the shape of pharmaceutical research, was important to the success and profits of the drug industry, and the need for a rapid response was shown by the Covid pandemic. The degree to which technology may unlock solutions to problems, for example nuclear fission, is far from clear, but is clearly worth pursuing. More immediately, energy-efficient technologies, as in manufacturing and transport, are important in both cost and environmental terms. The rapid growth of solar electricity generation in the 2020s, a major triumph for technological innovation, offered the prospect of overcoming earlier energy constraints, and notably so at a modest cost.

ABOVE: Opioids became one of the leading causes of death in the US, with fentanyl the prime contributor.

BELOW: Bitcoin.

CRYPTOCURRENCIES

These are digital currencies using computer systems as a medium of exchange that are not directed by a centralized authority. After discussion and initiatives in the 1990s, this came to the fore in 2009 with the creation of Bitcoin as a currency. As with other technological innovations, there were very different responses by governments and, indeed, political movements. Bitcoin was adopted as legal tender by El Salvador in 2021, alongside the US dollar, but, three years later, authoritarian China totally banned its trading. In 2024, Donald Trump, who presented himself as the 'crypto president', suggested that cryptocurrency was able to challenge the dominance of 'the big banks and financial elites'.

CONTAINERIZATION

The focus on paradigm-shifting technologies has meant that others that have been easier to introduce generally lack sufficient attention, and readers will have their own suggestions to make. Disputes over election results, as in America in 2000 and Brazil in 2022, for example, in part rested on the deficiencies of the voting machines in use.

Containerization was a key aspect of transport change, one that was more insistent than, say, jet aircraft as it affected transport on land and at sea and, to a degree, in the air. Closed container boxes and the carriage of containers on flatcars were both the case before World War II, but in 1951 a Western European railway standard was developed for containers. Container ships followed from the 1950s, and then the double-stacked rail transport of containers from 1977, with the US the innovator and China a key copier.

BELOW: A Cadillac in a shipping container, 1962.

ABOVE: A modern container ship.

As with other technologies, containerization required investment. In this case, it was in new freight facilities, but containerization increased the speed and cut the cost of freight movements, greatly raising labour productivity on the railways and changing the nature of marshalling yards. Interoperability with ships and trucks rapidly improved. Containers can readily be moved from ship and train to lorries, although as ships move containers in greater bulk and are more energy-efficient, it is ships that are most important for trade.

So also with trade routes, which indicate the convergence of technology with economics and geopolitics. From the growth of Japanese exports and the increased sophistication of the Japanese economy, in the early decades of our period, to the comparable growth of China from the 1990s, the major trading routes have been maritime ones from East Asia to the Americas across the Pacific, and from East Asia to Europe. These routes have seen a heavy reliance on canals, those of Panama and Suez respectively. There have also been key routes linked to the movement of oil, notably from Iran to China and from the Middle East to Europe.

Scenes in the Panama and Suez canals have captured the varied timetables of technology at play in the present, as the canals were late-19th-century technology being now used to

ABOVE: A container ship on the Suez Canal.

move container ships, and with the Panama Canal widened to that end. At the same time, the environment played a role. Lower rainfall and greater evaporation caused a fall in the late 2010s and 2020s in the level of Lake Gatun, which makes up two-fifths of the Panama Canal, and thus has threatened the depth of the ships that can transit, as well as plans for upgrades. Panama's income and water supply are both threatened.

In contrast, politics has closed or affected the Suez Canal route from 1956, with successive Arab–Israeli conflicts leading to closure, as in 1956–7 and 1967–75. There have also been closures due to shipping problems, as in 2004 and 2021. Looking to the future, it is unclear how far long-endurance, heavy-loadbearing drones will overcome existing constraints and transform logistics.

TECHNOLOGIES OF THE FUTURE

By its very nature the future is unknowable, but it is also more than simply a matter of speculation. Instead, much of the present is a preparation for the future. The basic technological changes are always in process. At present the resolution of energy issues are crucial, and this is leading to solar energy improvements and to development in the use of hydrogen. Greater energy availability will be important to the desalination of water, but, in contrast, there is no breakthrough yet in terms of the synthetic production of fresh water. That is different to the situation with food, as factory-farm production is now possible, which potentially frees up land otherwise used for agriculture, for example making it available for housing.

Biomedical technologies open up previously futuristic possibilities about genetic understanding and improvability for individuals. How far these will be taken forward at the level of communities as a whole is unclear, but the potential of such technologies for public health is considerable. Gene editing will probably lead to extended lifespans.

There is currently no possibility of technological development through contact with advanced life elsewhere in the universe. As a result, human ability, as well as the resources of the Earth and from the Sun, are crucial. Neither have been exhausted. If a world war can be avoided, for such a conflict, thanks to scientific innovation and technological application, will be far more destructive than previous ones, then it is probable that scientific ideas and research will create the possibilities for a greater degree of change in the human context and condition.

Today's digital revolution cannot begin to compare with the love affair with science of the early 1950s. And the encroaching AI is today's seeming 'boogeyman', a version of science's zombie.

BELOW: Gene editing is one technology that can be expected to play a greater role in the future, with the potential to extend human lifespans.

5 Economies

Our period was an era where the command economies of the Communist bloc faced the free-market ideology of the developed world.

Underpinning it all was the 'Long Boom' of 1945–73, a time of postwar prosperity and growth in the West. It could not last, though. Borrowing against the future and spending on the present squandered the prospects for coming generations, weakened fiscal restraint, and undermined good government. Living within one's means became a discredited concept for many states and individuals. By the end of the century, there had been serious debt crises across Latin America, Africa, much of South Asia, for example Indonesia and Thailand, and Russia.

Significant economic growth in the second half of the 20th century created expectations, notably of social welfare and healthcare, that it was difficult to meet in the first half of the 21st, especially after the financial crisis of 2008 and the debt crises that followed.

In the coming years, it should become clear whether authoritarian regimes, specifically China, will successfully be able to spread their economic models, and how, elsewhere, governments, markets and economies will handle the opportunities and challenges of globalization.

AGRICULTURE

The continuing rapid rise in the world's population has only been successfully handled as a result of a major increase in agricultural production. This increase was very necessary to confront malnutrition, food insecurity and even famine. This continues to be the case, as in war-torn Ethiopia and Yemen in the early 2020s.

This increase in agricultural production arose in part from the extension of the cultivated area, notably as a result of deforestation, as in Amazonia and Indonesia, but not the West. Not all of this land was cleared for human food crops; a large proportion of it was given over to grow animal feed or to produce vegetable oils.

More commonly, however, the increase in agricultural productivity has been due to the widespread use of chemical fertilizers and pesticides, mechanization and the selective breeding of animals and crops, for example high-yield and disease-resistant strains of rice. Water management improved, with agricultural machinery and tillage practices adapted to dry soils, as on the Argentinian pampas. The result of enhanced productivity was a significant rise in activity per agricultural worker, and a major increase in food

BELOW: Agriculture in Indonesia.

production, especially in India, but more generally across much of Asia, and with some African countries, for example Malawi and Zambia, producing a food surplus. Indeed, new food supply links included agricultural exports from Zambia to wealthy Saudi Arabia. Such export cash crops earned revenue but also could decrease the local availability of inexpensive food.

ABOVE: Norman Borlaug with the strain of wheat he developed.

THE GREEN REVOLUTION

'These and other developments in the field of agriculture contain the makings of a new revolution ... I call it the Green Revolution.'
William Gaud, administrator of US Agency for International Development, 1968.

The Green Revolution attracted much praise. In 1970, the American agricultural scientist Norman Borlaug, who had played a key role in extending it to Mexico, received the Nobel Peace Prize for his efforts. However, there was also a vulnerability in the need for water and fuel for these processes, as well as in the environmental problems arising from fertilizers and pesticides, and the relative decline of biodiversity, as in the number of tree species in Britain. These issues became more acute in the 2020s as climate warming affected crop yields and greatly underlined the need for sufficient water by altering the established equations of provision, availability and requirements; there was more need for irrigation and, due to climate warming, more evaporation of water.

So also with concerns about the health implications of some forms of 'factory farming', for example of chicken, salmon and prawns. Such concerns underlined the question of whether food production would increasingly become a branch of manufacturing, not least with the use of synthesized products, a course that posed regulatory, ethical, health and

LEFT: Genetically modified maize in Kenya.

other issues, notably in energy requirements for the manufacturing of food.

At the same time, genetic engineering reduced the vulnerability of crops to pests and, therefore, the need for pesticides. Such instances demonstrate the trade-offs involved in developments and therefore the inherently political nature of regulation, both at a national and an international level.

Globally, there were major shifts in consumption, as greater wealth led to increased meat consumption in Japan from the late 20th century and in China from the early 21st. So also with urbanization ensuring that food was increasingly purchased from urban outlets, rather than consumed in rural communities. Eating habits were an expression of social position and expectation. At the same time, traditional patterns in consumption remained important in many countries and acted as a constraint on change.

The impact of politics was often far more direct. This was particularly seen with China in the late 1950s and early 1960s with the 'Great Leap Forward', an attempt at rapid industrialization which carried forward an earlier effort to transform agriculture that had seen violent, often murderous, land seizures – frequently from peasants who owned only small plots. The collectivization of farming did not produce the anticipated output, a situation also seen in other Communist countries, and the endeavour to focus resources on industry led in China to an agrarian crisis in which millions died. In contrast, in the Soviet Union, after the earlier homicidal stage in the interwar period, postwar collectivization was instead associated with low agricultural productivity and a failure to transform the situation by ploughing up the Steppe.

RIGHT: Tractors on a Chinese farm during the Great Leap Forward.

ABOVE: Wheat fields, Île-de-France.

Fiscal trends can also be significant in food availability, not least with food being priced in dollars and thus becoming more expensive, as in Egypt and Sri Lanka, when the dollar was strong. In turn, the war from 2022 in Ukraine, a major grain exporter, greatly affected those who imported that grain, notably many African countries. Higher energy costs hit the prices of fertilizer and transport that are very important to the agricultural economy. Combined with climate disruption, these elements helped ensure higher world food prices in 2024, and this put particular pressure on the poor, and increased public disaffection.

There were also long-term changes in agriculture in Europe. Small farms became uncompetitive, so that in France, the most important agricultural economy in the European Economic Community, the forerunner of the EU, the number of farms fell from about 1.6 million in 1970 to around 700,000 in 2005. What were left were increasingly agri-businesses, such as the large cereal producers of the prairies of the Île-de-France and Poitou, mechanized and using much chemical fertilizer. The uncompetitive nature of small farms contributed strongly to rural depopulation and the move to the cities, as in Italy and Portugal, and was also seen in the US.

Protectionism was a problem for many exporters. Thus, the EU protected its sugar-beet production, hitting Caribbean sugar-cane exports, while banana exports were hit by its tariffs. Australasian food exports to Britain, notably New Zealand lamb, were affected by Britain's entry into the European Economic Community. As a result of protectionism, free trade agreements were significant. So also with the expansion of trading blocs. In particular, the expansion of the EU provided opportunities for agriculture for new entrants, notably Spain and Poland, but also challenges to existing producers, especially France.

THE ECONOMICS OF THE COLD WAR

The US dominated the world economy after the cataclysmic costs of the world wars. The international economic order was very much under the US aegis, with the Bretton Woods System, the International Monetary Fund, the World Bank, and the World Trading Organization all designed to ensure international free trade and capital markets on the American model – and hopefully lead to stability, encourage growth and limit political radicalism. Under the Bretton Woods Agreement of 1944, US-supported monetary agencies the International Monetary Fund and the World Bank, both of which had US headquarters, were established in order to strengthen the global financial system. Fixed exchange rates were seen as necessary to stability, not least by preventing competitive devaluations. The General Agreement on Tariffs and Trade, signed in 1947, began cuts in tariffs designed to help free trade. The US also supported decolonization as a way to end imperial trade preference systems and therefore help its exports. The prosperity of US workers, and the lower costs made possible by mass production, ensured that the average American household owned a car from 1950. By 1973 there was one car for every 2.25 Americans, while the automobile industry provided a sixth of all jobs.

RIGHT: The Bretton Woods Conference of 1944.

ABOVE: The Esso Tower in the La Défense business district, Paris, 1970.

THE LONG BOOM

In 1955, the general manager of the Ford Motor Company, Robert McNamara, informed graduates: 'The test of your generation will not be how well you stood up under adversity, but how well you endured prosperity.' McNamara was later Secretary of Defense during the Vietnam War.

US finance, markets, organizational models and technology were to the fore, with the US setting standards for new techniques, products and processes, and for ensuring productivity, notably the use of machines on production lines, but also agricultural machinery, that provided more profit and higher real wages, and thus financed new consumption. This model influenced the rest of the capitalist world. It was no surprise that the first tower to open in the new business district of La Défense in Paris in 1964 was the Esso building. This district, with its skyscrapers, was a counterpoint to the traditional power structures – physical and commercial – of the city centre.

Widespread economic growth after World War II benefited from a rising world population able to provide workers and consumers, and from relatively low prices, low inflation, low unemployment, falling protectionism, the dissemination of advanced industrial technology and techniques, and stable finance. There was particularly

ABOVE: A Japanese shipyard in 1965.

pronounced growth in the US, Japan, West Germany, France and Italy, but less so in Britain. In 1955, Japan replaced Britain as the world's leading shipbuilder. In Western Europe, the European Economic Community established in 1958 encouraged a tariff reduction that helped growth. Western Europe and Japan saw a considerable economic catch-up with the US and a move toward greater industrialization.

The early 1970s, however, saw a reversal of this situation, with 'stagflation', the inflation encouraged by the decision of the US to pay for the Vietnam War by borrowing rather than taxation. This contributed to the US, where individual borrowing was also higher, having higher inflation than Japan and West Germany. The US ran its first trade deficit of the 20th century in 1971, the year in which the convertibility of the dollar into gold was suspended. In turn, economic problems came to owe much to a major increase in oil prices in 1973. At the same time, that increase brought to the fore already existing structural flaws in the global economy and financial system, and, in particular, in US public finance.

The economic downturn of the early 1970s was not accompanied by a comparable decline in public spending. The consequence was an expansion of the impact and role of government. This put pressure on the productive economy, lessening growth rates, and led to greater state borrowing, which distorted investment priorities.

In turn, there was significant revival in the 1980s, notably in the US under President Ronald Reagan (r.1981–9), but not the Soviet Union. Falling energy prices, structural reforms and growing productivity greatly benefited the US, although there was also regulatory looseness that built up major problems for the future, notably in loan policies. The US was clearly outperforming its Soviet rival and this helped encourage the movement of international money into America, enabling it to borrow cheaply and avoid higher taxation,

THE PERSONAL VIEW: EAST GERMANY IN 1980

Working in East German archives in 1980, I spent time in both Dresden and East Berlin. I had anticipated that I would see few cars on the roads and a limited range and quantity of goods in the shops, but I was struck by the poor quality of public services. This was readily apparent in terms of street lighting and paving, railway and postal collection schedules, and atmospheric pollution due to the reliance on lignite coal and to the inadequate nature of regulation.

ABOVE: A sugar cane farm in Cuba, *c.*1960.

and to produce a degree of domestic political harmony, which helped Reagan win easy re-election in 1984 and ensure success for his vice-president, George H.W. Bush, in 1988. Whereas the annual growth rate of US GNP had fallen from 3.5 per cent in 1947–73 to 1.6 per cent in 1973–82, it rose to 2.8 per cent in 1982–90, and the base was now far larger. Between 1970 and 1990, the number of cars on American roads increased by 60 per cent.

American neo-liberal economic policies were introduced elsewhere, with the Structural Adjustment Programs advocated by the World Bank and the International Monetary Fund seen as the ways to cope with crises.

Economic development, more generally, was heavily affected by politics. Having taken over Cuba in 1959, Fidel Castro pushed through a socio-economic revolution, notably nationalizing assets, including land. The largest foreign ownership of nationalized assets was American. The regime's inefficient planned economy, combined with a US economic blockade, soon led to an economic crisis, as well as the beginning of rationing, with people subsisting on a diet of rice and beans. In the Soviet Union and Eastern Europe, low productivity helped make Communism unappealing, and there were few consumer goods for workers to purchase. It was also difficult to get housing. Bribery and connections were generally necessary to obtain goods and privileges. Soviet tractors sent to Mexico tended to break down whereas US ones worked.

The contrast between Communist states and Japan was particularly dramatic. Resource-poor, notably in oil, Japan benefited from US technology and production techniques, and from the US market in which the Japanese made increasing inroads from the 1950s. The Japanese, moreover, soon proved far more innovative on the production line, notably in the prestigious field of car manufacture. Japan also benefited from the enforced abandonment, due to defeat in World War II, of militarism and international aggression. South Korea and Singapore shared in this economic expansion, prefiguring the later route of China and Vietnam.

CHINA–THE US AND THE ECONOMICS OF THE 1990s–2010s

Having triumphed in the last stage of the Cold War, the US dominated the postwar world economy of this period, with a rise in its percentage of the world's GDP and exports, the latter to 17.7 per cent in 1999. The US also took a central role in handling international fiscal crises, particularly those of the late 1990s and that of 2008, although the latter was largely due to poor US lending and regulatory practices.

In turn, notably with the collapse of the Soviet bloc in 1989–91, the US operated as a market for the rest of the world and provided investment accordingly. At the same time, the growth in the world economy saw many of the politically stable low- and middle-income countries enjoy significant catch-up growth. US models of economic and fiscal organization were to the fore, with public monopolies privatized and protectionism lessened.

Japan had been a key beneficiary of US markets during the Cold War, but, from the 1990s, this was increasingly the case for China, whereas Japan, where labour rates were higher and labour availability less, was hit by declining growth. The Chinese Communist regime had

PRIVATIZATION AND 'CRONY-CAPITALISM'

Privatization could operate to the benefit of the consumer, but, as in Russia in the 1990s, was frequently a matter of corruption, the acquisition of state assets at very low prices, and the creation of new pseudo-monopolies. Privatization also created greater opportunities for profit from lobbying government, as influence could determine who took control of these newly privatized companies. Thus greater funds were devoted to acquiring political control and influencing government. Many regimes did not bother to limit the corruption from which they profited. Other governments found it very difficult to limit corruption and addressed the problem with periodic purges, as in China under Xi Jinping from the early 2010s.

To a degree, politics could become a matter of competition between political-entrepreneurial groups, which indeed was an element in the 2024 US presidential election. This process encouraged public dissatisfaction and cynicism, as expressed for example in the South African election of 2024, but also led to major issues in the misallocation of resources. In particular, the 'constructive destruction' seen in the US, as more efficient companies succeeded others, was not present in systems of 'crony capitalism'.

ABOVE: A disused steel plant in Bethlehem, Pennsylvania. The so-called 'Rust Belt' saw a major decline as manufacturing moved abroad.

long sought to support industrialization but had been adversely affected by the rigidities of doctrinaire central planning, while the industrialization pursued had been for heavy industry and not for goods for consumers. In contrast, liberalization from the 1980s, and more particularly the 1990s, saw prices freed, private businesses encouraged and foreign investment sought. Indeed, by 2000, China attracted the second-largest inward investment in the world after the US, much of this investment American.

Helped by protectionism, including a manipulated exchange rate, as well as by cheap labour, China enjoyed important comparative advantages over other exporters. This hit US manufacturers, for example of steel, producing serious decline in the 'Rust Belt' of the Midwest and northeast, but benefited American consumers by keeping prices for Chinese goods cheap, while also ensuring that many Chinese were lifted out of poverty. The multiple facets of globalization were clearly shown.

At the same time, as with the modernization of Eastern European economies, and in part reflecting a reallocation of resources and profits that freed up expansion, there was the ending in China of Maoist social politics. These had included full employment and universal housing and healthcare. Instead, uncompetitive factories closed, causing unemployment and poverty. State-owned enterprises declined in profitability and relevance, and many closed, for example in the heavy industrial region of Manchuria.

In their place came an entrepreneurship that searched out market opportunities, notably

RIGHT: Workers at a Chinese factory in Shenyang, China, 2000.

in the US. Low wages gave China an important advantage in labour-intensive areas of manufacture, such as textiles, shoes and toys. In turn, Chinese expansion made the country a major market, notably for Pacific Rim states, and as part of a degree of commercial liberalization. Exports to the US also helped South Korea, Taiwan, Malaysia and Vietnam, all encouraging growth, and notably so after recovery from a severe regional financial crisis in 1997. In practice, however, China continued to face many of the serious problems with financial systems seen in that crisis.

By 2005, the US trade deficit with China was $202 billion, and this was only manageable due to substantial net capital inflows into America. US interest rates were kept low to cut the cost of borrowing, encourage growth and ease the public mood, albeit at the cost of American manufacturing. Low US interest rates proved acceptable, as the dollar was, and remained, the world's principal reserve currency, and Asian central banks bought dollars to keep the value of their own currencies low and help their exports.

At the same time, industrial transformation ensured that Asian manufacturing produced a greater range of goods for export and at a good price. For example, in the 2000s, the export of engineering and petrochemicals by India increased greatly, while Vietnam, with labour rates lower than China, came to compete with it from the 2010s in pursuing export-led growth, notably in consumer goods.

Consumer borrowing in the US was encouraged by cheap credit and social norms, and, by 2005, imports were responsible for about 37 per cent of domestic purchases. Americans in work benefited from the lower consumer costs made possible by the poor conditions of Chinese workers, which, in turn, helped restrain US wages, and thus assisted American companies. US shops, such as the many supermarkets of the Walmart chain, were full of Chinese products. In December 2005, Alan Greenspan, chairman of the American Federal Reserve, referring to the ability to borrow to finance the current-account deficit of the US, claimed 'deficits that culminate to ever-increasing net external debt, with its attendant rise in servicing costs, cannot persist indefinitely'. That year there was a $319 billion government deficit.

ABOVE: Alan Greenspan, chairman of the American Federal Reserve 1987–2006.

The strains of fiscal overreach, both in the US and elsewhere, were lessened by 'quantitative easing', an increase in the money supply, that became widespread in response to the financial crisis of 2008. The latter was a product of poor risk management, and assets of questionable value, notably in US subprime mortgages. Quantitative easing, however, while a stimulus, also amounted to a loose monetary policy that posed serious long-term problems in terms of disguising an underlying lack of viability in many assets and risks, as well as of policies such as expensive state pensions and generous social welfare schemes. The economic and financial valuation of the policy of quantitative easing must be set alongside socio-cultural pressures and political risks. In the US, pressure on the federal debt limit became a political football, with the Republicans willing to risk a shutdown of the federal

FINANCIAL TIMES

Tuesday September 30 2008 | £1.50

Meltdown Monday

NEWS: Pages 2-10 The crisis spreads in Europe Pages 8-9 The problems of small countries with big banks Page 9 COMMENT: GIDEON RACHMAN Asia is not immune Page 19

Global crisis House shocks investors . . . S&P 500's worst day since 1987 . . . Banks saved

Stocks dive on bail-out rejection

S&P 500
Intraday movements Sep 29 2008
1,213.23
1,106.42

The day in summary

Global markets

Bradford & Bingley

LEFT: The front page of the *Financial Times* reports on the financial crash of 2008.

government in opposition to raising the debt limit. More continually, and despite investing in infrastructure, government action could not replace a widespread shift from long-term investment in industrial assets to shorter-term speculations resting on easy credit. The volume of money in circulation became far greater than that of goods.

In Europe, there was comparable pressure on traditional manufacturing regions from areas nearby able to compete, particularly Eastern Europe. This process was aided by the expansion of the European Union, especially in the 2000s, although not limited to that. Thus, Slovakia, Poland and Serbia became major centres of car production, hitting that in Italy where Fiat had been the leading European producer. The Italian production of washing machines was also battered by that in Poland, as well as by competition from Turkey and South Korea, while the last became a major competitive force in shipbuilding and car production.

The industrial transformation of France was more generally symptomatic of the West. Traditional heavy industrial sectors and areas, notably iron and steel, Lorraine and the Nord, were hit hard; while light sectors, such as electronics, and new industrial areas, for example the Toulouse region, did well. So also in Germany, where Bavaria and Baden-Württemberg grew faster than the traditional heavy industrial centre of the Ruhr. In Belgium, another heartland

BELOW: Protest against US government shutdown, January 2019.

ABOVE: Toulouse, a region focused on the newer industries of electronics and aerospace, did well with the economic transformations of the late 20th and early 21st centuries.

of heavy industry, Walloonia suffered, while Flanders, traditionally more rural, developed new industries. Industrial transformation was linked to a decline in trade union membership, from 22.3 per cent of US workers in 1950 to 14.1 per cent in 1996–7.

In guiding transition, the skill of political and economic management was important. Countries afflicted by poor government and fiscal mismanagement did badly. Thus, Argentina and Venezuela have declined, the latter becoming increasingly chaotic from the 2010s. In 2019, the official poverty and inflation rates in Argentina rose to 35 per cent and 43 per cent respectively.

On the global level, fiscal instability remained a problem, one that reflected the relaxation of strict controls on domestic and international capital transactions and banking regulations that had become significant from the 1980s. This caused particular problems when there were banking crises, as in Indonesia, Thailand and Japan in 1997–8 and Britain in 2008.

The 2008 financial crisis greatly accentuated economic and political difficulties, notably in Greece, Italy and Spain, with unemployment rising rapidly to more than 27 per cent in Spain and 28 per cent in Greece (and with a higher rate of youth unemployment), which put serious strains on the politics, finances, economics and cohesion of the European Union. The debt-to-GDP ratio of Italy, Greece, France and Spain were still over 100 per cent in 2022. There was no comparable fiscal union in the North American Free Trade Area created in 1994; while Vladimir Putin's 2011 argument for a 'Eurasian Union' – the economic integration of the former Soviet Union – went nowhere.

'THE DAGGER THAT FINALLY IMMOBILIZED APARTHEID'

Barend du Plessis, South African Minister of Finance, 1984–92.

The demand of major banks, notably the major US bank Chase Manhattan, for the repayment of government loans was a key point in a divestment process of asset sales, trade bans and sanctions that hit South Africa hard from 1985. This encouraged the moves and negotiations from 1989 that led to a 1992 whites-only referendum approving a multi-racial transitional government. This was followed by the election of an African National Congress government in 1994, with Nelson Mandela, who had been released from long imprisonment in 1990, becoming president. Apartheid was dead.

CRISIS FOR GLOBALIZATION, THE 2020s

The global political tensions of the 2020s damaged economic prospects, not least by challenging trade and the related offshoring of manufacturing, with the comparative advantages that were thereby offered. This was particularly seen in rising tension between the US and China, such that there was strong encouragement in the US to bring manufacturing back there and shorten the supply chain. This led to protectionism, not least with the Inflation Reduction Act of 2022 involving $369 billion of government support for clean energy and manufacturing, for example of electric vehicles, support which was viewed in China and Europe as a form of economic warfare. Exports of electric-powered cars from China, the world's leading manufacturer of them, were a particular source of protectionist pressure in 2024, with both the US and the European Union adopting tariffs accordingly.

This rivalry was made more acute by the degree to which it sat on an already precarious fiscal situation. In the US and elsewhere, government deficits increased. By 2019, foreign investors held $6.2 trillion in US public debt, and, by 2023, the federal deficit of the US was 6.3 per cent of GDP. This was part of a fundamental mismatch in the global financial system and economy. Currency inflows are in large part a matter of sustaining consumption. Indeed, since 2000, foreigners, notably the Chinese central bank, have invested in US bonds, particularly Treasury bonds, rather than, as previously, in US companies. This means a lack of underpinning for long-term US economic growth. Despite considerable US economic growth, there is a shortage of exports to help service the foreign debt. By the early 2020s, more than 80 per cent of jobs in the US were service-oriented, and most were not earning export dollars, a problem found more generally across the West.

The combination of heavy borrowing with a loose monetary policy is such that by the mid-2000s there were more than 1.3 billion credit cards in the US, and the design of wallets, and therefore of jackets, had to respond to the large number of credit and charge cards owned by individuals. In the US (and more generally), personal and governmental indebtedness interacted in a disturbing synergy carried forward by the heady drug of low interest rates and the ability to borrow. Successive presidential election campaigns saw these issues ignored.

Other parts of the world, nevertheless, might have very much relished sharing US economic and fiscal problems. Indeed, the US was able to borrow so much precisely because it was seen as a good credit risk, in the sense of being a safe one, with its borrowing linked to strong economic growth. This contrasted with what was regarded as the lack of safety and clarity in the financing of those states able arbitrarily to discard or alter obligations, as so many did. US growth was particularly notable in comparison with that

ABOVE: President Biden signs the Inflation Reduction Act on 16 August 2022.

of Europe, with the EU's GDP moving from similar to that of the US in 2014 to only two-thirds the size in 2023, in part due to greater US population growth and currency appreciation, but also due to economic strength. In 2019–22, average annual wages adjusted for inflation fell in Britain, France, Germany and Italy, but rose by 6 per cent in the US. The financial resources of American society and the liberal regulatory context underpinned investment, as in 2023 when venture capitalists invested $170 billion in start-ups in the US.

The BRIC (Brazil, Russia, India, China) economies of major growth, a term coined in 2001, sought to alter the international order. Meeting in Russia in 2009, their leaders called for 'a greater voice and representation in international financial institutions'. However, the BRIC economies have gone in very different directions, with China and India much more successful (although differently so) than the other two. Russian industry could not match international competitors and the Russian economy relied on energy sales. Brazil struggled to meet expectations and, as with South Africa, which was invited to join in 2010, its divided politics is matched by a marked degree of dysfunctional government, weak finance and economic underperformance. Both have sought to be politically influential, Brazil doubling the number of its embassies in Africa in 2003–9 to 30, and South Africa seeking to act as the regional power in its part of the continent.

China, in contrast, is a key provider of markets and investment, and therefore of great importance to other countries. Thus, Latin American copper and lithium, Iranian and Russian oil, and Australian coal, iron and natural gas all flow to China. It has energy needs met by imports, but its growth rate makes it easier to deal with the situation than is the case with Europe. The size and growing wealth of its population also makes China a significant market, buying in 2021 more than a third of the world's cars and about a

RIGHT: The BRICS summit of 2012.

quarter of its clothing and shoes. This became a key market for Chinese industry, which gave its companies particular strength.

In manufacturing and service terms across the world, the likely implications of new technology are unclear, but there is probably going to be a lower need for labour in some areas, notably due to automation including AI, and it is unclear how far it will be possible to make changes without causing considerable disquiet. There are related issues in generational opportunities, which are much greater for young workers. Yet, they are under pressure from population growth and their prospects affected by trade union-linked restrictive practices on behalf of existing workers. Moreover, the need in recently expanded labour spheres, such as care work, is predominantly for female workers. As a result, opportunities in labour markets for poorly skilled men have greatly deteriorated, and this helped provide a social basis for the upsurge in populism in the 2010s and, even more, the 2020s, notably in the US and Europe.

These and other issues can be seen in social dynamics, as well as in divisions in economic activity within individual countries, some of them as significant in economic terms as those between them. Thus, both prosperity and growth rates in rural India and China are far lower than those in urban areas. In India, the north and east has failed to match the prosperity of the south and west. Bangalore, a centre of the Indian tech industry, and Mumbai, of finance and media, are worlds away in experiences and assumptions from the low-efficiency agriculture of much of the heavily populated Ganges Valley. In China, the rural west sees poverty, whereas agricultural areas in the east are helped by the market of nearby growing cities. The same rural–urban divide is the case in Japan, Europe and the US, but, in each case, much of the population left the land in the late 20th century. Nevertheless, rural poverty is a problem in each, and, in turn, the resulting impact on consumption hits other aspects of the local economies of agrarian areas.

LEFT: Bangalore, heart of the Indian tech industry.

The geographical approach to economies draws correct attention to factors in physical and human geography, notably resources and politics, that lead to contrasts within, as well as between, national economic performances. However, there are other common strands to consider. These include the need for appropriately skilled labour, the value of social capital, the costs of expensive social welfare systems, the value of government support and the difficulties that arise from protectionism. These, and other factors, award skill and nuance in economic management, but those are often in limited supply.

The pressures of international competition in the 2020s, and the resulting risks and costs, are not likely, as they should, to encourage an emphasis in political leadership on informed economic management and the pursuit of fiscal stability; and that failure will probably contribute to the developing international crisis.

LEFT: Threshing in Punjab. The rural–urban divide in India has never been greater.

LOOKING AHEAD

The international crisis of the 2020s was accompanied by an unravelling, or at least weakening, of existing supply chains, notably those linking the US and China, and those joining Germany and Russia. However, this process underlined the extent to which China was already dominant in emerging technologies and, therefore, best placed to control their development and, probably, successors. Thus, by 2022, China controlled more than 80 per cent of world solar panel manufacturing and, in 2023, was responsible for 75 per cent of the world's clean energy manufacturing investment. It was the leader in the production of electric vehicles, solar cells and lithium batteries. The Chinese model will probably continue to be successful. It is one of state support, easy credit, the manipulation of commercial law and trading relationships, for example the under-pricing of exports that was, in practice, a form of protectionism, and relatively low-cost labour.

The Chinese will use their economic heft to strengthen existing supply chains and create new ones, especially seeking raw materials from Africa and Latin America. If China seizes control of Taiwan, then it will increase its control over the production of advanced semiconductors. The major development of the Chinese navy and of anti-ship weaponry from the 2010s, so that it can challenge its US counterpart, is designed both to make it easier to intimidate,

BELOW: Solar panel manufacturing, Jiangxi, China, 2021.

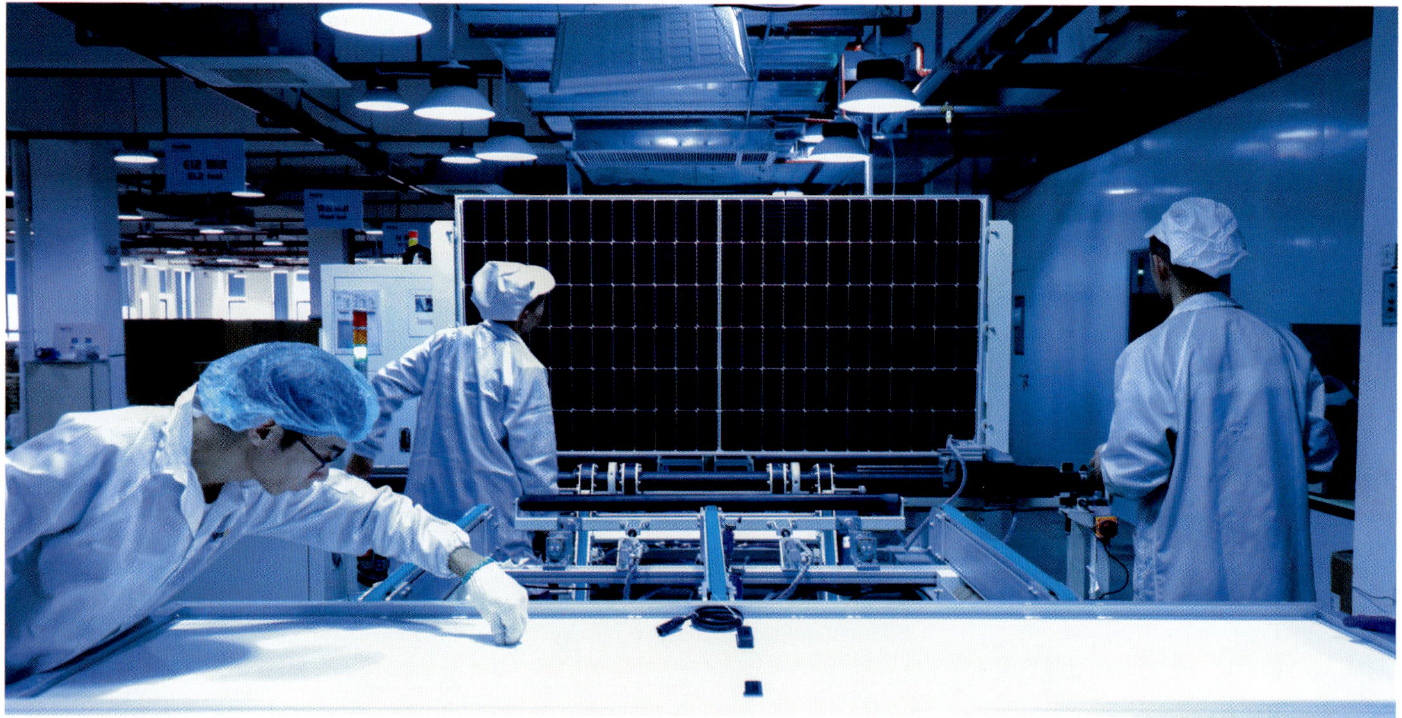

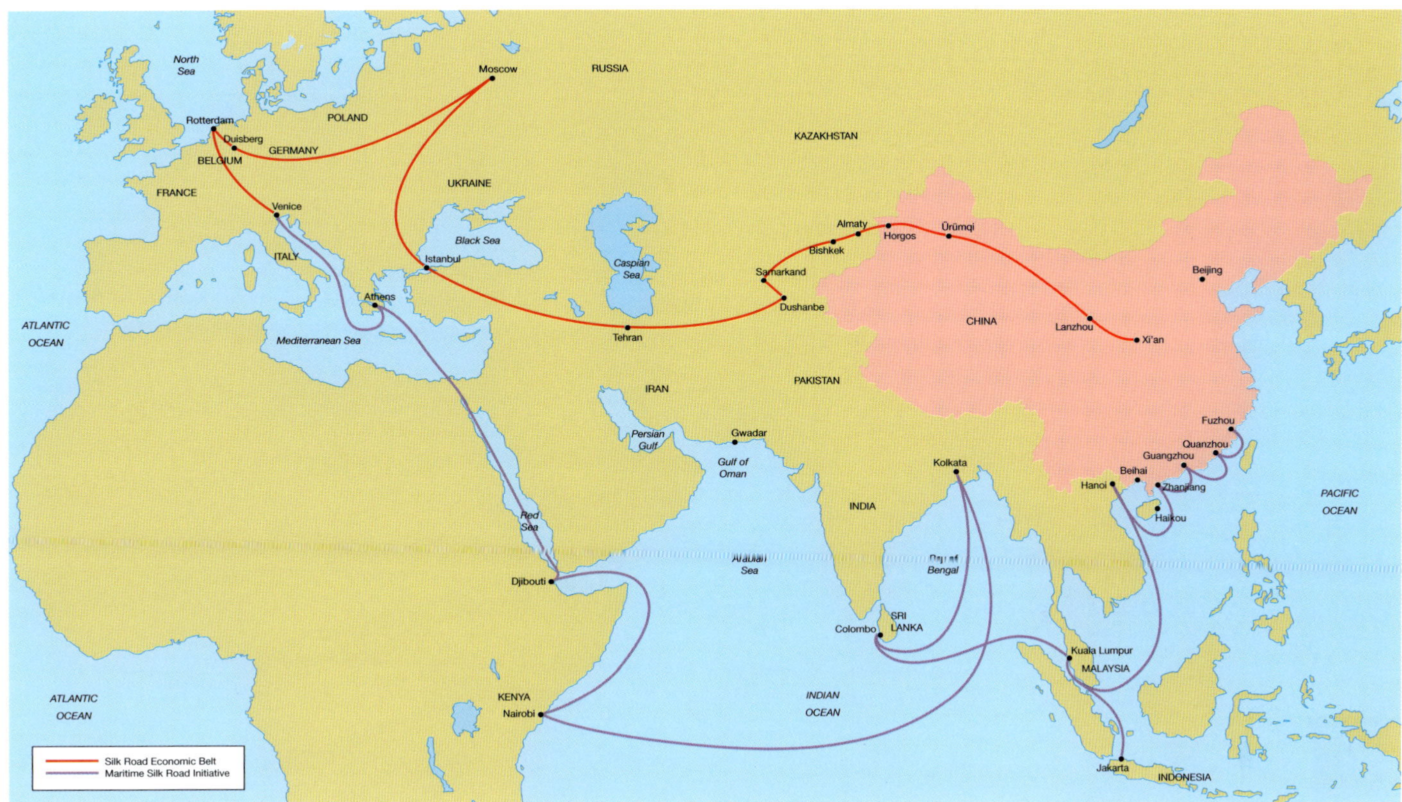

ABOVE: The Belt and Road Initiative.

blockade and seize Taiwan, and to protect the maritime routes that serve to provide resources for China, for example oil from Iran, and link it to markets. China has one of the lowest amounts of per capita arable land. Its energy and food imports largely come by sea, including more than half of its oil imports and half of its gas, while it is the largest coal importer in the world, mostly from Indonesia and Australia. China is seeking security for its existing maritime routes and pursuing new maritime links, notably to Western Europe, as a result of the melting of Arctic ice.

China is also seeking to develop rail connections across Asia. Under President Xi Jinping's 'Belt and Road' initiative adopted in 2013, international aid for infrastructure is linked to the development of 'rail corridors' that provide geopolitical and economic capabilities. Thus, in 2015, Xi launched the China–Pakistan Economic Corridor, a bilateral project that envisaged the modernization of Pakistan's transport systems, including an overland rail route from China to the deep-sea Indian Ocean port of Gwadar. In practice, such distant links have proved more elusive than shorter lines, notably to Vientiane, the capital of neighbouring Laos, opened in 2021, and a new link to neighbouring Mongolia opened in 2022. Cost, terrain and politics are all factors inhibiting the delivery of planned routes, for example to Kathmandu in Nepal and to more distant Singapore.

In addition, the relationship between military preparedness and economic position remains important. From the late 1940s, and even more 1950, this relationship ensured that the economic expansion of Western Europe, Japan and South Korea was part of a US system. The extent to which the Western economy is now more multi-centred is one change, especially from the late 1960s, but so also is the rival determination of China to establish a strong and defendable basis for its economic reach.

The ability of the US and Europe to match the Chinese position through protectionism

ABOVE: A container ship at the deep-sea port of Gwadar in Pakistan, 2016.

and government support is unclear, as is the likely nature of India's trajectory. Debt is about 120 per cent of GDP in the US, 115 per cent in France and 100 per cent in Britain, and the share of GDP needed to service government debts is rising in all three. The room for public investment for the future is lessened by current commitments, notably in social welfare. Nevertheless, it is clear that a 'market decides' policy will not be followed in a West increasingly confrontational towards an ascendant China. As a result, notably of the unravelling of some global supply chains, 'free market' policies will be sidelined, and notably so at the international level.

Furthermore, concerns about domestic stability, notably in the face of populist pressures, will encourage the pursuit of full-employment policies, in so far as these are possible. Where they are lacking or not possible, there are clear problems for political stability, not least where there are many young men, as in South Africa, Algeria and Egypt.

Many of the current constraints on economic activity provided by energy availability and cost will be overcome by the major expansion in solar power. But it is unclear that sufficient jobs can be created. This is a particular issue in Africa, where the median age is young, 40 per cent of the population being under 15 in 2023.

SHOPPING AND SELLING: A RETAIL REVOLUTION

Thessalonika in Greece, with its still-active crowded historic central market and yet also its more recent car-thronged suburban supermarkets, is typical of a major change that is significant both in economic terms and with reference to patterns and assumptions of social activity. In place of long-established personal links at markets and on high streets, with shoppers purchasing individual goods from specialists, notably the butcher, the baker, the greengrocer, and so on, came the mass purchasing of economies of scale. As a result, shopping chains could undersell independent shops. Furthermore, supermarket shopping was encouraged by car culture. Larger volume outlets encouraged advertising, by justifying the outlay and with advertising focusing on entire national markets.

Advertising also changed as a result of technological change and intensification: by radio, television and the internet. These replaced or at least overshadowed more traditional methods: in newspapers, shop windows, on billboards, the sides of buses, and by means of 'sandwich men'.

Advertising helped branding, both national and international. Products now had a global range, made possible in part by the growth of branding. New materials and technologies, such as synthetic fibres and colour photography, made advertisements more compelling than ever before. Selling and buying became key elements of social style, and of the particular styles of specific groups, notably in age, class and gender. Design was linked to this, but it was the consumerism that came first. The branding of cars by desired purchaser group was a key element of this by the early 21st century. Thus, like the whole concept of 'influencers', advertising served to sustain the distinctiveness of social groups while also seeking to redefine their preferences.

Style was central to tourist preferences and choice, and these have become more significant for economies. Thus, economics in Pacific Islands increasingly means tourism. This is now New Zealand's chief source of foreign income, but is an extremely unstable one.

BELOW: The central market in Thessalonika, Greece.

6 Culture

The cultural life of the 1950s reflected many prewar tendencies, styles and contexts, not least the contrasts between the idealized 'Socialism Realism' of Communist states, the consumerist hedonism of the US, characterized by Hollywood and jazz, and the intellectualized élite culture of Western Europe, which embraced Modernism and the abstract.

These contrasts continue in the present, and, alongside globalization, has come the vitality of this range. To think in terms of key events or themes can be unhelpful, as national contexts are so different.

Culture is a sphere that is capable of many different classifications. Whereas the word was once synonymous with 'highbrow' pursuits, it now encompasses a wide range of leisure activities within a 'culture industry'. Today, indeed, culture can in many respects be defined – if it can be defined at all – as that which consumers spend their free time and money on.

LES

THE GLOBALIZATION OF CULTURE

In the 1950s and 1960s, culture was largely regional. This was a tendency driven very much by the Cold War, which for political and commercial reasons made it difficult for movements in art, music, literature, films and television to gain traction internationally. Indeed, the term the 'Cultural Revolution', for the intensification of Chinese Communism in the late 1960s, was particularly appropriate.

POP CULTURE: 'ALL YOU NEED IS LOVE' (1967)

Our World, the first live global television link, broadcast via satellite on 25 June 1967, was watched by 400 million people in 26 countries. The Beatles' song, commissioned by the BBC as the British contribution to the programme, was designed to present a simple message that could be understood by all. As a single, the song went to number one in the British and US charts. Censorship meant that it could not be listened to in most of the rest of the world.

ABOVE: The Beatles prepare for the *Our World* television performance in 1967.

For a long time, Western commentators thought of culture in terms of the expansion of their norms and models. Never convincing, this account increasingly looks fanciful. Instead, the understanding now is of culture flowing from many areas of origin. Thus, Asia has offered K-Pop and Korean TV shows, Bollywood, Kung-Fu and international food. Yet, there has also been influence from many other directions. Popular music has proved a particularly important type and means of influence, with Nigeria being an important source in the 2020s, with musicians such as Wizkid. The Nigerian film industry, Nollywood, is highly productive and particularly important in sub-Saharan Africa. That it was not so earlier exemplifies the extent to which there are changes across time; although, as in other branches of culture, influence can be difficult to quantify and thereby to date.

At the same time, there have been many attempts to limit the spread and expression of culture, a situation that has continued and became stronger from the 2010s. Communist states proved particularly repressive, with critics and those who were different treated as dissidents, and often harshly so. In Soviet Russia, the composer Dmitri Shostakovich (1906–75), whose work was denounced in 1948, was described as waiting 'for his arrest at night out on the landing by the lift, so that at least his family wouldn't be disturbed'. He and his work were only rehabilitated in 1956. Many artists defected or were allowed to emigrate, for example the Estonian minimalist composer Arvo Pärt (1935–) who had been criticized by the Soviet regime and was allowed to leave for Austria in 1980.

In Cuba, Decree 349, issued in 2018, meant that permission had to be obtained from

BELOW: A Nollywood movie poster.

CULTURE IN ALBANIA

Ismail Kadare (1936–2024), Albania's leading writer, described the Gorky Institute of World Literature in Moscow, where he was sent for training, as 'a factory for fabricating dogmatic hacks of the socialist-realism school. In fact, they took three years to kill every creativity, every originality they possessed.' His poem 'The Red Pashas' (1975), in which officials wore the bloodstained coats of the murdered, led to his being sent to a re-education camp.

ABOVE: Ismail Kadare.

the Ministry of Culture before artistic works could be shown in public, and banned 'anything that violates ... the normal development of our society in cultural matters'. Protests against the new law led to violent arrests. Thus, repression continued alongside a loosening of economic restrictions. It was symptomatic of the situation that the artist Tania Bruguera was repeatedly arrested in 2014–15 after, as part of a performance art, she invited people to speak freely into a microphone in Cuba's Plaza de la Revolución. Many Cuban artists left for the US and Spain.

At present, China very much polices opinion, but so also do other authoritarian states, as well as Islamic ones.

Key changes in the context of culture in our period include rising literacy rates around the world, with developments in China playing a major part in the diminishing percentage of the illiterate in the late 20th century. India was less to the fore in tackling illiteracy. There has also been an increased standardization of language, with the number of distinct languages falling, Manchu being one that died out in the 2010s. This decline is linked to the pressures of globalization and the strength of English in information transmission. At

LEFT: Journalists waiting at Revolution Square for Tania Bruguera, 30 December 2014.

ABOVE: A McDonald's in Tokyo, 2023.

the start of 2008, Wikipedia contained more than 9 million entries in 250 languages, but over 2 million were in English. The impact of English can also be seen in the content of pidgin and creole forms of language, for example in the Caribbean.

The global branding of food chains, notably McDonald's (in France which by 2024 had 1,500 branches, a counterpart to Disneyland Paris) is a particular form of cultural globalization. In 2014, 87 per cent of French adults ate pasta, rice or noodles at least once a week.

Across the range of culture, there was a degree of novelty with the production of popular 'lowbrow' works, as in the manipulation of images through digital enhancement. Nevertheless, compared to much 'highbrow' culture, there was often a reluctance to experiment with form and style. This contrast sustained the differences seen with the earlier impact of Modernism, ensuring that there were dissimilar understandings and experiences of culture and the arts. These understandings and experiences reflected not just stylistic pluralism, but also the wider cultural politics of societies containing very different levels of income, education and expectation. One clear contrast is that offered by age, with the young more committed to new technologies for transmission and consumption, and readier to welcome new styles, idioms and ideas.

SPORT

Sport shifted into high-value economics, notably so from the 1980s, becoming a mass commodity worth hundreds of billions of dollars internationally as a form of universal consumerism. As a key element of globalization, football became the world game, with British clubs having foreign owners, including from the US, and being very attractive to East Asian supporters and gamblers, and not only there. Latin American countries and African players increased their presence and success rates in football, even if the Africans tend to be trained in France where facilities are far better.

Other sports had a global coverage. Born Cassius Clay, the US heavyweight boxer Muhammad Ali (1942–2016) was undisputed champion from 1974 to 1978, and had famed bouts in Kinshasa (1974) and Manila (1976). The former, 'The Rumble in the Jungle', was one of the most watched television events of all time, with, it was claimed, 1 billion viewers, about a quarter of the world's population, although that was probably an exaggeration.

Sport very much reflects international links, baseball being important in Cuba and the Dominican Republic, and cricket in Australasia, South Asia, and the former British West Indies, but not in former French colonies. In 2023, 87 per cent of sports advertising, sponsorship and endorsements in India went on cricket. Football also has a strong following in former colonies, particularly former French colonies, notably Senegal.

There has been a movement in relative success. In 1984–6, West Indies cricket teams won 5-0 victories over England in Test match series that were known as 'blackwashes', with West Indies' bowlers devastating British teams.

BELOW: The 'Rumble in the Jungle' fight between Muhammad Ali and George Forman in Kinshasa, 1974.

As a form of culture, sport works across societies, encompassing professionals and amateurs. Television has greatly served to encourage its reach, and has further commercialized sport so that some cannot afford access to it. This is a key element of the link between technology and culture. Sport has also served as a political weapon, as with boycotts of South Africa under apartheid, as well as controversy over sports representation, as with Russia's participation in the 2024 Olympics.

CINEMA

Cinema is a classic instance of the development of a more globalized appreciation of culture. At the same time, trends are more complex. There was a difference between a global system in 1950 dominated by American products, and that of today in which not only are there several different sources, but also no one model of production. The 1950s saw US films and film technology to the fore. In the 1957 hit *Silk Stockings*, Fred Astaire and Janis Paige in the song and dance number 'Stereophonic Sound' sing about how film audiences now expect such sound as well as a 'glorious technicolor' and 'breathtaking cinemascope'. The role of American models was seen in Disney theme parks, at Anaheim in California (1955) followed by Orlando in Florida (1971), and, further afield, Tokyo (1983) and, in 1992, EuroDisney in France (now called Disneyland Paris) – which by 2022 had received 375 million visitors.

RIGHT: Disneyland Paris, opened in 1992.

Yet, a contrast in content and tone in cinema was present from the outset, as in Italian 'neo-realist' films from the late 1940s, while the *Nouvelle Vague* (New Wave) of the late 1950s saw French films that differed from the standard fare of Hollywood in accepting the complexity of life. In turn, however, differences between national cinema traditions have become more apparent, and understandably so. Cinema is crucial to the propagation of identities, the understanding of experience and the framing of aspirations. It offers the apparent accuracy of photography, but employs it to present alternative realities. *La Haine*, which won Mathieu Kassovitz the Best Director prize at the 1995 Cannes Film Festival, depicted the consequences of police brutality in Paris's poor suburbs.

It is always unclear where to put the emphasis. For West Germany, the New German Cinema movement of 1962–82 included creative figures such as Werner Herzog, Wim Wenders and Rainer Werner Fassbinder, and their works enjoyed international attention. Yet, high culture scarcely exhausted the range there. Genre directors were also very successful. Active from 1958 to 1984, Alfred Vohrer turned out a large number of mystery films based on the novels of Edgar Wallace, such as *Der Hexer* (*The Warlock*, 1964). There were also the films of Karl May novels, and, both set in New York, the Jerry Cotton and Kommissar X series. The New Wave directors attacked these films as *Opas Kino* ('Grandpa's cinema'), and there was definitely a reaction against the escapist *Heimatfilme* ('Homeland Films') of the 1950s, with Social Realism more to the fore by the late 1960s. Yet, most of the New Wave Cinema had limited commercial success or artistic legacy. In addition, the films shown in East Germany included many Westerns.

ABOVE: Werner Herzog.

Films captured a mood, but could also seek to make it normative. Thus, in the US in the 1970s, an anti-authoritarian theme, critical of government, was seen in many films, such as *All the President's Men* (1976), an account of the Watergate conspiracy. As part of a tendency to believe in conspiracy that became more prominent in American culture, authority, at all levels, was also presented as corrupt and dangerous in a range of films, from *Chinatown* (1974), a portrayal of 'Old Money' as evil, to *Apocalypse Now* (1979), a searing portrayal of the Vietnam War. The vacuous quality of affluent society was a theme of *Shampoo* (1975), and a wider alienation was displayed in films such as *Taxi Driver* (1976).

Bollywood became a key producer of films in India, producing more than 800 a year by the late 1990s, while Nigeria's Nollywood did the same for sub-Saharan Africa. The norms and even the tunes of Bollywood musicals were more widely influential, for example across South and Southeast Asia, the Middle East, and Latin America. Chinese films, in contrast, were more attuned to government ends, not least in presenting an account of history in which China was assailed by the West and Japan, as with Xie Jin's film *The Opium War* (1997). This was an aspect of a potent cultural nationalism. In 1991, the General Secretary of the Chinese Communist Party, Jiang Zemin, wrote that patriotic education would 'let the Chinese people, especially the youth, enhance their pride and self-confidence in the nation' and thus avoid 'the worship of the West'. The number of films produced annually in China rose from more than 40 in the 1970s to about 100 by 2004.

Governments could criticize films they disliked. The US-made *300* (2017), an account of the heroic Greek resistance at Thermopylae to a major Persian invasion in 480 BCE was described as 'insulting to Iran' by Mahmoud Ahmadinejad, that country's prime minister. *Argo* (2012), a US account of the Tehran hostage crisis of 1979–80, was similarly condemned. As with most film accounts of history, *Argo* was simplistic, not dealing with the political dimensions of the hostage crisis within the US.

ABOVE: A poster for the 1979 movie *Apocalypse Now*.

The profitability of cinema has been affected by the rise of television and, subsequently, of cable television and then of streaming, such that streaming companies selling subscriptions, for example Netflix, did well, only, in turn, to be challenged by new rivals, notably Apple TV and Amazon. Film producers have

RIGHT: *Westworld* (1973) was the first movie to use computer-generated imagery.

responded with Disney launching a streaming service, Disney+, in 2019, and some movies went straight to streaming. Online film-watching hit traditional cinemas, a comparable move to the impact on bookshops of the online purchase of books.

The production techniques of film have been greatly affected by the potential resulting from digitization. CGI (Computer-Generated Imagery) has had a major impact, with CGI used with live action from *Westworld* (1973). The scope increased greatly from the 1990s with the development of 'virtual cinematography' techniques.

CONSUMERIST PRESSURES

'I do feel that independent producers should take note of public demand and make films of entertainment value. The public has clearly shown that it does not want the dreary kitchen sink dramas.'
Sir John Davis, managing director of the Rank Organisation, owners of the important Odeon cinema chain in Britain, 1963.

'These people are not brash or stupid. They know exactly what they're aiming at, what their audiences want, and they're just striking a different balance between entertainment and content. And they're very proud of that.'
Mike Bartlett, the writer of the BBC series *Press*, after a research visit to the *Sun*, the leading British tabloid. Quoted in the *Sunday Times*, 19 August 2018.

TELEVISION

The 'box in the corner' represented what was superficially a far more individualistic consumption of culture than the dominant film screen watched by a large audience. There is considerable choice in what is watched when multiple channels are present and, even more so, when programmes can be stored and watched whenever the viewer chooses. However, in many countries, choice is severely limited by government, while even when there is a market, that is restricted by the exigencies of financing. In this way television is not simply driven by consumers, however important that might be in some countries, notably those with capitalist economies and advanced technologies.

Consumers are particularly important when there is advertising revenue at stake, as their choices of programme provide opportunities for television companies to sell advertising space. However, that model only existed in some national systems, notably the US, with regulatory processes often a consequence of particular national political cultures. This includes the decision as to whether to have a national broadcaster, as with the BBC (British Broadcasting Corporation). There is no national broadcaster in America.

Following the earlier interwar pattern with radio, television ownership became far more common from the 1950s, with mass production manufacturing less expensive models in North America and Western Europe, while rising real wages and consumer fashions encouraged this trend. In particular, television in large part replaced or minimized the role of both radio and cinema because of its ability to act as a family medium for entertainment and cohesion. This was seen in the programmes of the period, such as *Leave it to Beaver*, an American situation comedy of 1957–63 with a perfect suburban housewife and perfect bread-winning husband discussing their troublesome son, Beaver, round a well-provided dinner table.

ABOVE: A family watching television in the 1950s.

Individual programmes, as well as the very process of watching the television, acquired an iconic force, expressing values and encouraging the sharing of experience that was

THE 24-HOUR NEWS CYCLE

Day-round news and opinion has transformed the culture of politics, economics and much else. The time available for research, reflection, and strategic analysis and recommendation has been brutally foreshortened. Bullet points and instant opinion have come to the fore.

ABOVE: A news broadcast. With television channels created to present news around the clock, there was less time for researching and analyzing stories.

particularly pronounced when there were relatively few channels. For both families and individuals, mealtimes were organized round the television, which, in turn, provided copy for newspapers. Television stars followed cinema counterparts in winning fame.

American programmes helped make aspects of life elsewhere appear unattractive. Thus, in Britain, beards and moustaches seemed out of place given the clean-shaven men on US programmes. So also with living in terraced housing and coal fires. Television also became more attractive to consumers as it adopted colour, developed more channels, and attracted more investment in programming. The rise of television culture was dramatic, not least with longer broadcasting hours and rising viewer numbers.

In turn, in the early 21st century, television companies lost market share as entertainment and news became more diverse with internet provision and new providers more important, and notably so for the younger generations. Despite the possibilities offered by 'on demand' asynchronous television, terrestrial television has been diminished in importance by satellite and cable services, which are all now being diminished by streaming services such as Netflix, which greatly expanded viewing, and, even more, by YouTube and social media. Indeed, in democratic, capitalist societies, there were serious problems for traditional service providers, as they lost market share, relevance and profitability. Ironically, there was also the rise of television nostalgia, notably in the US and Britain with channels such as Talking Pictures TV and Rewind TV, which show programmes from the late 20th century.

History, itself, in the sense of the presentation and understanding of the past, was greatly influenced, with television a key element in the shift from literary to visual exposition; a process also seen with news reporting. Fluency, but also simplicity, characterize visual accounts, with a unitary account of the past (and present) that offers little nuance in explanation. It is necessary to have pictures. This is an aspect of the 'surface' and often moralizing nature of visual culture. Furthermore, it was also more individual, with software-based products providing platforms for user-generated content.

IDEAS OF IDENTITY: TO POSTMODERNISM AND BEYOND

Philosophical ideas of relative values and of the subjective nature of experience and understanding became more important in the West from the 1960s, at least in so far as fashionable academic theory was concerned. Paris was the centre of an intellectual world that felt able to offer an important cultural alternative to that of an unwelcome American influence which was unfairly stereotyped as consumerist.

Radical intellectual influences contributed to a sense of flux and also to established norms and values being seen as simply passing conventions. In the two decades after World War II, fashionable European culture was greatly influenced by Existentialism, a nihilistic Continental philosophical movement, closely associated with Martin Heidegger (1889–1976), Søren Kierkegaard (1813–55) and Jean-Paul Sartre (1905–80), that stressed the vulnerability of the individual in a hostile world, and the emptiness of choices. Novels affected by these notions, such as those of Albert Camus (1913–60), for example *The Plague* (1947), had an impact, as did plays, most obviously the work of Sartre, for example *No Exit* (1944). Their influence in the US, in contrast, was minimal.

This approach connected with the non-realist 'Theatre of the Absurd' associated with the works of Samuel Beckett (1906–89), such as *Waiting for Godot* (first performed in 1953), and Eugène Ionesco (1909–94), author of *The Bald Soprano* (first performed in 1950), both of whom settled in Paris. The extent to which these ideas merited much attention was inherently contentious, but, more significantly, the nature of economic activity and personal experience, and the role of material culture, did not match this apparent suggestion of an inherent unreality.

BELOW: A performance of *Waiting for Godot* in Paris, 1953.

Structuralism, a movement that looked in particular to the anthropologist Claude Lévi-Strauss (1908–2009) and the literary critic Roland Barthes (1915–80), treated language as a set of conventions that were themselves of limited values as guides to any underlying reality, Barthes focusing, for example in his *Mythologies* (1957), on semiotics, the study of signs, arguing that they had mythic weight. Although links (like definitions) were far from clear-cut, this situation looked towards the Postmodernism that became influential in the 1980s.

Information as an objective ideal and progressive practice was affected by the problematizing of meaning and power by Jacques Derrida (1930–2004) and Michel Foucault (1926–84), respectively. Each emphasized the subjectivity of disciplines and categories, and the extent to which they reflected and sustained

ABOVE LEFT: Jacques Derrida.
ABOVE RIGHT: Michel Foucault.

social norms. This approach encouraged a degree of intellectual introspection and of scepticism, notably in terms of the values of categories such as nations. Ironically, in critiquing power, these thinkers and their supporters gained and deployed considerable academic power of their own. Even though philosophically the theory was problematic, the notion of fluid identities became more potent, at least in the West in the early 21st century, and especially so from the 2010s.

There was scant equivalence in China, the Islamic world, or indeed for most of human society. Instead, for most people, ideas of shown and felt experience as real within a context that did not rest on individual perception alone, but, rather, of essential truths of existence, were dominant. The principal division was that between religious belief or secularism. In that respect, there was no essential variation during the period, or between it and earlier periods.

Looking to the future, ideas of identity will become more pressing with the genetic modification of humans, an emphasis on robots, the extent to which machines become properly conscious, and the degree to which virtual reality will become pretty indistinguishable from reality. Many people may find these prospects attractive, and even addictive.

POP MUSIC, FROM THE BEATLES TO THE PRESENT

The sound of the century was pop music. Popular music had always been important, but now it was a major and highly profitable commodity, largely produced in studios and disseminated by radio, tapes, discs, and via the internet. Commercialism, in the form of the entrepreneurial packaging and presentation of performers, was to the fore. Moreover, many performers were global in their aspiration, with world tours a marketing choice of particular significance. This did not preclude from significance musicians who had an essentially national market, but, in these cases also, there was an emphasis, compared to the earlier age, on the transmission of recordings, often from a distance, rather than on performance in person.

Stylistic changes at first reflected the dominance of US models and performers, with rock and roll a key trend of the 1950s, as was bebop, improvised jazz with complex rhythms. British musicians such as The Beatles became of consequence in the 1960s because they were able to make an impact on the US market and more widely, although Bob Dylan (1941–), an American singer-songwriter whose debut album appeared in 1962, was a fundamental influence, symbolizing the transition from folk to accepted rock and producing iconic songs such as 'Blowin' in the Wind' (1963), 'The Times They Are a-Changin' (1964) and 'Like a Rolling Stone' (1965). He was awarded the Nobel Prize in Literature in 2016.

The range of successful musical types available for the British and US markets was shown with reggae. This Jamaican style,

ABOVE: A record of *Sgt. Pepper's Lonely Hearts Club Band* by the Beatles, 1967.

POPULAR MUSIC AS REVOLUTIONARY

Love and aspects of consumerism were to the fore in popular music, but there could also be a revolutionary dimension, or at least an assault on existing conventions. John Lennon of The Beatles argued in 1971 that songs such as 'Give Peace a Chance', 'Power to the People' and 'All You Need Is Love' were propaganda songs, adding 'I'm a revolutionary artist. My art is dedicated to change.'

ABOVE: Bob Marley.

beginning in the late 1960s, built on a range of musical genres, including calypso, jazz and African folk music, and was characterized by a heavy bass sound, Jamaican patois lyrics and offbeat rhythms. Bob Marley (1945–81), the leading figure, a Jamaican singer-songwriter, became an international icon. Like rap, reggae reflected the ethnic contribution to Western music; a process later to be seen with the electronic dance music of the 2000s known as grime and dubstep, in both of which syncopated rhythms are to the fore.

There was also the contribution of the working class, with popular music helping their language and mores become more significant in mainstream culture. This was the case with The Beatles and their successors in the 1960s, but, in the more divided 1970s, this process proved more difficult. In Britain, the violence of the punk aesthetic, as in the Sex Pistols' debut single 'Anarchy in the UK' (1976) and their album *Never Mind the Bollocks, Here's the Sex Pistols* (1977), was mirrored by 'Oi!' music, that of skinheads, mostly working-class Londoners, that was often misogynistic.

As with film, there was a challenge with an attack on Western-dominated globalization in the early 21st century. There was a determined rejection of Western styles in a range of countries, a pattern that will continue to be the case. Non-Western tendencies and examples have become more influential in recent decades, notably Afrobeats from Nigeria and Ghana,

LEFT: Flavour N'abania and Victoria Kimani, two leading Afrobeats artists.

and Congolese rumba. Afrobeats is a fusion, from the 1960s, of different West African music including Juju, a Nigerian style that was particularly popular in the 1990s. Afrobeats became newly coherent and vigorous from the 2000s. Drum-beat rhythms play a major role, and drummers such as Nigeria's Flavour N'abania (real name Chinedu Okoli) took a major role. In 2021, Congolese rumba, which developed from the mid-20th century, was added to the UNESCO list of intangible cultural heritage. Guitars are the key instruments, and the rapid chord changes of the music helps make the rhythm arresting.

At the same time, the continued salience of American popular music was seen with the success of Taylor Swift's Eras tour in 2023–24. The standard theme of her songs was very much a traditional one, and this success was echoed in the revival of many 'heritage bands' in the 2020s.

LEFT: Taylor Swift, one of the most successful modern singers.

MODERN ART

Tattoos are the most vivid demonstration of the prevalence of art today, possibly followed by graffiti. Far more people are involved in tattooing than in what are more traditionally seen as the arts, while graffiti has become the prime public art of the modern city, one connecting more particularly with the young than the statuary erected in a very different way of recording current norms. Statuary is official, graffiti unofficial, if not illegal.

To a degree, however, there is overlap as well as contrast. The break with conventional artistic approaches that characterized the 1960s was seen in graffiti as much as theatre or painting. So also with a reaction towards a degree of realism. And yet, as with much art, both tattoos and graffiti are culturally very specific, with tattooing long favoured in Oceania and more recently increasingly prevalent in parts of the West, such as Britain; but this is not the case for Asia or the Islamic world. In 2016, it was estimated in Britain that one in five people and one in three young adults there had tattoos, and these percentages were higher by the mid-2020s.

More generally, the person became more clearly a work of art, with previous conventions in hairstyles and make-up abandoned, as were restraints on piercings and unusual jewellery

BELOW: Graffiti on a New York subway train, 1973.

in the shape of studs and chains. Noses, tongues, eyelids, tummy buttons, breasts and genitals were among the parts of the body embellished with studs, rings and other objects. Rather than being limited to women, as with jewellery, most men were part of the process, for example with their earlobes and eyelids thus decorated. At the same time that fashion helped set the tone for appearance and behaviour, so both tattoos and graffiti, and the arts in general, were deliberately unconventional in content and presentation. Graffiti is the artform of particular urban milieux but is not seen in many non-Western cities.

Approaching modern art from the popular dimension avoids the somewhat modish concentration on particular styles and methods that have scant impact on the bulk of the population, at the national and still less global level. In practice, there can be crossovers between these approaches, as in advertising which is both functional and yet stylistic. This level of utilitarian art very much interacts with the public, as also, for example, does the artistic design seen in fields such as car manufacture. These aspects, however, tend to be underplayed in the formal discussion of modern art.

So also for the specific arts. Thus, to take literature, the most popular novelist has been the British writer Agatha Christie (1890–1976). By 2016, beaten only by the Bible and William Shakespeare, her sales exceeded 2 billion books in more than 100 languages, including 100 million copies for *And Then There Were None* (1939). There have been over 7,000 translations of her work, and the impact has been worldwide. For example, 1.1 million people saw the film *Murder on the Orient Express* (1974) when it was shown in West German cinemas in 1975, while the film *Death on the Nile* (1984) was shown 54 times between 2015 and 2020 on German, Austrian and Swiss television.

No painting, play or sculpture has had this impact, and to focus on critically well-received but unpopular works is to downplay the significance of those works that have been more influential, and continue to be so, notably by remaining in print. Like other commentators, Christie could also comment on other arts. Thus, in her novel *Endless Night* (1967), the conservative landowner Major Phillpot, a self-proclaimed 'bit of an old square', nevertheless likes a new house: 'It's got shape and light. And when you look out from it you see things – well, in a different way from the way you've seen them before – very interesting.'

In the early 21st century, there was some recovery of realist themes in Western culture. For example, in reaction to the atonal music that lacks a key, avant-garde composers such as Olivier Messiaen (1908–92), Iannis Xenakis (1922–2001), and Pierre Boulez (1925–2016) rediscovered melody, as with Joan Tower's *Made in America* (2005).

At the same time, there was a continuity in the situation that had become insistent from the 1960s, that of the importance of the views and interests of the young. Youth culture was a key element of consumerism and helped make many earlier preferences appear redundant.

BACK TO BARBARISM

'The burning wreckage of the island' was a consequence of the mayhem described in William Golding's 1954 debut novel *Lord of the Flies*, which described the murderous breakdown of civilization among a group of British boys stranded on an uninhabited Pacific island. The quest for power and a joy in savagery triumphed all. This was a profoundly pessimistic account of the human condition.

MODERN ARCHITECTURE

Architecture, like art or music, sees an interaction of technology, style, entrepreneurialism, theory and criticism, all played out in different national and social contexts. The need to construct large numbers of buildings was a key driver, as, particularly during the 'Long Boom' of 1945–73, was the disposable wealth, public and private, that made this possible. Expenditure was concentrated in the wealthier countries, notably in the West, but subsequently for example in the Gulf states, with functional design issues to the fore for housing and business purposes.

ABOVE: Le Corbusier in 1964.

There were global design trends, notably linked to the Modernism espoused by Le Corbusier (Charles-Edouard Jeanneret, 1887–1965), whose first public commission was for postwar housing in Marseille. He also played a major role, alongside the Brazilian Oscar Niemeyer (1907–2012), in designing the United Nations headquarters. In his design for Chandigarh, the capital city of the states of Punjab and Haryana in India which was built from 1951 to 1962, Le Corbusier used the raw concrete he favoured, describing it as a 'new art'. In practice, his schemes were overly domineering, with the individual works often off-putting by their scale as well as destructive of the complexities of human society and cultural heritage. His 'Cities in the Sky' often ended up as unattractive public housing.

Modernism, ironically, could underplay the significance of functional considerations, such as the problems that flat roofs posed in the face of heavy rainfall. Separately, the production of cement used to bind concrete is, for chemical as well as energy-using reasons, a major source of carbon dioxide emissions.

Alongside Modernism as a global style, there were particular regional and national emphases to Modernism, as in Afro-Modernism, such as the Hôtel Ivoire and La Pyramide in Abidjan, Côte d'Ivoire, as well as reactions to it, and often against it. Public bodies are generally the biggest commissioners of buildings. This is the case both of large individual works, such as universities and hospitals, and of multiple units, especially council houses. The importance of public commissions encouraged the production of designs that were believed likely to appeal to government advisers, and this moulded the profession more widely than the actual commissioning process itself. Approved techniques and styles were reinforced through the planning process. The requirement for planning permission provided many and insistent opportunities for the propagation and enforcement of specific agendas. Proscriptive and prescriptive governmental pressures are readily apparent.

A reaction against Modernism, and against the Postmodern after-echo of the 1980s and 1990s, became more apparent in the early 21st century, in particular with a concern

LEFT: Brasilia, the new capital of Brazil, built in 1956 as a symbol of modernity.

BRASILIA: THE CITY AS MODERNIST MONUMENT

Built from 1956, the only 20th-century city to become a World Heritage site, Brazil's federal capital of Brasilia celebrated its 50th anniversary in 2010. Symbolizing the country's mission to modernize and to spread Brazil inland from the coast, the city, which replaced Rio de Janeiro as capital in 1960, was located in an area of tropical savannah. Its planner, Lúcio Costa (1902–98), gave it the outline form of an aircraft, with a long axis that included the governmental buildings designed to represent a fuselage, and residential section wings. Oscar Niemeyer, a protégé of Le Corbusier, designed many of the buildings. In a comment on the social politics of Le Corbusier's ideas of cities, Brasilia is now surrounded by shanty towns, the population of which provide much of its workforce.

with comfort as an aspect of functionality. Classical design features again came to the fore in a rejection of the minimalism seen with Modernism and its ally Brutalism. New Classicism is linked in many contexts to an interest in new traditional architecture that emphasizes particular traditions and materials, as with the Neo-Andean style developed by the self-taught Bolivian architect Freddy Mamani (1971–). The International Network for Traditional Building, Architecture and Urbanism was founded in 2001, and the Driehaus Architecture Prize followed in 2003. It is awarded to a living architect whose work 'promotes and encourages architectural excellence that applies the principles of traditional, classical and sustainable architecture'.

RIGHT: La Pyramide, Abidjan.

THE FUTURE CHARLES III ASSAILS MODERNISM

As Prince of Wales, speaking at the Royal Institute of British Architects, Charles praised signs of a Neoclassical revival – 'at last people are beginning to see that it is possible, and important in human terms, to respect old building street plans and traditional scales' – and in 1988 attacked Modernism, describing cities littered with 'huge, blank and impersonal' buildings, the Brutalist National Theatre as 'a clever way of building a nuclear power station in the middle of London', initial plans for the extension to the National Gallery as a 'monstrous carbuncle' and those for the new British Library as 'a dim collection of brick sheds and worse'.

TRENDS IN WESTERN CULTURE

In the US, there was a degree of homogenization, notably thanks to the sway of television culture, as well as the significance of national brands, which included the assimilation of traditions. This was part of the 'melting-pot' practice of American culture, as with Leonard Bernstein's successful musical *West Side Story* (1957). At the same time, there were signs of difference. These ranged from the rap music which developed in the Bronx in the 1970s to the popularity in 2004 of the film *The Passion of Christ*, an attempt to recreate the last days of Christ's life that was designed to elicit religious fervour. Nevertheless, a decline in the distinctiveness of particular parts of the US was to the fore, notably with desegregation in the South.

In the 2010s and 2020s, there was, in contrast, a strong sense in the US that the national culture was suffering increased division, with bitter political differences a symptom of a wider national malaise. This approach might exaggerate the bitterness, but captured the degree to

BELOW: A performance of *West Side Story* in 1957.

ABOVE: The Grande Arche at La Défense.

which there was a significance to culture that owed little to the arts that tend to dominate attention. Alongside the 'culture wars' of different values and norms, American society continued to emphasize the importance of material possessions, and social status remained closely reflected by the objects one owned.

Cultural change in Europe was a reflection of social and political developments, with both urbanization, and, more specifically, the eventual fall of Communism major changes. The state as patron of the arts played a greater role than in the US. Cultural patronage could be large-scale, as in the very expensive *grands projets* of François Mitterrand, France's president from 1981 to 1995. In Paris, these included the 'People's Opera', the new National Library, and the Grande Arche at La Défense. Containing an exhibition centre as well as a library, the last, finished in 1989, was described as a modern equivalent to the Arc de Triomphe, one focused on humanitarian ideas, not war. Sport was catered for in a new national stadium, the Stade de France, which was extensively used in the 2024 Paris Olympics.

In Europe, it was only in Communist countries that state patronage extended to close control over cultural content. Under the Communists, 'Socialist Realism' was both theme and content. As a result, there was a major change in Eastern Europe in the early 1990s, although it was one in several directions, including globalization, Americanization, an attempted emulation of Western Europe, and what was presented as a rediscovery of native roots. The last was taken furthest in Russia under Vladimir Putin, in part as a deliberate rejection of Western models, a rejection closely linked to an endorsement of Russian nationalism and Orthodox belief.

'CULTURE WARS'

Cultural conflict focused on values, ideologies and collective memories is scarcely new, but has become insistent in recent decades as this element both of politics and of culture has been seen as of great significance. They are an aspect of identity politics that encompasses the presentation of history, social policy, and what is more conventionally regarded as culture, in terms of forms, content and patronage. The extensive mobilization of culture by state authorities during the Cold War has now become a multi-layered process of assertion. Indeed, the number of actors in cultural assertion is an aspect of the tensions involved, with questions of authority as well as opinion very much to the fore. 'Cancellation' is used against those who are disliked.

7 World Politics

International rivalry and conflict have defined too many lives since 1945. The change in some states' fortunes since then has been dramatic. In 1950, Britain, France, Belgium, Portugal, Spain and the Netherlands were still imperial powers, controlling much of Africa, Oceania, the West Indies and Southeast Asia. Most of those colonies are now independent states.

During and after decolonization, struggles between imperial-ideological blocs came to the fore, first with the Cold War, and then, from the 2010s, with a revived Cold War. At the same time, the large number of newly independent states ensured that there were more 'players' in international relations, which therefore became more complex.

As ever, it is necessary to accept that there is no one perspective and no one account that can cover every aspect of this period. There is the need to weigh relative significance and also the problem of treating as separate developments what in fact were both simultaneous and interacting events.

THE UNITED NATIONS

A new international order derived from the Anglo-American United Nations Declarations of 1941 and the United Nations Conference on International Organization held in 1945. Its subsequent success was a matter of controversy, not least because of Cold War disputes over representation and decisions. Similarly, the idea that the International Court of Justice could use international law to ensure harmonious international relations was not realized.

Yet, the UN did no worse in preventing conflict than older systems of collective security. Ending aggression proved impossible, but there were successes, especially in the development and use of economic sanctions and arms-control diplomacy, and in integrating newly independent states into the international system. Moreover, with time, the General Assembly became larger and less dominated by the Security Council, providing a different international sounding board. States such as Brazil, Germany, India and South Africa pursued membership of the Security Council, dominated by the victors of 1945, as a sign of their significance, while claims were also made about the role of specific states as representing regional constituencies.

BELOW: The UN General Assembly in 2017.

DECOLONIZATION

Decolonization as a subject ranges from the initial independence movements, to longer-lasting legacies, not least in terms of debates about existing elements of empire that remain and shape the world today. Decolonization had many older roots but acquired a new urgency from the late 1940s. The colonial empires of Britain, France, the Netherlands, Portugal and Spain were greatly lessened within three decades. The pursuit and framing of this process led to a series of conflicts, but in the long term it proved difficult to muster continued enthusiasm for the imperial project, a marked change in European attitudes. Linked to this comes the problem of deciding how far decolonization was the product of pressure from the colonized and how far from changes in the attitudes of the colonial powers. In many cases, for example France in sub-Saharan Africa or Britain in West Africa and the West Indies, the process was peaceful, but this was not the case elsewhere, for example for France in Vietnam and Algeria, Britain in Malaya, Kenya, Cyprus and Aden, and Portugal in its African colonies.

In Vietnam, the French were defeated in 1954 at Dien Bien Phu by the nationalist Viet Minh and, although they still controlled the major centres of population, France's will was broken. In the Geneva Conference of 1954, Vietnam was divided between a Communist North and an anti-Communist South, although this was not to be a lasting settlement.

LEFT: The battle of Dien Bien Phu.

THE WIND OF CHANGE

'The wind of change is blowing through this continent, and whether we like it or not, this growth of national consciousness is a political fact.'
Harold Macmillan, speech to South African Parliament, 1960.
Macmillan, British prime minister from 1957 to 1963, oversaw widespread British decolonization, notably in Africa.

ABOVE: FLN fighters in the Algerian war, May 1955.

THE VIOLENCE

Violence came from all directions in wars of decolonization. In Algeria, the *Front de Libération Nationale* (FLN) launched an insurrection in 1954, initially with terror operations, the French army fighting back. In 1961–2, the *Organisation Armée Secrète* (OAS), a terrorist movement that wanted to keep Algeria French, attempted to disrupt the independence the de Gaulle government sought. In 1961, de Gaulle told a press conference, 'Algeria is costing us, this is the least one can say, much more than it brings us.'

Jean-Jacques Susini, a key OAS figure, defended terrorism: 'On a side street in the centre of Algiers there was an Arab who sold eggs for a living. Every day you would see him there with his tray of eggs. One day he was blown to smithereens ... are we going to [use tactics like the FLN], yes or no? The egg-seller was the first to go. Now they'll understand.'

The OAS failed and in 1962 Algeria became independent.

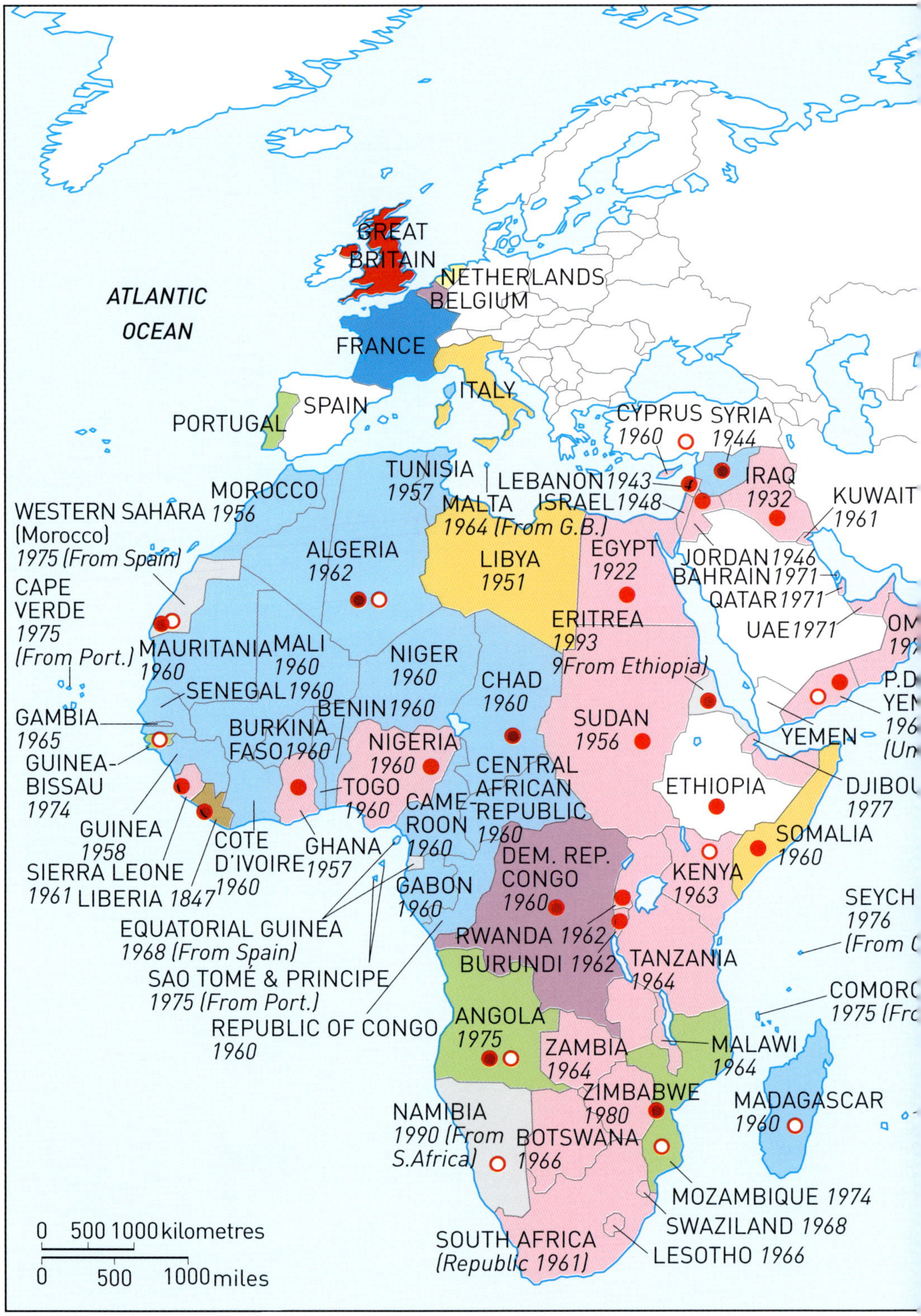

In contrast, in Malaya, where the military challenge was weaker and the Communists lacked adequate Chinese support, the British were able to contain and then beat the insurgents, while moving Malaya towards independence in 1957. The British were also able to contain and then defeat the Mau-Mau uprising in Kenya in 1952–6. The harshness of British policies of separating the guerrillas from popular

LEFT: Decolonization in the second half of the 20th century.

support, notably by large-scale detention, has since attracted much attention, but at the time appeared an appropriate response. In 1956, in response to the pan-Arab nationalism of Egypt's dictator Gamal Abdel Nasser, Britain, in the Suez Crisis, unsuccessfully sought to intimidate Egypt, only to fail totally, not least due to a lack of US support. This led to a marked speeding up of the pace of imperial retreat.

ABOVE: Gamal Abdel Nasser announces the nationalization of the Suez Canal, 26 July 1956.

Decolonization was also hastened by a strong upsurge in colonial nationalist movements, which caused problems, particularly in Ghana in West Africa. Policy-makers did not know how to confront these, as they sought to rest imperial rule primarily on consent, rather than on force. The combination of nationalism and the mass mobilization of people and resources that had characterized industrializing nations in the 19th century spread to the non-Western world and helped to undermine the logic and practice of colonial control: it was no longer practical to rely on local consent. The Western 'right to rule' colonial peoples could not be sustained in the political climate of the later 20th century. There were examples of successful military counter-insurgency, but the political contest was lost as imperialism came to seem ideologically and politically bankrupt. This factor indeed was to be more important in the collapse of Western control over most of the world than changes in military capability and effectiveness. Loss of political will, and the related unwillingness to pay the necessary political and military costs of empire, were different from the inability to maintain control; but all played a role. The hope that something would turn up was, by the late 1950s, increasingly focused on granting independence.

This process was made easier, for Britain and France, because decolonization was presented (however complacently and even misleadingly) as a benevolent process, with empire being transformed into a new relationship, in the British case the Commonwealth. Thus, imperial missions responded to the condition, needs and opportunities of the moment.

France also gave most of its sub-Saharan colonies independence in 1960, although without comparable disorder, and it maintained considerable political, economic and military influence in some, including Mali and Niger, until the 2020s. The *Communauté financière africaine* (African Financial Community), a common currency established as legal tender in 14 French African colonies in 1945, was continued and is now supported by the Euro to France's interest.

LEFT: Patrice Lumumba under arrest, 1960.

BELGIUM'S EMPIRE

Belgium controlled Congo, Rwanda and Burundi. An independence movement in 1959 pressed hard for immediate autonomy, and, abandoning hope of a gradual transition, Belgium withdrew from Congo in 1960, although some Belgian interests supported independence for the mineral-rich province of Katanga. The conflict in Congo was exacerbated by Cold War concerns – when the radical prime minister Patrice Lumumba turned to the Soviet Union for help in suppressing the growing rebellion in Katanga, going against the advice of the Congolese president, Joseph Kasavubu, it drew the United States and its allies into the conflict. The CIA developed plans to assassinate Lumumba, but before they could put their plans into action, Lumumba was captured and killed by the Katangese with Belgian connivance. Katangese secession was suppressed in 1963 and Kasavubu replaced in a military coup that brought the Belgian-backed Mobutu Sese Seko to dictatorial power in 1965, a position he held until his death in 1997. The Congo example helped drive nationalism and instability in Ruanda-Urundi, which became independent as two states, Rwanda and Burundi, in 1962.

The British and, even more, Portuguese and Spaniards were still ready to fight to retain particular colonies, the British doing so as late as the Falkland Islands in 1982. In Britain's colony of Aden, nationalist agitation, which had been increasingly strident since 1956, turned into revolt in 1963. The British position was undermined by their failure to sustain local support. The British were reduced to holding on to Aden, a base area that had to be defended from internal disaffection and where the garrison itself had to be protected, which largely nullified its value. The only initiative left to the British was to abandon the position, which they did in 1967, bringing to an end a rule that had begun in 1839.

The major effort to retain a colonial empire after the French withdrawal from Algeria was made by Portugal, whose conservative government under António de Oliveira Salazar, prime minister from 1932 to 1968, saw Portugal's long-standing imperial position as its national destiny and Christian duty. Guerrilla movements in Portugal's colonies began in Angola in 1961, Guinea-Bissau in 1963, and Mozambique in 1964.

Some earlier uprisings, such as the Mau-Mau in Kenya in the 1950s and that among the Bakongo in northern Angola, displayed many facets of old-style peasant uprisings or militant tribal identity. Although these elements still played a part, the uprisings from

BELOW: The Langata Detention Camp a few miles outside Nairobi where suspected Mau Mau rebels were held, 1954.

ABOVE: Guerrilla soldiers in southern Sudan, 1971, during the civil war that lasted from 1955 to 1972. South Sudan eventually achieved independence in 2011.

the mid-1960s were more explicitly located in a different ideological context, that of revolutionary Socialism. There was direct reference to the revolutionary war principles of the Chinese leader, Mao Zedong, training by foreign advisers, especially from the Soviet Union, China and Cuba, and a provision of more advanced weapons, although many did not arrive in any quantity until the early 1970s.

A successful left-wing revolution in Portugal in 1974 proved the catalyst to independence for the colonies. This demonstrated the crucial role of events 'at home' in the metropole, the colonial power. This had also been seen in the case with British and French decolonization. Yet, at the same time, these events in Portugal were greatly affected by the Portuguese Colonial War (1961–74), for the revolution owed much to military dissatisfaction with the intractable nature of the conflict, as well as to civilian hostility to military service: in response to long tours of service in Africa, there was desertion and large-scale emigration by young men. The change of government led to the granting of independence to the colonies the following year, and most of the settlers returned to Portugal.

Formal independence was not always coterminous with its economic and cultural counterparts. Thus, former colonial powers could remain economically dominant, as with much of French Africa, but not Algeria or Guinea. In cultural terms, there were educational and linguistic legacies of colonialism, while indigenous believers had to gain control of churches from Western missionaries.

In contrast to decolonization, the consolidation of US power in Alaska and Hawaii, both of which became states in 1959, was a reflection of late-19th-century imperial expansion that helped underline the US position in the Pacific, as did the retention of Guam, Wake and Midway islands, and American Samoa.

Anti-imperialism became more complex when it was applied to states that were non-Western and did not consider themselves imperial, for example India in Kashmir and Punjab, Egypt in Yemen, China in Tibet, Ethiopia in Eritrea and the Ogaden, Nigeria in Biafra, Congo in Katanga, Oman in Dhofar, Indonesia in northern Sumatra, East Timor and western New Guinea, Pakistan in East Pakistan and Baluchistan, Myanmar in tribal territories, Turkey and Iraq in Kurdish areas, Sudan in southern Sudan, and Serbia within Yugoslavia. In addition, separatists in Europe were apt to decry what they saw as imperial rule. This was the argument in Northern Ireland against the British, Corsica against French rule, and the Basque country and Catalonia against Spain.

The list, which can be very readily expanded, reflected the extent to which international relations were complicated but also greatly overlapped with domestic politics. In each case, the political causes, course and consequences were different, but, in each, force was very much involved in the struggles both to maintain and to overthrow control. Indeed, non-violent resistance was more common as a concept than a reality. There was total failure for the rebels in Kashmir, Tibet, Biafra and Katanga, but eventual success of a sort in the other cases, notably with independence for Eritrea and South Sudan.

In discussing decolonization and much else, there is a tendency to focus on countries as units. However, whereas decolonization in the shape of independence itself was achieved as a national unit, subsequent politics frequently saw tensions within such states. In part, these reflected differences over the terms of decolonization, but there was also the attempt at autonomy or indeed independence within the new states, as with Sudan, Nigeria and, later, Ukraine. There is no reason to anticipate an end of this process.

There is also the more subtle control stemming from the dominance of particular parts of countries and/or differential rates of prosperity and growth. Thus, coastal China benefits over inland and northeastern China, while west and south India does far better than east and north.

A post-colonial alternative to countries as units was provided by larger, federal entities, some of which were discussed by imperial powers as a way to retain influence and preserve stability. There was scant success. The idea for an Indo-China Federation among former French colonies failed, as did that for an ex-British Central African Federation and for British-backed Caribbean integration. However, although Singapore left the newly established federation of Malaysia, it otherwise survived.

THE COLD WAR: MEANING AND DEVELOPMENTS

The struggle between the Soviet-led Communist bloc and the US-led anti-Communist bloc was the major rivalry in international relations between 1949 and 1989, with this struggle also having significant domestic aspects. The struggle was military, political, ideological, social, economic and cultural. It ranged from rivalry in space exploration to the support of opposing sides in regional struggles in East and South Africa, Central America, and Southwest, South and Southeast Asia.

From 1945, despite shared military limitations, each side increasingly felt threatened, and seriously so, by the other, both militarily and ideologically. This sense of threat helped define and strengthen the sides. Fear, indeed, was a driving element in the causes and escalations of the successive stages of the Cold War, while also being a unifier of state and society, or, at least, a would-be unifier from the perspective of governments and commentators that sought accordingly to impose discipline and maintain ideological control. This fear was to be seen across societies, including in popular culture, from films to youth organizations.

Internal surveillance was presented as an aspect of conflict, as in Communist Albania, where thousands of individual pillboxes were constructed as part of a defence system. In many countries, the security services were boosted as part of an active front in the ongoing conflict. To a far greater extent than Western counterparts, Communist states controlled

ABOVE: The Hungarian Revolution, 1956.

LEFT: The so-called 'Prague Spring' of 1968, when mass protests occurred across Czechoslovakia until they were brutally suppressed by Soviet forces.

ABOVE: American troops on the move during the Korean War, September 1950.

information and they made major efforts to block radio transmissions from the West. Secret police forces, such as the KGB in the Soviet Union and the AVO in Hungary, routinely used torture. In Hungary in 1956 and Czechoslovakia in 1968, the suppression of Communist reform movements by Soviet forces was followed by the reimposition of police states. In contrast, in the US, Japan and Western Europe, the rule of law operated in democracies in which governments changed peacefully.

Aside from the missiles, the Cold War indeed saw multiple competitions, notably in supporting protégés, in arms races and rivalry, across what was called the Third World, in espionage, and in cultural and intellectual opposition. While some of the rivalry interacted with decolonization struggles in the Third World, many other factors were involved. In the 1980s, there were major struggles in sub-Saharan Africa and, to a lesser extent, Central America, as well as in the Islamic world, notably Afghanistan.

The years up to 1954 saw the territorial clarification of the two sides, with the Communists coming to control China, Eastern Europe, North Korea, and, finally, North Vietnam, while the anti-Communists did the same in Western Europe, South Korea and South Vietnam. The Communist invasion of South Korea in 1950 was fought to a stop by a US-centred United Nations coalition in the Korean War of 1950–3, a conflict that was important to the militarization of the West: it was already the case in the Communist bloc. The West organized alliance systems, notably the North Atlantic Treaty Organization (NATO), founded in 1949, the Baghdad Pact in 1955, and SEATO (the Southeast Asia Treaty Organization) in 1954, in an effort to contain Communism.

The boundaries of the two blocs continued to be uncertain with the next major conflict being the Vietnam War. More generally, a sense that the situation might slip out of control through a 'domino effect', as the fall of one country to Communism led to that of others, encouraged the US government to take a greater interest in the course and consequences of the Western retreat from empire. This interest was especially shown in the Middle East and in Southeast Asia.

Although nationalism was crucial to the 'liberation struggles' there, and elsewhere, they were also characterized by Communist exploitation as the Soviet Union and China sought to challenge the US indirectly by encouraging supporters to attack American allies, such as Israel and South Africa. These attacks brought together notions of popular warfare, nationalism and revolutionary Communism, in a programme of revolutionary struggle in which success was believed to be inevitable.

Conversely, Western governments feared that Third World anti-colonial movements and nationalism would be exploited by the Communist powers, and this fear encouraged a view that the West's front line ran round the world and that Communism had to be contained. Committed to 'containment', America was determined to keep the front line not only away from the Western hemisphere, but also as close to the Communist bloc as possible.

From 1957, South Vietnam faced a Communist rebellion by the Viet Cong, which led to more overt and widespread US intervention. From 1959, forces from North Vietnam were infiltrated into South Vietnam in support of the Viet Cong. The Americans, in turn, were concerned that a failure to support South Vietnam would lead to the further spread of Communism in Southeast Asia. In response, the commitment of US 'advisers' to South Vietnam, including the foundation, in 1962, of Military Assistance Command, Vietnam, encouraged pressure for increased support. Although President John F. Kennedy (1961–3) increased American activity in Vietnam, it was his successor, Lyndon B. Johnson (1963–9), who escalated US involvement from a small 'advisory' role to large-scale direct combat. US forces in South Vietnam peaked at 541,000 in January 1969.

BELOW: Viet Cong soldiers, 1966.

RIGHT: US soldiers disembark from a helicopter during the Vietnam War, August 1965.

In the face of North Vietnamese and Viet Cong determination and morale, the Americans cracked first, after an inability to secure victory had resulted in an attrition that led to apparent stalemate. Viet Cong morale, which owed much to coercion and indoctrination, was apparently sustained despite heavy casualties.

While the Americans, however, could, as the 1968 Tet Offensive showed, repel mass attacks on their strong points, and could drop thousands of bombs from a great height without much opposition, their will for the war was worn down by its continuation, while they could not deny control of the countryside to their opponents.

The US, however, greatly strengthened its diplomatic position by a *rapprochement* with China in 1972, a step that exploited serious rivalry between China and the Soviet Union and made it less serious strategically for the US to abandon South Vietnam, which it did in 1973.

In 1975, South Vietnam was overrun by an invasion from the north. The Vietnam War demonstrated that being the foremost world power did not mean that a state could win.

The next major change was in the mid-1970s, with the former Portuguese empire in Africa taken over by left-wing liberation movements. In the 1980s, there were major struggles in the Islamic world.

BELOW: Henry Kissinger.

REALPOLITIK AS AMERICAN STRATEGY: HENRY KISSINGER

As National Security Advisor, Kissinger advised President Richard Nixon in 1972:

'I think in 20 years your successor, if he's as wise as you are, will wind up leaning toward the Russians against the Chinese. For the next 15 years we have to lean toward the Chinese against the Russians. We have to play the balance of power game totally unemotionally. Right now we need the Chinese to correct the Russians and to discipline the Russians.'

This was seen as a way to get North Vietnam to terms.

NUCLEAR CONFRONTATION

The nuclear monopoly enjoyed by the US in 1945 was rapidly lost as the Soviet Union followed suit, and the same was to be the case also with thermonuclear weaponry, the more powerful hydrogen bombs. These weapons were not used after the bombing of Hiroshima and Nagasaki in 1945, but the threat of their use caused alarm throughout the Cold War. The prospect of imminent extinction was constantly in everyone's mind, a psychological burden almost too much to bear for many. This inner terror was exacerbated because nuclear war appeared a close possibility on a number of occasions including 1953, 1962, 1973 and 1983.

In 1962, the US took military steps to prevent the Soviet Union from basing nuclear weaponry in Cuba. Both sides prepared for war, but the US blockade deterred the Soviets, who agreed to remove their missiles in return for a US promise not to invade Cuba and, later, to remove its nuclear missiles from Turkey. The crisis revealed the importance of restraint by the leaders, Kennedy and Khrushchev, but also the risks of unforeseen circumstances. The ideas and equations of nuclear threats proved important to military planning, while the availability of nuclear weapons and guarantees was important to the dynamics of alliance

ABOVE: A PGM-19A Jupiter Intermediate Range Ballistic Missile, of the type deployed in Turkey in 1961.

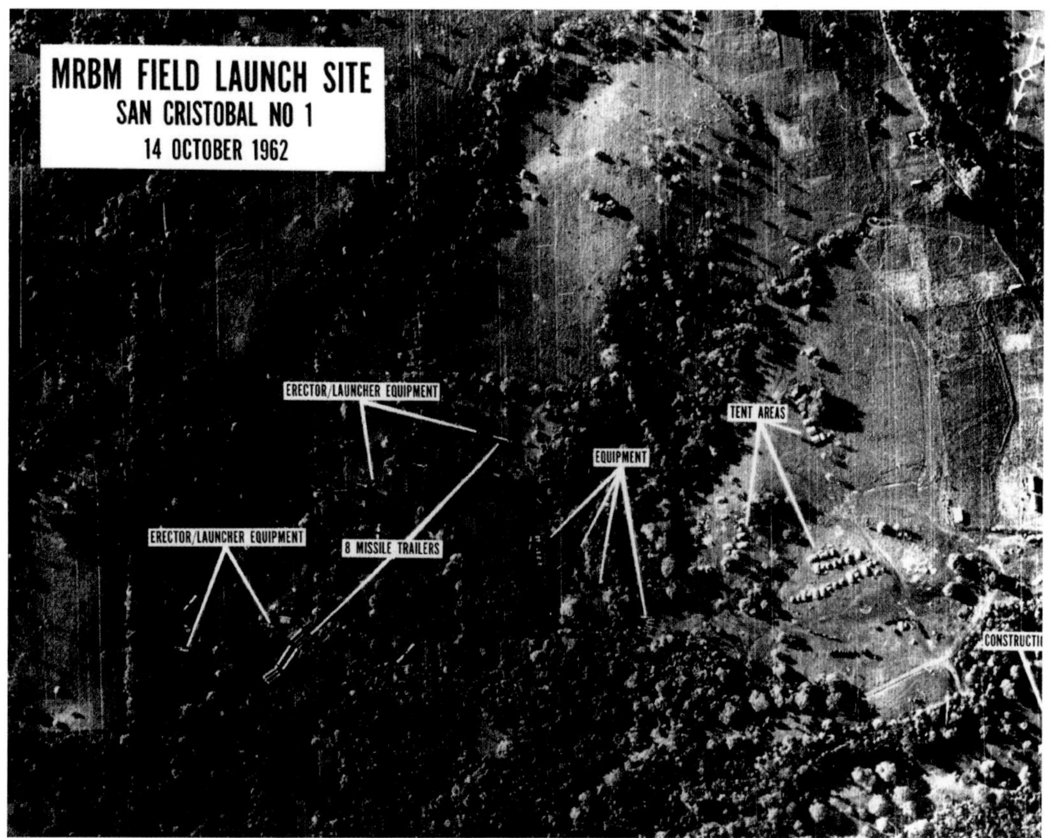

LEFT: A missile base under construction in Cuba, seen in a photo taken by an American U-2 spy plane.

systems. There was also a new military geography. Under a 1951 agreement with Denmark, a major US airbase was completed at Thule in its colony of Greenland and became a centre for aerial reconnaissance and deterrence of the Soviet Union.

There was a tension between a possible stalemate borne of Mutually Assured Destruction (MAD) and innovations in weapons delivery and planned usage. Thus, subsequent attacks were designed to deter rivals from a first strike or surprise assault. To that end, having initially been carried by aircraft and then on land-based rockets, nuclear warheads were also mounted on rockets fired from submarines, which were mobile and therefore hard to detect. So also with the intermediate- or limited-range weaponry, notably lorry-mounted nuclear rockets and cruise missiles, that were increasingly deployed in the 1980s. These increased the uncertainty bound up in any resort to attack.

The MAD threatened by massive nuclear stockpiles and by the increased vulnerability following the development and deployment of intercontinental missiles eventually brought a measure of stability, in part by giving substance to the use of the concept of deterrence. However, it was only in hindsight that this was to be seen as a success. At the time, there was a great risk that deterrence would not work, and, instead, that the danger that the other side would strike first would encourage a move to war. The Berlin Crisis of 1961 and, even more, the Cuban Missile Crisis of 1962, highlighted this risk. The deployment in the 1970s of rockets with multiple independently targeted re-entry vehicles increased the danger. Yet, enhanced capability on both sides was matched by attempts to lessen the possibility of nuclear war. The US–Soviet Anti-Ballistic Missile Treaty of 1972 (SALT I) limited the construction

BELOW: A Soviet attack submarine near Cuba during the Cuban Missile Crisis.

of defensive shields against missile attack to two anti-ballistic missile complexes, one around a concentration of intercontinental ballistic missiles and the other around the capital. By leaving the US and the Soviet Union vulnerable, the treaty was designed to discourage a first strike, as there would be no effective defence against a counterstrike. Thus, atomic weaponry was to be used to prevent, not to further, war. At the time of the Arab–Israeli War in 1973, however, the Americans put their forces on nuclear alert in response to the threat of Soviet intervention. The SALT I treaty also served as the basis for further negotiations, which resulted in the SALT II treaty in 1979. Meanwhile, in 1975, the Helsinki Agreement ratified Europe's frontiers and therefore the territorial division between West and East.

ABOVE: Jimmy Carter and Leonid Brezhnev sign SALT II.

THE ATOMIC THREAT

President John F. Kennedy (r.1961–3), who used the concept of 'The New Frontier', also declared in his Inaugural Address that 'Man holds in his mortal hands the power to abolish all forms of human poverty and all forms of human life.'

Other states also developed nuclear weaponry and delivery systems, notably Britain, China and France. India, Pakistan, Israel and North Korea did so subsequently. Attempts to limit nuclear proliferation, especially to prevent Iran and North Korea developing capabilities, proved of only limited effectiveness.

THE END OF THE COLD WAR

The Cold War that began with the Russian Revolution had been suspended when Germany attacked the Soviet Union in 1941, leading the latter to ally with Britain and the US. It resumed after World War II and continued until there was a crisis in Soviet power, stability and authority in the late 1980s. The Soviet system had become sclerotic under the leadership of Leonid Brezhnev (r.1964–82), while Yuri Andropov (r.1982–4), an authoritarian, was too ill to push through his attempt at revival. Konstantin Chernenko (r.1984–5) proved an elderly makeweight of no consequence.

ABOVE: Mikhail Gorbachev.

A sense of failure and anxiety that this might threaten the interests of the Communist élite provided the opportunity for an attempt to modernize the Soviet system through economic and political reform, the two seen as linked. However, this led to a crisis of cohesion, first among the Soviet allies in Eastern Europe and then in the Soviet Union itself. Mikhail Gorbachev (1931–2022), Soviet leader from 1985, was committed to *perestroika*, reform at home, as well as to defusing the Cold War by arms control agreements with the US, and his liberalization was not ended by his overthrow by rivals, as had happened with Nikita Khrushchev in 1964. This reform policy, which sought to modernize and humanize Soviet Communism, saw competitive elections to the Supreme Soviet as well as the televising of its debates, all in pursuit of *glasnost* (openness). Communist Party control disappeared. Gorbachev's policies, however, unravelled the precarious domestic basis of the Soviet Union, and, at the same time, failed to provide sufficient food, let alone reasonable economic growth. Furthermore, his pressure on Soviet satellite states in Eastern

RIGHT: The fall of the Berlin Wall, 10 November 1989.

Europe for reform resulted in their fall, as Gorbachev was unwilling to use the Soviet military to maintain their governments in power when they faced pent-up popular pressure for change. These governments themselves had totally failed. East Germany – apparently the most successful, but its economy in fact wrecked by ideological direction – was on the edge of bankruptcy in the autumn of 1989: it had only been able to continue that long thanks to large loans from the West, especially West Germany. The fall of the Communist regimes in Eastern Europe led to the dissolution of the Warsaw Pact in 1990 and, subsequently, to the withdrawal of Soviet forces.

The end of the Soviet Union, when it came, in 1989–91, was rapid and accompanied by little fighting. The fall of the Soviet Union was at once a stage of the Cold War and also an important stage in decolonization; the Soviet Union, after all, rested on a powerful degree of Russian, as well as ideological (Communist), imperialism. Counter-reform attempts by the Soviet military, keen to preserve the integrity of the Soviet Union, led to action against nationalists in Georgia (1989), Azerbaijan (1990), Lithuania (1991), Latvia (1991) and Moldova (1992), and there was an attempted coup in Moscow by hard-line Communists in 1991, but they were unable to prevail.

ABOVE: The Baltic Way in Lithuania, 23 August 1989. This demonstration for independence involved a human chain that extended for more than 400 miles (650 km) across Latvia, Lithuania and Estonia.

The growing weakness of the Soviet state and the division and confusion of the government's response was accentuated by the strength of nationalist sentiment, especially in the Baltic republics, the Caucasus and western Ukraine. Nationalism in the republics, including Russia, led to their peaceful independence, and thus to the collapse of the Soviet Union. Gorbachev resigned on 25 December 1991. With Soviet Communism in ruins and Chinese Communism increasingly market-orientated and looking in particular to the US market, the Cold War was apparently over.

Soviet power collapsed over the different peoples of what in theory was a federation, as did that of the Communist Party. The two were aspects of rapidly developing economic and political crises that it proved impossible to stall let alone stop.

THE UNIPOLAR WORLD, 1990–2005

The combination of the fall of the Soviet Union with the US–Chinese alignment underlined an apparent American dominance of global politics and economics. This dominance also rested on control of the world fiscal system by the US and on the degree to which American-led coalitions rapidly defeated opponents that challenged its views, notably Iraq in 1991 and 2003, Serbia in 1995 and 1999, and Afghanistan in 2001. With Russian weakness in the 1990s, the arithmetic of deterrence, underlined as it was by the risk of mutually assured destruction, no longer discouraged overt Western intervention.

The defeat of Iraq in 1991 was dramatic. In 1990, the Iraqis rapidly overran oil-rich Kuwait, but this provoked a US-led response in which the Iraqi forces were crushed the following year. Kuwait was liberated, but there was no overthrow of Saddam Hussein, the Iraqi dictator, until war was resumed in 2003, when Iraq was conquered.

In the meanwhile, the US sought to stabilize areas that appeared dangerous, imposing settlements in 1995 and 1999 to limit the wars that had broken out in the former Yugoslavia. The brutal slaughter of civilians by the Serbs (and, to a lesser extent, by their opponents) was an all-too-familiar feature of conflict in much of the modern world and reflected the extent to which ethnic groups were seen as units of political strength, and thus as targets. In 1995, the Bosnian Serbs murdered more than 7,800 unarmed Muslim males in Srebrenica, which had been designated a safe zone by UN representatives whose peacekeeping force, however, was too weak and too focused on self-preservation to prevent the massacre.

This action was termed ethnic cleansing – the expulsion, with considerable violence, often murderous and on a considerable scale, of members of an ethnic group. It was generally associated with the Serbs, but was also used by the rival Croats. Although its use by others does not excuse Serb actions, it helps explain the paranoia that characterized their policymakers. In turn, such action against civilians led to pressure on outside powers to overcome earlier hesitations about action and adapt existing views on peacekeeping to adopt a proactive policy of peace enforcement focused on humanitarian goals.

Regimes that had hitherto looked for Soviet support found themselves exposed. US force-projection was not challenged by a revived Russia because the collapse of the Soviet Union was not followed by a stronger Russia. Instead, it faced serious economic difficulties as the dismantling of the old command economy exposed the uncompetitive nature of much Soviet-era industry, while it proved difficult to establish effective monetary and fiscal mechanisms, and, instead, became a system of rampant corruption. Western loans were necessary to prevent a total collapse of Russia in the 1990s. Even so, debt payments caused a severe crisis in 1998, leading to default and devaluation, although, subsequently, the rise in the price of oil and natural gas helped underwrite Russian assertiveness and a

ABOVE: Operation Desert Storm during the Gulf War, 1991.

military build-up, a situation that from 2022 made it easier to launch and sustain a war with Ukraine.

In the meanwhile, former Russian allies had joined NATO: Poland, the Czech Republic and Hungary becoming members in 1997. They were followed by former members of the Soviet Union, in the shape of the Baltic Republics, Estonia, Latvia and Lithuania. Eastern Europe presented itself as part of Europe and its Cold War links with the Global South were sidelined.

There was talk of an 'End of History' because of the dominance of the American model of democratic capitalism, with the argument that there would be no future clash of ideologies to destabilize the world. In practice, aside from a range of sources of opposition, there were political, military, economic, and fiscal weaknesses in the US position, and, having been apparent in the 1990s, notably with unsuccessful US intervention in Somalia, these were to become more obvious in the 2000s as America pursued the 'War on Terror' announced in response to al-Qaeda terrorist attacks on New York and Washington DC on 11 September 2001. Yet, earlier, the idea of a unipolar world had been widely voiced.

REVIVED COLD WAR, 2006–

America's problems in Iraq and Afghanistan engaged much attention from the mid-2000s. However, it was the shift in international relations that was more significant. Having consolidated his position in Russia, Vladimir Putin readily used force to forward his interests in nearby regions, notably attacking Georgia in 2008, seizing Crimea from Ukraine in 2014, and launching a full-scale invasion of Ukraine in 2022. At the same time, and creating more room for manoeuvre for Putin, relations between China and the US seriously deteriorated, more especially from the late 2010s. This ensured not only acute tension in East Asia and the Western Pacific, most particularly over the status of Taiwan, but also a more general challenging of US interests and concepts. Talk of a new Cold War came to the fore from 2022.

ABOVE: Ukrainian artillery fires in defensive action against Russia, July 2022.

BELOW: A rebel fighter fires against government forces in Aleppo, November 2012.

The Russian invasion of Ukraine was the culmination of years of political pressure and episodic military action designed to reverse the consequences of the collapse of the Soviet Union, for Ukraine was the most economically and politically damaging of the Soviet losses to democratic nationalism in the early 1990s and the one that most vexed President Putin of Russia, challenging his view of Russian identity and historical destiny.

The Ukraine crisis led to a NATO response that was more resolute than might have been anticipated. The failure to discourage Russia from acting encouraged a shift to greater NATO preparedness, not least with the development of more high-readiness. This response was particularly marked in Eastern Europe where there was anxiety about Russian expansionism, but not only there. The major Norwegian submarine base at Olavsvern, carved into a mountain near Tromsø and closed in 2002, was reopened in 2020 in response to US requests. Meanwhile, Putin sought to strengthen alliances, notably with China and North Korea. In 2024, Kim Jong-un referred to a new North Korean–Russian treaty as 'a driving force accelerating the creation of a new multipolar world'.

In 2009, Osama bin Laden, the head of al-Qaeda, pressed for *jihad* (religious war) over Gaza, where Hamas was in conflict with Israel. However, in practice, conflict between Muslims was to the fore in the 2010s with the instability of the Middle East centred on Syria and Iraq.

The attempt to reform Syria in the 'Arab Spring' of 2011 led to a brutal response by President Assad, including highly indiscriminate bombing and shelling, the use of poison

PIVOT TO ASIA

Disengaging from Iraq and, from 2021, Afghanistan, US policymakers became more concerned about China. In 2011, President Barack Obama told the Australian Parliament, 'As a Pacific nation, the United States will play a larger and long-term role in shaping this region and its future.'

ABOVE: Palestinian refugees return home to Rafah, Gaza, 20 January 2025.

gas, and the blockade of rebel-held areas. Russian and Iranian support for Assad and rebel divisions left him in control of much of Syria, but with millions of its inhabitants refugees within or outside the country. However, the foundations of the regime were weak. It was totally dependent on controlling the means of violence and when, in late 2024, the flow of conflict abruptly changed, Assad fell rapidly in the face of an Islamicist insurgency that offered a new start.

In 2023, this instability switched to Israel as a result of an attack from Gaza by Hamas through the Israeli border fence (the defence of which failed) on Israeli settlements. Some 1,400 people were killed, more than 240 taken prisoner, and Israel's security doctrine gravely weakened, in both domestic and international eyes.

In response, having called up 360,000 reservists, the Israelis launched a large-scale invasion of Gaza, designed to root out Hamas. This was a densely settled urban terrain in which the population had risen from less than 50,000 in 1948 to 2.4 million in 2023, and the Israeli advance caused heavy civilian casualties. Many more followed as a consequence of the breakdown of any stability, not least a rise in death from disease and hunger. Hamas took losses, but was not destroyed. The conflict expanded to include Lebanon's pro-Iranian Hezbollah movement which saw a military invasion by Israeli troops in October 2024 before a ceasefire was agreed two months later.

ENDURING EMPIRES

The Russian seizure of Crimea in 2014 was a reminder that imperial themes and ambitions recurred. Russia had first acquired it in 1783 (from the Crimean Tatars), had faced resistance there during the Russian Civil War of 1918–21, lost it to Germany in 1942–4, and saw it become part of an independent Ukraine with the dissolution of the Soviet Union. That also led to the loss of Estonia, which had been ceded by Sweden in 1721 as well as other 18th-century gains including Latvia, Lithuania, Belarus and western Ukraine. Looked at differently, all of these and more freed themselves from Russian and later Soviet imperialism.

No such freedom was gained by Tibet and Xinjiang, both conquered in the 18th century by China. The freedom of Taiwan, and all that remained of Nationalist China when the Communists took over in 1949, was precarious and Chinese military intimidation of the territory markedly increased in the 2020s. To a degree, Myanmar, Cambodia, Sri Lanka and Nepal appear as parts of an informal Chinese empire.

On a smaller scale, other states inherited earlier imperialist acquisitions, notably Ethiopia, which had greatly expanded at the same time as the major bout of European imperialism in Africa in 1880–1914.

Other states maintained the bold boundaries of conquest that the Europeans had imposed. In South America, the dominant scale of Brazil reflected earlier Portuguese imperialism. In Africa, the consequences of ethnic rivalry helped cause civil war, as in Nigeria in 1967–70 when the Igbo failed in their separatist drive to create the new state of Biafra.

The slaughter of substantial numbers of Igbo – possibly 30,000 – in the massacres that followed the second military coup of 1966 in Nigeria led to a collapse of Igbo support for the notion of a federal, multi-racial Nigeria. The new Nigerian government, composed of officers that had taken part in the coup, was unsympathetic to the Igbo demand for a looser confederation, while the Igbo leadership challenged the legality of the federal government.

After the Igbo republic of Biafra was proclaimed in the southeast of Nigeria, the federal government launched a 'police operation' in July 1967 that became a civil war. The federal forces benefited from overwhelming numerical superiority, including an army of 120,000 troops, and from the availability of British and Soviet weaponry, while France sought to support Biafra. The Nigerian navy was crucial, both in imposing a debilitating blockade of Biafra and in enabling the seizure of ports and coastal positions, notably Port Harcourt, which increased the number of fronts on which the Biafrans were under attack.

Unlike the Viet Minh and the Viet Cong in Vietnam, the Biafrans were swiftly cut off from foreign land links and this exacerbated their lack of food and military supplies. The Nigerian government felt no hesitation in using starvation to help destroy the Igbo, and hunger and devastation helped cause many civilian deaths. The hard-pressed Biafrans finally collapsed after their airstrip at Uli was overrun in 1970, severing their remaining supply link.

ABOVE: Igbo soldiers during the Biafran War, 1968.

The theme of enduring empires was played down due to the emphasis on nation states, but such nationalism frequently reflected imperial bounds, politics and legacies. Most clearly, this was the case with language, which helped explain this sensitivity. Political movements, especially nationalist and separatist ones, could be associated with supporting particular languages as official ones. Thus in Canada, Quebec separatists favoured the use of French rather than English, while in India, the BJP backed the use of Hindi rather than English. Riots in New Caledonia in 2024 about the terms of continued French colonial rule fed into a conventional decolonizing narrative, but the same in practice was the case elsewhere for states that were no longer ruled by European imperial powers.

WAR FROM 1945

The lack of any conflict on the scale of World War II led many who were not directly affected by war to argue that the subsequent period was peaceful. Such a view would have appeared absurd to most of the world's population, for China, Southeast Asia, South and Southwest Africa, and sub-Saharan Africa all saw much warfare in the period following 1945. Struggles between India and Pakistan were particularly significant, and the Indian conquest of East Pakistan in 1971 helped to create the independent state of Bangladesh. The Middle East saw a series of conflicts between Israel and Arab neighbours notably in 1956, 1967, 1973 and 1982. In casualties, however, the Iraq–Iran War of 1980–8 was far more deadly. Furthermore, there were international conflicts elsewhere, even if large areas, notably in Latin America, did not suffer. International warfare was also experienced by several states who participated in expeditionary conflicts by states – such as the Americans in Vietnam in the 1970s, the Russians in Afghanistan in the 1980s, or the British, French and Americans in Afghanistan in the 2000s – that otherwise did not directly experience warfare at home.

If conflict is enlarged to consider civil wars then its range expanded, not least to include most of Latin America, for example Colombia and Peru, and more of Africa. Indeed, the maintenance of authority was often a matter of force, and notably so in authoritarian states

LEFT: Bangladeshi guerrilla fighters during the Bangladesh Liberation War, 1970.

ABOVE: Congolese soldiers in March 1997.

with scant experience of the peaceful transfer of power, or for democracies facing violent separatist movements. With the state frequently the arm of the military and the military the arm of the state, the nexus and means of politics could in part be a matter of coups and repression, as in Argentina, Brazil, Chile, Myanmar, Pakistan, Thailand and many other countries, for parts or much of our period.

To exclude this activity from any discussion of war would be misleading. Indeed, the politics of the military helped not only determine promotion and weapons procurement, but could also determine or at least influence policies, both military and non-military. Much of the military history of our period can be told in terms of decolonization, the Cold War, and other major trends; but there were also specific clashes between states, for example Ethiopia and Eritrea, or within them, as in Congo and Somalia, that had their own causes and narratives however much they might also become engaged in bigger themes, not least due to great power intervention.

At every point, it is necessary to remember the lives lost. The war in Congo in 1996–2003 saw about 400,000 people killed, but maybe another 5 million dying due to wartime disease and starvation.

THE MEANS OF MODERN WARFARE

Weaponry after 1950 long maintained the essential goals, forms, and patterns of what had been employed to fight World War II. Indeed, albeit with significant changes, weapons and platforms introduced in the first two decades of the 20th century remained significant, including manned aircraft, tanks and aircraft carriers.

Yet, the changes in the widespread use of these systems from the 1990s, notably in the shape of the application of advanced electronics to provide rapid and accurate guidance systems, increased the potential lethality of weaponry. The 2003 defeat of Iraq saw the American use of satellite surveillance linked to target acquisition and firing on the ground to achieve a high strike ratio. Bomb and missile guidance systems meant the replacement of 'dumb' air power dropping free-fall bombs in favour of the new, 'smart' option.

By the 2020s, the emphasis instead was on a miniaturization provided by drones which offered surveillance and strike means very much less expensive than those from aircraft. And yet the Ukraine war also saw a reliance on artillery and the related use of trenches that was similar to the Korean War of 1950–3.

WAR AS STALEMATE

General Valery Zaluzhny, the Ukrainian Commander-in-Chief, was pessimistic, in November 2023: 'Just like in the First World War we have reached the level of technology that puts us into a stalemate... There will most likely be no deep and beautiful breakthrough ... Russia has lost at least 150,000 dead. In any other country such casualties would have stopped the war.'

LEFT: Guided 'smart' bombs and missiles have increasingly been used in warfare since the 1990s.

THE NEW DIPLOMACY

The new diplomacy in part involved many more independent states, and the active search by the major powers for allies among them. Aligning this search for cooperation with the ideological suppositions of the particular bloc created difficulties. In addition, the newly independent states sought their own alignments, as with the establishment in 1955, with the Bandung Conference held in Indonesia, of the Non-Aligned Movement. This, however, was seen by the Soviets as providing an opportunity to break free of what they regarded as encirclement by the West.

Relations between competing blocs was handled by summitry, but there was also complication as the result of the development of transnational activism. Radicals attempted to ensure links in what they saw as a common struggle against capitalism and US imperialism.

A NEW WORLD

'Vientiane is, I agree, a post with an unpleasant climate, few amenities and a limited social life. But there are unfortunately many such places – some even more unpleasant and restricted – in places like the Persian Gulf and West Africa.... Nowadays reputations are made in the back-of-beyond and no longer in the comfortable but unimportant posts of Western Europe.... However, I wish that we did not keep having to open up Missions on the Equator.'

Sir Francis Rudall, chief clerk at the British Foreign Office, to John Addis, ambassador to Laos, 1960.

Meanwhile, new international idealistic codes, especially on environmental matters and what were defined as human rights, came to the fore, advanced by humanitarian groups, such as the London-based Amnesty International and the New York-based Human Rights Watch. Violations against human rights were pursued through the European Court of Human Rights or by appeals to the Declaration of Human Rights passed by the UN General Assembly in 1948 and complemented in 1976 by an international covenant on social, economic and cultural rights, and also by one on civil and political rights.

ABOVE: The Bandung Conference, 1955.

8 National Politics

There are no typical states, and no uniform development of countries. All share in the global natural and socio-political environments, but experience them differently, in part due to the accidents of war, international relations, and leadership. This chapter focuses on a number of countries and regions that, together, include much of the world's population.

Divisions within states varied very greatly depending on general trends, such as population pressure and the specifics of particular countries, notably their constitutions, politics, ethnic mix and history. Also, the means of political division varied from electioneering to violence. Where this activity took place was less varied, with cities playing an increasingly important role in each country's social, political and economic life throughout our period. This has consequences for how those states were policed, how societal issues developed and were addressed, and how crime and its consequences were handled.

At the same time, as cities grew and changed, the act of transformation became itself an expression of political control – as seen in the remaking of Beijing in China in the run up to the 2008 Olympics, when many of the city's traditional neighbourhoods, or *hutongs*, were simply bulldozed out of existence.

CHINA FROM THE COMMUNIST TAKEOVER

State control to the ends of the dictatorial party was the theme throughout the period, even though the particular goals adopted varied considerably. Under Mao Zedong, there were differing attempts to jump-start mass Socialism (i.e. Communism) and overcome the 'backwardness' of the past, notably the attempt at modernization in the 'Great Leap Forward' and at ideological purity in the 'Great Proletarian Cultural Revolution'. These efforts involved much cruelty and very many deaths, but without there being any significant challenge to Party rule. The 'Cultural Revolution' included an abrupt and striking attack on diplomatic norms, an attack matched in the treatment of Western diplomats and embassies. Chinese policies could also be seen in one of its only allies, Albania, where the Communist model of totalitarian state control, personality cult, collectivization and state atheism were also insulated from reformist pressures elsewhere in the Communist world.

ABOVE: The Cultural Revolution.

After Mao, and notably under Deng Xiaoping, the dominant figure from 1978 until 1989, there was a process of liberalization in economic and social affairs but not in Party controls. Market reforms were announced in 1978 at the third plenum of the Central Committee of the Communist Party. A Socialist market economy was the goal. In turn, once Xi Jinping had become the Supreme Leader in 2012, there was a drive to increase Party control and social direction. The central theme was control. The relative freedom of Hong Kong was crushed.

By 2023, China was responsible for 31 per cent of global manufacturing. China, however, faces the problems of maintaining growth rates, not least as the global free trade from which it benefited greatly from the 1990s was hit by deteriorating international relations in the 2020s, deteriorating relations that owed much to a Chinese emphasis on rivalry, indeed struggle. In response, Xi sought to take control of the industries of the future, notably electric cars, artificial intelligence and biomanufacturing, emphasizing the value of 'high-quality development'. Western technology was no longer to be to the fore, but his model of Chinese prosperity depended on export-led growth, not consumer spending, and the continued viability of the former is unclear.

ABOVE: Car manufacturing in Linhai, Zhejiang Province, China, 2017.

Since the 2010s, there has been a resurgent Chinese nationalism, with an increasingly belligerent tone. Whereas in the 1960s the Chinese moved against the Soviet Union, and in the early 1970s into an alignment with the US, the focus has become clearly hostile to the latter. From 2012, Xi pressed for the fulfilment of a 'Chinese Dream' in which national self-assertion is linked to the end of what is presented as the country's historical humiliation at the hands of colonial powers. In 2021, the foreign minister, Wang Yi, declared that the rise of China was unstoppable. Moreover, under Xi, China has turned overseas to express its influence, attempting to gain allies in the Pacific, investing heavily in Africa and Central Asia, and using surveillance and spies to monitor its citizens abroad. The 'Belt and Road' initiative is a prime instance of ambitious Chinese geopolitics: launched in 2013, it was designed to support the development of infrastructure, primarily, but not only, in Asia and was seen as serving Chinese geopolitical interests, both strategic and economic.

Nationalism abroad was matched by that at home, with minority peoples, such as Tibetans, forced to adopt Han Chinese norms and Communist ideology, and the imposition of a harsh policy of cultural suppression in Xinjiang.

THE US, FROM TRUMAN TO TRUMP

It is easy to divide US history into its different presidents. They are indeed important, and notably so in foreign policy, where the constitution leaves them particular power; but the presidents are only part of the formal political process. The period was one of major population growth; of economic primacy, but with very differing benefits and costs; of social cohesion and yet also significant weaknesses; and of major regional and local differences. Indeed, it is this last history of the US that is of considerable importance in the appreciation of the tensions within the country. There has been a decline of bipartisanship and a rise in the polarization of US politics. It is not so much that the country is weak in civic virtue, as some claim, but rather that there are a number of competing visions of civic virtue. Thus, in 1970, in the Hard Hat Riot in New York, building workers attacked protesting anti-war students, which helped President Nixon to use the term 'silent majority' to sum up the idea that the consensus was naturally conservative.

ABOVE: Ronald Reagan, president of the US from 1981–1989.

The political balance in the US saw both Democrat and Republican presidents, while the electoral practices of its federal system could help ensure victory for the candidate with fewer votes, as with Donald Trump in 2016. Presidents needed widespread appeal. Ronald Reagan, president from 1981 to 1989, appeared particularly appropriate for an America increasingly aware of the pull of the Pacific Rim and the declining influence of Europe and the East Coast. But Reagan's success was not that of a narrowly regional candidate, and no subsequent president has come from the West Coast.

Foreign policy has had a great impact on US politics, as we have already seen. It was especially important for John F. Kennedy (r.1961–3) and Lyndon B. Johnson (r.1963–9); while the 'War on Terror' rapidly became central to the presidency of George W. Bush (r.2001–9).

These were not the sole elements that were significant to the international dimension. So also with the economic trends discussed in chapter five. For example, in 2004, the US imported 58 per cent of the oil it consumed, compared to 34 per cent in 1977.

Suburbanization, car culture and a conservative progressivism were all part of the mix. The Republican Dwight Eisenhower's re-election in 1956, with a margin of 9 million votes, was a product of widespread satisfaction with the economic boom and social conservatism of that decade. This conservatism

ABOVE: The Hard Hat Riot, New York, 1970.

RIGHT: John F. Kennedy in the limousine moments before his assassination.

THE KENNEDY ASSASSINATION

Shot dead in Dallas on 22 November 1963, Kennedy's fate launched a series of conspiracy theories that continue to circulate. These testified not only to the strength of paranoia, but also to a sense that the barrier to an alternative world, in which violence played a major role, had been surmounted. This was partly a matter of the apparent bridging of the division between international conflict and domestic politics, most obviously with reports that the Cuban government or anti-Castro Cuban exiles, disillusioned by a lack of support, had been responsible. There were also reports that Kennedy was the victim of organized crime, or of sections of the military or intelligence world who wanted a tougher anti-Communist stance. There is no conclusive proof for any of these interpretations, but the conclusion by the Warren Commission that the assassination was the work of a single individual was greeted by many with scepticism.

The shock of the only US president assassinated since William McKinley in 1901 (President Harry Truman was not harmed in 1950 in an attempt by Puerto Rican independence activists and Reagan was shot in Washington in 1981, but survived) was compounded by Kennedy's youth and a sense of optimism lost. Other assassinations followed, notably Malcolm X in 1965, and both Martin Luther King and Robert Kennedy in 1968, while George Wallace, the third party presidential candidate in 1972, was wounded by a would-be assassin. In 2024, an assassination attempt on Donald Trump as he campaigned for the presidency failed.

included an upsurge in religiosity as church membership and attendance rose. Popular culture reflected religious factors, and Eisenhower encouraged the ostentatious commitment of the addition of 'under God' to the Pledge of Allegiance and 'In God We Trust' on the currency. He also sought to preserve peace with the Communist bloc while deterring Communist expansion, and to keep inflation down.

Yet there were also social and racial sides to government policy. For example, the Interstate highway system approved by Congress in 1956, and particularly important in the South and the West, saw the federal government provide 90 per cent of the construction costs, allowing state revenues to be spent on secondary roads. However, in many cities, such as Chicago and New Orleans, the new highways wrecked or isolated established poor neighbourhoods, often Black.

Having narrowly won the presidential victory in 1960, beating the Republican Richard Nixon, Kennedy was less willing to support legislative action than might have been suggested by his language of hope, notably his use of the concept of 'The New Frontier'. Northern liberals and Black activists both felt a considerable measure of disappointment with his conduct.

Kennedy was succeeded by his vice-president, Lyndon B. Johnson, who, in 1964, convincingly won the presidential election with the highest percentage of the vote hitherto accumulated by a candidate, defeating the Republican Barry Goldwater, who was depicted as too extreme. Johnson's subsequent reputation has been far more mixed than that of Kennedy. In part, this is due to his role in greatly building up US participation in the unsuccessful Vietnam War, and, in part because, in hindsight, his looks and personality proved unattractive in a television age that, instead, gave posthumous plaudits to Kennedy.

Yet, in domestic politics, Johnson was willing, and able, to engage with profound inequalities that Kennedy had largely only proved willing to talk about. This reflected the legacy of Johnson's Southern populism. Johnson tapped into powerful iconic ideas with his talk of social improvement, affirming a possibility of national greatness and being willing and also able to link this to government action. He declared 'unconditional war on poverty' in his first State of the Union address in 1964. Johnson also backed desegregation (see chapter 3).

WATERGATE

The break-in in June 1972 at the headquarters of the Democratic National Committee, in the Watergate Building in Washington DC, was intended to discover the party's election plans. Unnecessary anyway, as the Democrats were doing very badly, and Nixon easily won, the break-in was the act that brought the Nixon edifice down. The long aftermath of the discovery of the break-in overshadowed Nixon's second term and he was forced in August 1974 to resign for his conspiracy to obstruct justice, thus avoiding impeachment on three counts, including violation of the constitution. Nixon was subsequently pardoned by his Republican successor, Gerald Ford, who, however, suffered politically as a consequence.

The Watergate scandal led not only to the fall of Nixon but also to a crisis of confidence in national leadership, one that left a powerful legacy in terms of the role of conspiracy theories in fiction and on the screen.

BELOW: Protestors against Nixon after the Watergate scandal.

RIGHT: Barack Obama, the first African-American president.

Johnson, however, ran aground on the Vietnam War, which also fractured the Democratic coalition. The Democratic presidential candidate in 1968, his vice-president Hubert Humphrey, was defeated by Richard Nixon, who was hit hard by economic and fiscal problems but able, as promised, to end US participation in the Vietnam War, although only after broadening it to include an invasion of Cambodia. Nixon was helped by serious divisions within the Democratic Party as it struggled to respond to a more radical agenda. He easily won the 1972 election, but, paranoid and convinced he was the target of conspiracies, Nixon encouraged a systematic campaign of illegality including telephone tapping and break-ins.

Nixon's successor, Gerald Ford, suffered from the serious economic problems of the period, and lost in 1976 to the Democrat, Jimmy Carter, the outsider candidate. However, Carter came to seem a less than competent director of government and, suffering from a sense of malaise and economic problems, lost to another outsider, the Republican, Ronald Reagan, whose deregulating zeal and attacks on 'big government' saw him easily re-elected in 1984.

His Republican successor, George H.W. Bush, an insider, lacked Reagan's charisma and popularity and lost to the Democratic candidate Bill Clinton in 1992. Clinton proved politically successful, winning re-election in 1996, but was unable to enact much meaningful legislation and was dogged by questions about his personal integrity. The succeeding presidency, that of the Republican George W. Bush (r.2001–9), was consumed by foreign policy, notably the 'War on Terror' and the invasion of Iraq. In 2009–17, Barack Obama, a Democrat, the first African-American president, again focused on foreign policy, but he was also hit by the financial meltdown of 2008.

Both factors helped the Republican Donald Trump (r.2017–21) to an unexpected win in 2016, but he was beaten in 2020 in a victory that showed the political differences of American society: Trump had the majority of voters among men, the married, Protestants, those over 50, and those who lived in rural areas, the Midwest and the South. His Democratic opponent, Joe Biden, had the majority of women, the unmarried, Blacks, Latinos, Asians, Catholics, Jews, those under 50, first-time voters, those in the East and West, urban voters and (narrowly) suburban voters. In 2024, Trump again won the presidency.

NIXON QUITS, 1974

'I no longer have sufficient political base in Congress to continue.... We must complete a structure of peace so that it can be said of our generation of Americans that not only did we end one war, we helped prevent others.'

Nixon's resignation speech, 8 August 1974. The war he refers to is the Vietnam War.

INDIA, FROM INDEPENDENCE TO MODI

The orthodoxies of Indian history under the Congress governments that ruled in the early decades of independence have long ended. Congress put its emphasis on an Indian form of Socialism, a powerful state taking a key role in the economy, and a social activism designed to incorporate all. However, there was economic inertia, certainly compared to the US and China, with state regulation to the fore, and much industry in the form of low-efficiency licensed monopolies able to avoid new processes. Hindustan Motors, the only significant car manufacturer, produced in a far less efficient fashion than the Japanese and South Korean companies such as Toyota, Honda and Nissan that came to play a key role not only in their national markets but also in world ones.

The Nehru dynasty ran India under the Congress Party banner, but came to adopt an authoritarian stance, in part based on entitlement but also in response to the difficulties of governance. Indira Gandhi, the prime minister from 1966 to 1977 and 1980 to 1984, enacted a totalitarian 'Emergency' in 1975–7, ruling by decree and imprisoning without trial about 140,000 opponents. Moreover, the forced mass-sterilization campaign by the government in 1976 scarcely accorded with most views of human rights.

The Indira Gandhi government also responded to separatism, notably in Kashmir and the Punjab. In 1984, the army stormed sacred sites in Punjab occupied by Sikh militants, especially the Golden Temple in Amritsar, as well as taking control of the entire Punjab, with many casualties. Martial law, troops, police and paramilitaries asserted control,

ABOVE: Indira Gandhi speaks to a crowd of supporters during the 1971 election campaign.

but about 25,000 people were killed. Indira Gandhi was assassinated later that year by two of her Sikh bodyguards, an episode that led to the mob killings of about 8,000 Sikhs, mostly in Delhi, with no intervention by the army to restore order. This was an instance of the more general use of force in India, against and by the government, notably in Kashmir by Muslim insurgents, and also in east-central India, by the Naxalites, a Maoist insurrectionary movement. In 2021, about half a million Indian troops garrisoned Kashmir, the population of which suffered from the highest unemployment in India. In contrast, the Sikh insurgency in the Punjab had come to an end by 1997, in part due to the more cautious stance of the central government in the handling of Punjabi politics, but also due to the absence of the external intervention seen with Pakistan and neighbouring Kashmir.

BELOW: The Golden Temple in Amritsar, India.

In contrast to Congress, the Bharatiya Janata Party (BJP), founded in 1980, was central to government in 1998–2004, and then won the 2014 and 2019 elections. The BJP is

ABOVE: Narendra Modi takes the oath of office for his second term on 30 May 2019.

more interested in Hindu nationalism and popular economic freedoms. The autocratic prime minister, Narendra Modi, presents himself as opposed to India's old establishment, and has certainly overseen the broadening out of the Indian middle class. At the same time, Indian economic growth has benefited from deregulation, rising domestic consumption, US concern about China, and the potential offered by solar energy.

In 2024, Modi's BJP lost its majority in a general election that reflected popular concern about the government's ability to generate sufficient jobs, as well as the continued strength of regional parties. Alongside lower-caste concerns about BJP preferences, these undercut the BJP emphasis on Hindu nationalism. In 2018, Ashok Bharti, head of the National Conference of Dalit Organizations, referred to 'an authoritarian regime', adding that 'India is divided ... between people who are humiliated and those who humiliate'. Modi had to resort to alliances with other parties to form a government.

Modi's Hindu nationalist project offers little to the 14 per cent of the population who are Muslims, while more generally economic growth has proved more elusive than anticipated, and notably so in manufactured exports. Nor has it been as easy to limit the size of government as anticipated.

EUROPE

Under the US nuclear umbrella, Western Europe enjoyed stabilization and growth after World War II, with no state fighting another. Alongside the 'Long Boom', there was the establishment of the European Economic Community, the forerunner of the European Union. More significantly, there was an ability to overcome the economic problems of the 1970s and to bring Greece, Portugal and Spain into the Western European order once their right-wing autocratic governments had fallen in 1974, 1974 and 1975 respectively.

ABOVE: The prime minister of Spain signs the treaty to join the European Economic Community, 13 June 1985.

The end of Communist rule in 1989–91 ensured that this process was extended to Eastern Europe, albeit only after war in the former Yugoslavia in the 1990s. Eastern Europe was integrated into the existing institutions, principally the European Union and NATO, with the former swelling to 27 members by 2009. There was a considerable degree of optimism about a future in which Europe would be able to deliver peace, prosperity and social capital to its people.

This optimism took a heavy series of blows from the late 2010s, and in both international and domestic affairs. In the first, the US 'pivot' towards Asia and a growing American irritation with European attitudes and institutions clearly expressed by President Trump ensured that there was concern about the degree to which the past reliability of US assistance was still present. This was thrown to the fore from 2022, with the crisis created by the Russian invasion of Ukraine and the fear that the Russians would press on to destabilize Eastern Europe more generally. Russian policy made a mockery of the previous German reliance on Russian energy. In turn, the failure of the German–Russian alignment, as well as concern about the US, re-energized France's long-standing quest to lead Europe via the European Union.

There were also serious domestic tensions, not least due to concerns about immigration and economic change. 'Populism', much in evidence from the 2010s in Italy, Germany, France, Spain, Britain, the Netherlands and Austria as well as other countries, was in practice a democratic response to a sense of slippage in stability, control and expectations.

Partly as a result, surveys of the national mood revealed great pessimism in many European countries. To some commentators, this was linked to the widespread fall in the birth rate. Against this background of geographical variations and political divisions, the Continent became more urban, car-ownership rose, women became more important in society and there were major changes in the fortunes of particular regions and localities.

AFRICA

Decolonization was the dominant note in the first quarter-century of the period, but it was rapidly replaced by conflict within and between states. There were many coups, frequent civil wars and significant international ones, and this situation has remained the case to the present, with many states consumed by reigns of terror, as with Ethiopia under Haile Mengistu, its brutal dictator from 1977 to 1991. Only a few states have been politically stable for most of the period, principally Botswana, Senegal and Zambia. Independent from France in 1960, Mauritania became a one-party state in 1964, leading to uncontested elections, but the dictator was overthrown by a coup in 1978, leading to military governments until a new constitution in 1991 allowed for democracy. Another coup in 2005 was followed by the first fully democratic presidential election in 2007, only for another coup in 2008. In 2019, a democratic election was not followed by a coup. Many states have been ruled by dictators, usually from a military background, for example Idi Amin in Uganda, who seized power in a coup in 1971 until he was thrown out by a combination of rebel forces and troops from neighbouring Tanzania in 1979. These dictatorships have extended to dynastic rule as sons succeeded fathers.

Alongside frequent political chaos has come economic development. This has been considerable. Much effort has focused on resource extraction, for example oil from Angola and Nigeria, but there has also been the development of agricultural exports, as well as the

LEFT: Idi Amin.

RIGHT: An election billboard for Jerry Rawlings, 1996.

GHANA: FROM CHAOS TO PROGRESS

Independent in 1957, Ghana, formerly a British colony known as the Gold Coast, did not have a peaceful and democratic change of government until 2001. Initial hopes of progress were dashed by economic mismanagement, leading to a series of military governments. Alongside high inflation and poor government there was discontent among the poor and coups, notably those in 1979 and 1981 that brought Jerry Rawlings, an air force officer, to power, leading to the execution in 1979 of three former heads of state. Instead of understanding that economic mismanagement was the problem, the focus was on corruption, and in 1979 Rawlings had the central black market in Accra blown up. After his second coup, Rawlings abolished the constitution and dissolved parliament, but in, 1983, he changed policy, turning from left-wing economic (mis)management to free market reforms. Coup attempts were suppressed in 1983, 1984, 1985, 1986 and 1987, and economic growth shot up, and, with it, stability. Rawlings returned to constitutional government, won elections in 1992 and 1996, and was cited in 1998 by President Clinton, alongside South Africa and Uganda, as evidence of an 'African Renaissance'. Retiring in 2001, Rawlings was succeeded by John Kufuor, president until 2009, and his successor, John Mills, formerly an opposition politician, who became in 2012 the first Ghanaian head of state to die in office. Subsequently, Ghana has continued to be a democratic state and a contrast with the instability in much of West Africa.

growth of industrial sectors. However, the ability to produce food for export is affected by rapid population growth, and industrial activity has been disrupted by lawlessness, notably in South Africa. Credit has been a major problem, with many states becoming heavily indebted in part due to the need to finance imports, particularly, as in Egypt, of food for their growing populations. In Kenya in 2024, proposed tax increases, including on bread and cooking oil to help tackle a very high level of public debt, led to 'TikTok protests' spread by social media and then serious rioting with parliament stormed. The government abandoned the proposals.

LEFT: Protesters campaign against the introduction of higher taxes in Nairobi, Kenya on 18 June 2024.

Corruption has also been a serious issue, for example in Nigeria, Gabon, South Africa and Zimbabwe, and this has sapped confidence in the government. It has proved very difficult to develop the social capital of accepting that power is not a prerogative for pillage. Thus, French-backed Paul Biya, prime minister of Cameroon from 1975 to 1982 and president since 1982, is an authoritarian who has won elections characterized by irregularities. Teodoro Obiang has held power in Equatorial Guinea, another oil exporter, since 1979 when, in a coup, he replaced his uncle, who was then executed. His brutal rule has been characterized by human rights abuses, including routine torture. The wealth of the country's oil goes to the president, his family and his allies, while little is spent on health and education. Obiang has described himself as in contact with God.

The former imperial powers long remained influential in their former empires. Thus, with the exception of Guinea which moved in a very left-wing direction, France dominated its former empire until the early 2020s, extracting raw materials, such as manganese from Gabon, maintaining bases, supporting Chad against Libya in the 1980s, and intervening in Mali, the Central African Republic and Niger in the 2010s. Britain retained considerable influence in Kenya and Nigeria, but this was not the case for some of its other former colonies, notably Tanzania and Zimbabwe, and was not the case for former Italian and Portuguese colonies. China became a major source of credit in the 2010s, for example in

BELOW: French president Emmanuel Macron meets with president of Niger, Mahamadou Issoufou, 2018.

CONFRONTING THE IMPERIAL LEGACY

'France, Get Out!' is a frequent social media meme in West Africa, and French leaders, especially Emmanuel Macron, president from 2017, have recently moved to apologize for aspects of French imperialism. In 2017, Macron called French policy during Algerian decolonization a 'crime against humanity', while there was acknowledgement of France's malign role in the 1994 Rwanda genocide. Macron abolished the elitist *Françafrique* summits proposing, instead, a more equal *Afrique-France* partnership.

RIGHT: Refugees from the Rwandan genocide in the Kirundo refugee camp, Burundi, 1994.

Kenya, which caused concern about a struggle for influence with the West. Meanwhile, the rapidly rising population of Africa remains a fundamental issue, as does environmental change, notably a shortage of water and grazing land.

The large number of Africans who seek opportunity in other continents is a sign of the failures of African economies to generate sufficient jobs. In 2023, about 380,000 migrants sought to travel from Ethiopia to Saudi Arabia. Many Africans also seek refuge and opportunity in Europe.

There are also more positive signs. The African Union has played a role in protecting democracy and stability, and intervening accordingly, as in military intervention in West Africa and Somalia. In 2008, suspension from the African Union was a response to a military coup in Mauritania, with mediation by neighbouring Senegal helping lead to an election process in which the head of the junta became president. Major African cities, such as Accra and Dakar, have been able to cope with their population rise without breakdown. Although South Africa is now in serious difficulties, and the Horn of Africa, Sudan, and the Sahel are even more violent and unstable, the situation for most Africans is better than in 1950. Yet, the genocidal violence seen in Rwanda in 1994, with probably over a million Tutsi and moderate Hutus killed by the French-backed extremist Hutus, who then controlled the government, continues, notably in neighbouring northeast Congo and in western Sudan.

There is also the danger that instability will spread. In 2020–3, there were coups in Mali, Sudan, Chad, Guinea, Burkina Faso, Niger and Gabon, while in 2021 Idriss Déby, president of Chad, was killed fighting Muslim rebels. The resulting instability threatens to exacerbate problems in neighbouring states, such as Nigeria. It is unclear how this situation can be contained.

LATIN AMERICA

The pressures of population growth, rapid urbanization, and socio-economic change posed major challenges to the institutions and politics of Latin American countries. So also did the tensions of international ideologies and power politics, as well as established political alignments and rivalries within countries. Economic growth was pronounced in some areas, but insufficient to meet employment needs. Alongside wealthy groups and enclaves, there was a degree of income inequality that interacted with the weakness of social welfare and the strength of political animosities.

American influence, political and economic was dominant after World War II, with the Americans frequently in alliance with corrupt dictators, as in Cuba, the Dominican Republic, Nicaragua and Venezuela, and encouraging coups to overthrow governments judged left-wing, as in Guatemala in 1954 and Brazil in 1965. Attempts by democratic governments in the 1950s and early 1960s, notably in Mexico and Brazil, to develop links with the non-aligned movement were weakened by their economic relationship with the US.

ABOVE: Fidel Castro, prime minister and then president of Cuba from 1959 to 2008.

US dominance was challenged from the 1960s, notably with the Cuban Revolution that took Fidel Castro to power and then saw him move into the Communist bloc. Alongside moves against racism, and campaigns in favour of healthcare and literacy, Cuba very much became an oppressive, one-party state, with the execution of critics and with a large number of political prisoners held in brutal conditions, while many others sought to flee. In an attempt to mobilize support from a widely discontented population, there was an active programme of political indoctrination, while Committees for the Defence of the Revolution provided surveillance of the people, by the people, for the dictatorship. While malnourished Cubans searched rubbish bins for food or queued for the few things available, Castro ate well, indulging his fancies for ice cream, quail eggs and baby eels. His dictatorship has also survived him, and remains highly repressive, leading to emigration as well as the protesting that is countered, as in 2021, with numerous arrests.

In response to Cuba's left-wing move, the US took a more proactive stance, establishing the Alliance for Progress (1961), intervening militarily in the Dominican Republic in 1965, and lending support to conservative military regimes, notably the Pinochet government that seized power in a coup in Chile in 1974, overthrowing the left-wing democratic Allende government.

Cuba, meanwhile, sent troops to advance Soviet Cold War goals in Africa, particularly in Angola and Ethiopia, but the Cuban attempt in Latin America to establish left-wing regimes in the Dominican Republic and Bolivia failed.

The lessening, and then end, of the Cold War led to a reduction in political tension and consolidated the move towards democracy already seen in the 1980s in South America

ABOVE: The Chilean coup of 1973.

with Peru (1979), Bolivia (1982), Argentina (1983), Brazil (1985) and Paraguay (1989) being prominent in moving to democracy.

In Central America, the situation in the 1980s was more troubled, with the US backing guerrilla opposition to the left-wing Sandinista movement that had taken over Nicaragua in 1978, supporting the conservative government of El Salvador against left-wing guerrillas, and intervening militarily to change the governments of Grenada (1983) and Panama (1989).

Cuba was weakened by the removal of Soviet support in the 1990s, but it, and its new ally Venezuela, sustained left-wing control in the face of US pressure in the early 21st century. Under Hugo Chávez, president from 1999 to 2013, and his successor, Nicolás Maduro, Venezuela took further the traditional left-wing Latin American opposition to the US, sought to create a regional anti-American movement, notably with Bolivia, Cuba and Ecuador, and aligned with other opponents of the US, especially Russia and Iran.

Political division was acute in many states, including Argentina, Bolivia and Peru; and economic growth failed to provide solutions to this or to the large-scale wish to migrate to America. In Bolivia, an unsuccessful coup in 2024 reflected the turmoil after the rule of Evo Morales, president from 2005 to 2019, a radical Socialist and the first president from the indigenous majority. Ethnic tensions are an issue in Peru and Bolivia, but not only there. In Guyana there is tension between Afro-Guyanese and Indo-Guyanese.

Changes in Latin America could be rapid. There was significant free-market economic growth in the 2000s and early 2010s. However, the Covid pandemic led not only to a very high fatality rate, but also to an economic crisis that, for example, pushed 20 per cent of Peruvians back into poverty. In 2021, Pedro Castillo, a left-winger, narrowly won the presidency there on the slogan of 'no more poor in a rich country'. The poor rural hinterland provided him with his core support, but it was not clear whether he had viable policies and in 2022 he lost power.

ABOVE: Contra forces, backed by the United States, in Nicaragua, 1987.

In Chile, there was significant economic growth after the end of the Pinochet dictatorship in 1990, leading to a great decline in poverty and significant expansion of the middle class. However, its economic growth slowed from 2014, while the ability of the political system to deliver results lessened. This helped cause a lack of confidence

SHINING PATH

The *Sendero Luminoso* (Shining Path) insurgency that began in Peru in 1980 drew on long-standing traditions of peasant activism especially in poor indigenous regions neglected by the élite, as well as Maoist ideas of social revolution and redistribution. There were many casualties. The capture of its leader in 1992 contributed to its decline.

ABOVE: Shining Path guerrillas, 1984.

ABOVE: Members of the Sinaloa Cartel are arrested in Mexico, 2010.

in institutions and a populist assault on what was seen as an unequal society run to the benefit of an élite who dominated much of the economy. Public order collapsed with rioting in 2020 and it proved difficult to restore cohesion.

Drugs proved destabilizing for many states, and notably when allied to powerful criminal networks, some of which had political ambitions, as in Colombia, Ecuador and Haiti in the early 21st century. A sense of social malaise saw its most abrupt demonstration in the scale of the killings by criminals, as in Mexico, where violent drug-trafficking gangs, such as the Sinaloa and Zeta cartels, fought each other and the government, with possibly 100,000 dead in 2006–14. By 2015, the Zeta Cartel dominated the underworld of much of Mexico, while the government increasingly turned to the military. In 2022, El Salvador responded to deadly violence by imposing a state of emergency.

Meanwhile, Guyana gained independence from Britain in 1966, and Suriname from the Netherlands in 1975. As an anomaly, Cayenne (French Guiana) remains under France, its largest overseas territory, but with an independence movement, founded in 1991, increasingly active and responsible for serious disturbances in 2017.

The US remained the dominant power in Latin America. Its markets were particularly important for neighbouring Mexico, not least after a free-trade pact with the US and Canada came into effect in 1994, boosting Mexican exports' percentage of GDP from 12 in 1993 to 40 in 2021. By then, Mexico was the world's 15th-largest economy.

Alongside the position of the US, China has become a major market, notably for raw materials, such as copper from Chile and Peru and soyabeans from Brazil. This represents a new stage of Latin America's role as a raw material source for the rest of the world, rather than a focus for trade and manufacturing within the region. Political cooperation and economic integration within Latin America, meanwhile, is limited, as are transport routes. Founded in 1990, Mercosur, a common market for Latin American nations, had scant impact.

THE MIDDLE EAST

But for oil and Israel, the Middle East would possibly not have had the prominence in world history that it has received. Other parts of the world, notably sub-Saharan Africa, have had more conflict and disruption, but have not attracted comparable attention.

Oil and Israel, which, after victory in the Six Days' War in 1967, controlled an unwilling Palestinian population, are scarcely the sole factors. There have also been significant divisions within the Islamic world, for example between Iran and Iraq from the 1950s to 2000s, as well as the role of great power rivalries, both during the Cold War and subsequently. Nevertheless, the degree to which the region's oil and natural gas production has played a key role in the global economy has comprised a central part in the attention devoted to it, as have Arab–Israeli Wars. Indeed, it is mistaken to treat oil solely in terms of energy use, because it is also politically fundamental, as well as divisive.

Azerbaijan, Iran, Iraq and Saudi Arabia were already producers by World War II, but much of the subsequent activity represented the bringing to fruition of areas in which oil

BELOW: Oil and gas refineries in Qatar.

ABOVE: Bahrain Minister of Foreign Affairs Abdullah bin Rashid Al-Zayani, Israeli Prime Minister Benjamin Netanyahu, US President Donald Trump and UAE Minister of Foreign Affairs Dr Zayed al Nahyan sign the Abraham Accords, September 2020.

was discovered in the 1930s (Saudi Arabia, Bahrain, Kuwait and Qatar), as well as finding new oilfields in these countries and in others: the United Arab Emirates from 1958 and Oman from 1962. The establishment of the Organization of the Petroleum Exporting Countries (OPEC) in 1960 was a major step, as was the massive growth in global demand, such that the US was no longer able to export oil.

The role of oil ensured US concern for the security of Saudi Arabia and the Gulf States, especially once Iraq (1958) and Iran (1979) had experienced regime changes that left them hostile to America. US support from the 1960s also greatly helped Israel, not least in arranging a peace treaty with Egypt in 1979. America also sought in the early 2020s to improve Israeli relations with Saudi Arabia as part of an anti-Iranian bloc and came close to success.

This reflected the tensions within the Islamic world that encompassed a variety of alignments including Shi'ites versus Sunnis, and fundamentalists versus moderates, as well as the competing regional ambitions of Iran, Iraq, Turkey, Syria, Israel, Saudi Arabia, the United Arab Emirates (UAE) and Egypt. Thus, the last in the 1960s sought to expand control or influence not only against Israel, but also in Libya, Sudan, Syria and Yemen, deploying its forces to support several of these goals, but without success. Pan-Arabist ideas to create a new identity, for example the Federation of Arab Republics established in 1971 and involving Egypt, Libya and Syria, gained limited traction. These tensions were seen in a range of disputes, such as the struggle for dominance in Libya from 2011, which led to Turkish, Egyptian and UAE intervention on behalf of competing protégés, and that in Yemen in the 1960s and the early 2020s.

At the same time, there were serious issues arising from population growth, intergenerational opportunity and income inequalities. These greatly contributed to the 'Arab Spring' that began in Tunisia in December 2010, a movement for political liberalization. Economic problems, notably a lack of work and income, allegedly caused a crisis of masculinity and certainly led to despair and anger. These were accentuated by economic mismanagement, particularly over subsidies and the price of bread. There was also anger about corruption, police brutality and authoritarianism, and these initially focused on Tunisia when Mohamed Bouazizi, a fruit seller robbed by the police, set himself alight. In 2011, the governments of Tunisia, Egypt and Libya were all overthrown, but the civil war that began in Syria in 2012 was brutally suppressed and, helped by Iran and Russia, the Assad dictatorship remained in power until 2024. A 'New Arab Spring' was discerned in Algeria and Sudan in 2019, but the reform movement in Sudan rapidly gave way to military dictatorship and civil war.

BELOW: Protests in Tahrir Square, Cairo, 9 February 2011.

ABOVE: Revolutionaries burn the US flag on the roof of the American embassy in Tehran.

EMBASSY POLITICS

The storming of the US embassy in Tehran in 1979 and the holding of the staff as hostages for over 400 days helped entrench the Islamic Revolution as an anti-American force and also provided a key issue in US–Iranian relations. When told that international law was being violated, Ayatollah Khomeini, the leader of the revolution, claimed that the observance of such principles should always be secondary to Islam and asked what international law had ever done for the people of Iran. Moreover, the fate of the 52 hostages became significant in US domestic politics, with the failure of President Carter's attempt to rescue them in 1980 serving as a symbol of his weakness, which contributed to his failure to win re-election. The attack on the embassy was both symbolic and an attempt to close down what was seen as a rallying point for those opposed to the Islamic Revolution.

AUSTRALIA

Often downplayed in global histories, Australia reflected wider international trends, such as Cold War concerns and the economic boom and subsequent birth of consumerism from the 1950s, but also experienced its own national trends. In particular, largely due to immigration from countries other than Britain, particularly Greece and Italy, Australia became multinational, indeed multi-ethnic, in its background, changing attitudes and making society more diverse. At the same time, Australia's indigenous peoples, the Aborigines, continued to be treated in a discriminatory fashion, not least with children taken from their families in a process of assimilation.

The late 1960s and 1970s saw a more troubled society, with economic problems, dissent about the Vietnam War, social fluidity, cultural innovation, and growing Aboriginal criticism. Many of these themes continued thereafter; but Australia benefited from economic growth and deregulation in the 1980s and from the more general economic expansion of Southeast and East Asia. Immigrants from China and India became more numerous, and Aboriginal activism increased. Relations with Britain became far less close, notably from the 1990s, although a republican rejection of the British Crown was voted down in a referendum in 1999. Contests over Australian identity played a significant role in 'culture wars' from the 2000s, while relations with China became tenser and environmental challenges more apparent.

In 2024, a referendum rejected constitutional change in favour of the Aborigines. New Zealand has followed a similar trajectory, although its indigenous Māori people are numerically and politically more prominent than Australia's Aborigines. In terms of economic resources, New Zealand does not have Australia's mineral wealth.

HEAT AND FIRES

The scale and intensity of the environmental problems of the 2020s were focused by drought and fires, and the legacy was seen in works of fiction:

'In her memory, bushfires of the scale and ferocity that seemed to occur in the south had never been a feature of this region. Until now. All the old certainties were coming to an end. The planet was finally calling their pestilent species to account.'

Dinuka McKenzie, *Tipping Point*, 2024.

SOUTH KOREA AND JAPAN

In a pattern more generally true of the 'Tiger Economies' of Asia, war and dictatorship dominated the history of South Korea after World War II. Yet, in South Korea, under US military protection, political activism and economic development brought change, with Syngman Rhee, the dictatorial president, stepping down in 1960 in the face of public demonstrations. A new constitution brought a parliamentary system, but a military coup in 1961 was followed by a new dictatorship behind the form of a republican system. Lasting until a transition toward electoral democracy in 1987, this repressive system saw 'Emergency Measures' that restricted freedom of expression but also major economic growth. In 1979, the dictator, Park Chung Hee, was assassinated, which was followed by another military coup as well as by popular opposition, notably in the harshly suppressed Gwangju Uprising in 1980. In 1987, more widespread opposition led to the fall of the regime and the introduction of a democratic order. This was scarcely problem-free and in 1997 the country faced a major foreign exchange and debt crisis. Nevertheless, that was rapidly overcome, and, as a capitalist democracy, South Korea offered its citizens a much greater quality of life than that in rival North Korea, which remained a Communist dictatorship. South Korea, however, was affected by a falling population.

ABOVE: Park Chung Hee.

Japan did not face the political instability of South Korea. Defeat in World War II led to US occupation, under which there was the creation of a democratic political system as well as land reform. Economic growth was accompanied by large-scale

A CHANGING SOCIETY

The Little Sparrow Murders (1971) by the highly successful writer Seishi Yokomizo (1902–81) is set in 1955 and begins by presenting the past as anachronistic:

'It was late July, in 1955, when Kosuke Kindaichi, accompanied by a letter of introduction from Inspector Isokawa, took a rickshaw over the Sennin Pass – astonishingly, this mode of transport was still in use in those parts.'

The social impact of change is clear: 'Like so many others, they lost practically everything in the land reforms.' There is also change between the generations, as in marital choices: '...ever since the war, people generally leave it to the young people to decide for themselves'.

movement from the countryside to rapidly expanding cities. While socially disruptive, this did not lead to political instability. Less positively, there was significant industrial pollution. Modernization was symbolized by the bullet trains introduced for the 1964 Tokyo Olympics.

Japan became the world's second-largest economy, only to be overtaken by the rise of China, which also posed a significant security threat from the 2010s.

ABOVE: A student demonstration for democracy in South Korea, 1987.

LEFT: Japan's first bullet train was inaugurated in 1964.

A WORLD IN DIVERSITY

The two Koreas act as an apt reminder that there was no inevitability in world developments. Two countries with similar geographies and resources have gone in very different directions. And so more generally, for example for the states created from the partition of British India, with Pakistan having the military dictatorships and low economic growth that India has avoided. Bangladesh, Myanmar and Sri Lanka have all seen ethnic conflicts and terrible instability, but, again, there are contrasts, with Bangladesh successfully becoming a democracy as Myanmar has failed to do.

This theme of diversity was present from the outset in 1950, but has become more so, in large part due to the accumulated occurrences of the intervening years, not least the impact of the Cold War. Politics rather than resources offer key contrasts, as in the differences between oil-rich Iran, oil-rich Iraq and oil-rich Saudi Arabia. The key contrasts here were the Islamic Revolution of 1978–9 in Iran and the succumbing of Iraq to adventurism, conquest and division, from 1980.

BELOW: Women wait to cast their votes, Bangladesh, 2024.

It is unclear how far these changes will become more or less pronounced. The differential demographic movements discussed in chapter two will certainly open up contrasts, as will related (but different) migration pressures and their consequences.

At one end of the spectrum are states characterized by stability and prosperity, for example Switzerland. At the other come those termed 'failed states', where political instability is such that society becomes primarily a matter for individual, family and communal security, or, indeed, survival. Over the last half century, this has been true of a number of countries, including Afghanistan, Myanmar, Iraq, Sudan, Rwanda, Congo, Mali, Niger, Sierra Leone and Liberia; as well as of parts of countries, such as northern Mozambique and northern Uganda.

To leave out these countries from the discussion of world history is as mistaken as to exclude states that do not match 'regional trends', for example North Korea. What is clear is that while there can be consistency in circumstances, success and failure, it is also possible that there will be abrupt changes. War is a classic instance of this and may indeed affect developments in Taiwan or the Baltic republics if they are attacked over the next decade. At the same time, there can be significant changes without war occurring, as with the collapse of Communism in Eastern Europe.

The consistent element of 1950 to the present is in part a matter of continuous circumstances, for example the internal peace of Australia and Canada, and in part one of inconsistency.

ABOVE: An Afghan minister gives a speech in January 2025. While some countries have moved towards greater democracy and tolerance in the last 75 years, others have gone in the opposite direction.

9 Looking to the Future

Future trends in world history understandably invite debate and are very important to choices made during our period, for every decision reflects a sense of the future. The trends currently under discussion are different to those in 1950 for example, when climate change was not an issue. These trends pull together themes in the chapters of the book, notably climate change, migration, changing political systems, and the risks of war, and invite consideration of how present concerns are actually different to earlier anxieties (as opposed to being perceived differently) and how far the present presents a similar set of challenges to the late 20th century.

The future is comprised of many elements, notably inherited ideas of the future, those derived from past predictions and perceptions in the present, both optimistic and pessimistic. In practice, these perceptions vary by group and are affected by the combination of the pressures of the moment and more long-term ideas.

posco

SCIENCE FICTION

Science fiction poses a powerful counterfactual to the real world, expressing hopes, anxieties, and paranoias. Science fiction invites speculation about suspending or transforming the laws of matter and other scientific fundamentals, speculation which can overlap with discussion by physicists of such concepts as parallel universes.

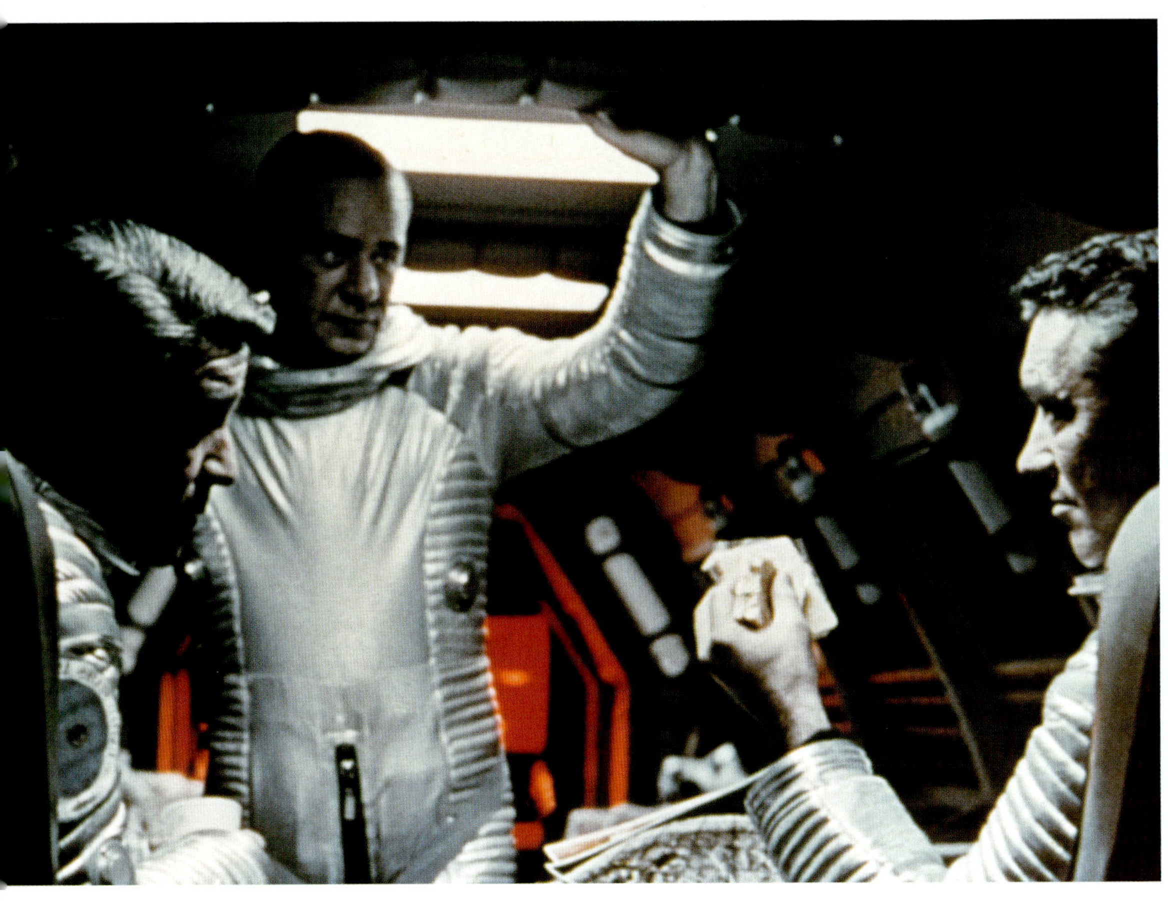

ABOVE: A scene from *2001: A Space Odyssey.*

There has been a fascination with extraterrestrials, as in *Alien* (1979), and with the creation of new and artificial life forms, the latter a theme also in engineering, computer science and biology. In *2001: A Space Odyssey* (1968), a monolith watching over human development on behalf of an alien force broadcasts the news of prehistoric man acquiring the ability to use weapons across the universe, providing a new history of Humanity: past, present and future, in which time is reconceptualized. There was an ironic jibe in the American film *Mars Attacks* (1997), in which the presidential science adviser explained, on more than one occasion, that the approaching Martians were bound to be peaceful because no advanced culture would wage war. This view was in keeping with a progressive account of diplomacy, one that presented it as an aspect of the improvability of society, if not mankind. In that film, the Martians, once arrived and greeted, prove coldly violent as they seek to take over the world.

The fictional treatment of relations with aliens has encompassed both conflict but also other elements. Television series and films such as *Star Trek* and *Star Wars* offered a number of different alien societies with their own goals and cooperative international organizations at the stellar level, notably the Federation, which was the key organization in *Star Trek* and in part a response to concerns about the 'colonization of space'. Both space for agreement and opportunities for conflict were portrayed.

PREDICTIONS MADE

The future in the 1930s appeared bleak. Published in 1934, Dennis Wheatley's novel *Black August* was set at some time in the future where there was: '...starvation rampant in every city in Europe.... Balkan and Central European frontiers disintegrating from month to month, while scattered, ill-equipped armies fought on broken fronts for whom, or for what cause, they now scarcely knew.'

The changing fate of World War II produced fresh gloom, and the late 1940s saw the greatest of dystopian novels, George Orwell's *1984* (1949).

TOWARDS WORLD WAR?

In a speech given on 15 January 2024, Grant Shapps, the British Secretary of State for Defence, argued that the world had moved to a 'prewar' phase:

In five years' time we could be looking at multiple theatres involving Russia, China, Iran and North Korea... Back in the days of the Cold War, there remained a sense that we were dealing with rational actors. But these new powers are far more unstable... Put it all together, and these combined threats risk tearing apart the rules-based international order established to keep the peace after World War II. Today's world, then, is sadly far more dangerous... The era of the peace dividend is over.'

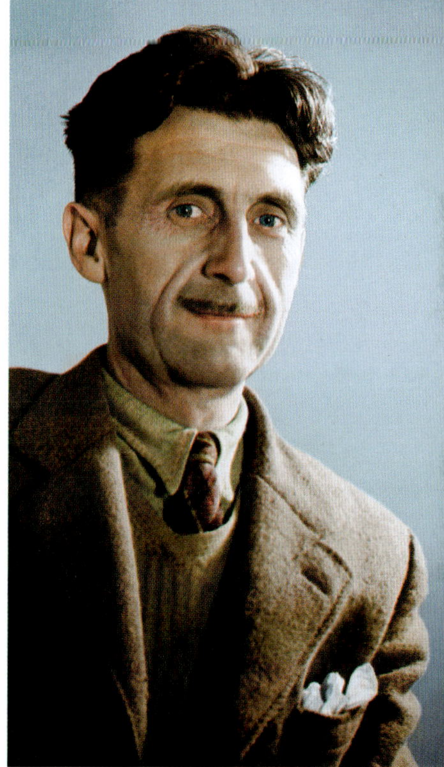

ABOVE: George Orwell, author of the dystopian novel *1984*.

Nevertheless, the theme of dystopia was to appear relatively distant in the 1950s, when economic growth matched recovery from World War II. Despite nuclear confrontation, it proved possible to shelve disputes, such as in Korea in 1953 and Vietnam in 1954, and also to address many issues without conflict, such as the Soviet suppression of popular discontent in East Germany in 1953 and of Hungarian nationalism in 1956. In the 1960s, the greying of the American dream induced greater caution, as did the apparent proximity of war over Cuba in 1962.

The future has been predicted and contested repeatedly in our period. In part, this is due to the degree to which progress towards a better future has been seen as validating the politics of the present. This was notably so as an aspect of teleological and progressive philosophies and prospects, whether of the Left, Right or Centre. This process can be seen in elections, governmental announcements, commentaries and fictional discussions. To a degree, there is what the American author Richard Grusin in his 2010 book of the same name calls 'premediation' and which he defines not as anticipation or 'getting the future right' ahead of time, but as 'making futurity present'. Grusin argued that socially networked media worked to that end.

There is a general tendency to think about the future in a linear version, as in the 'because of x now it will be the case of x plus five in a year's time'. That approach, however, is flawed. It fails to allow for the degree to which the past, and therefore what in the future will be the past and therefore now is the future, is non-linear. Indeed, there are a series of unpredictabilities. Looking to the past, it was far from clear that either the Russian invasion of Ukraine in 2022 or the Hamas attack on Israel in 2023 were inevitable, or, indeed, any election results, for example the US ones in 2000, 2016, 2020 and 2024.

This is the perspective from which to consider past assessments, including predictions of environmental disaster, nuclear war, political chaos and social breakdown. All have been to the fore. Ideological and religious predictions are also part of the equation. For Communists, these ranged to the triumph of the proletariat, while on the Right, and increasingly so from the 1980s, as it became more doctrinaire, there was a conviction of the inherently contradictory nature of the Left, and the inevitability of its fall.

The nature of prediction encompassed a generational element, with the young likely to anticipate a future involving the triumph of their values and the overthrow of those of the then-dominant generation. History is presented as on their side, the future therefore as knowledge. Indeed, wish-fulfilment was a key element of predication.

However, so also was apocalypticism, notably with predictions of climate catastrophe, atomic conflict, population overrun and inter-space invasion, all parts of the collective imagination of our period, though to differing degrees. Fiction was a classic form of these predictions. In his novel *The Sixth Commandment* (1979), the popular American writer Lawrence Sanders had the character Dr Thorndecker set out to 'make humans immortal', remarking:

'We are so close. You'll see it all within fifty years. Human cloning. Gene splicing and complete manipulation of DNA. New species. Synthesis of human blood and all the enzymes. Solution of the brain's mysteries, and masters of immunology.'

Not yet.

And so to the present. There is no set pattern for dystopia, but environmental catastrophe and human folly are key elements. Predictions of collapse are frequent, whether military, political, governmental, economic, social or ethnic. As a result of a sense of pessimism, there has been a rise in official interest in social resilience, while 'preppers', those preparing for life in a situation of chaos, social breakdown and shortage have become more common, notably in the US.

BELOW: John Perry Barlow.

A CYBERSPACE FUTURE

'...Cyberspace consists of transactions, relationships, and thought itself, arrayed like a standing wave in the web of our communications. We will create a civilization of the mind in Cyberspace. May it be more humane and fair than the world your governments have made before....'

The 'Declaration of the Independence of Cyberspace' by the American essayist and cyberlibertarian John Perry Barlow (1947–2018), was published online and was a critical response to governmental attempts, especially in the US, to control the internet.

ABOVE: The Garuda Palace, a presidential palace built in 2022–4, at the intended future Indonesian capital, Nusantara. The Garuda is a Hindu deity depicted as the king of the birds.

Pessimism is the prevalent tone in a lot of commentary about the future, more particularly in much independent commentary. In contrast, propaganda, the official line of governments, institutions and companies, was particularly prone to offer optimism, although the ideological context, content and tone varied greatly.

Governments and electorates alike tend to focus on short-term problems and solutions. When they look to the long term, governments often spend heavily on grandiloquent projects, such as new capitals, as in Brazil, Nigeria, Myanmar and Indonesia. In many states, there is much less interest in economic and environmental policy reforms that are viable, incremental and that do not require significant debt.

AN OPTIMISTIC NEAR-FUTURE

Yet, alongside these factors, there were reasons for contained optimism in many respects. The experience of those in emerging economies is of a life that is wealthier, healthier and better informed than that of former generations, and most people live in such economies. In part, this rested on the human capacity to attempt and devise solutions, to pursue innovations and to implement policies. These rested on a number of factors, including the desire to devise solutions, as well as the widespread wish to engage with the future and to pursue improvement.

Urban life, the condition of most, poses major problems of management, but the ability to devise solutions, notably for housing, sanitation and security, are not insuperable. Key are not only resources, but also social and political capital. Neither have been exhausted, and each can be replenished from existing societies and current or new ideologies, practices and policies. It is possible that new equilibria will emerge, not only in terms of population and, more generally, with reference to the environment, but also regarding economic activity, social organization and governmental practice. Some of the conditions may be unacceptable by current standards, but that does not determine the response or context in the years to come.

Public need, state strength, governmental interest in survival and the drive by the young for betterment, are all significant factors.

The means to improvement are diverse. In part, there will be the attempt to create new factors of production, especially through enhanced technology, as with the pursuit of nuclear fission. The application of recently developed technology will also be significant, not least the use of Artificial Intelligence (AI) for administrative tasks and, increasingly, problem-solving. There is a dystopian aspect to the last, as with 'machines taking over', but techniques and technologies of this type may well be used to pursue optimal accounts in multiple contexts, for example by helping the elderly, an increasing percentage of the population, to continue to live independently rather than in care. AI and other control techniques are also necessary to make the best use of resources, such as fresh water, that are in short supply.

Repeatedly, the balance of judgement is significant. It is appropriate to dwell on climate change, and its dangerous consequences, but also to point out that much of the world remains convenient for human life and settlement, and that there are possibilities of greater crop yields from higher temperatures, as well as of settlement in more northerly latitudes. Neither, however, will be easy.

ABOVE: Singapore is one country that managed to overcome a number of problems in the second half of the 20th century to emerge as one of the wealthiest and most successful nations of the 21st. What other states might follow in its footsteps over the coming decades?

THE YOUNG WILL LIVE THE FUTURE

More of the young than the current old will live to 2050, and indeed 2100, and their aspirations and experiences will clearly help frame the future. Yet, complicating the situation at the global level, the position varies greatly in different regions.

	Percentage under 15 in 2023	Percentage over 65 in 2023
World	25	10
Africa	40	3
Latin America and West Indies	23	9
Oceania	23	13
Asia	23	10
North America	18	17
Europe	16	19

ENVIRONMENTAL TRUTHS

It is all too easy to forget that the impact of the environment is inexorable and can be dramatic. The Mid-Atlantic Ridge, the border between the American and European tectonic plates, is unstable as the plates move apart about 3 cm (1.18 in) annually, with new seafloor produced. Linked to this, there is much volcanic activity and earthquakes, notably in Iceland, where there is destruction, as by a volcano on the nearby island of Heimaey in 1973 and on the main island itself in 2024, as well as the creation of the new island of Surtsey, thrown up after an eruption in 1963 and named after a fire monster.

Yet, it is the increase in temperature that is the environmental element currently to the fore. Despite much international diplomatic effort to tackle climate change, the impact has been limited, although it is unclear what would have happened if no efforts had been made. In practice, with the exception of the Covid 19 lockdown period, global emissions have risen since agreements were first made to limit them, and it is likely that the rise by 2030 will be at

BELOW: The cost of wind power has fallen rapidly, providing a real alternative to fossil fuels.

LEFT: An artist's impression of the *Voyager 1* space probe leaving the solar system.

BEYOND THE SOLAR SYSTEM

Launched in 1977, the *Voyager 1* and *Voyager 2* unmanned space probes, still operating in 2024, became, in part as a result of using the gravitational pulls of planets to provide power, the first human-made objects to cross the heliopause (the boundary of our solar system) and enter interstellar space. *Voyager 1* achieved this feat first, in 2012, and by 2024 was more than 24 billion km (15 billion miles) from Earth. Included in its payload is a time capsule that includes greetings from our planet to the universe.

least the 1.5°C above pre-industrial levels agreed as the target at the Paris climate agreement in 2015 and perhaps even higher (see pages 25–6). This raises the danger of approaching the 2°C above pre-industrial levels that was seen then as a high risk for the environment.

The best way to respond is one that links together themes in many of the chapters. Some favour new energy technologies, notably in the form of hydrogen usage and carbon capture, taking forward the themes in chapter four. Others focus on a linkage between themes in chapters four and five, with the costing of existing technologies being the key theme. This is focused on the falling real cost of renewable energy, notably wind and, even more, solar, due in particular to work with solar cells, and, as a linked point, rises in fuel efficiency.

Yet, as chapters two and three underline, rising global population, as well as changes in social structures that will lead to an increase in consumption, mean that there is more pressure on the environment. So also with consumerist trends, notably for more foreign travel, larger cars, homes with more electronic devices and demands for social welfare.

There are also pressures on resources caused by existing governmental priorities (see chapters 7 and 8). The distribution of spending on conflict and debt, and on current social policies (rather than long-term improvements), is one that poses issues, irrespective of the more specific point of the quality of the spending on particular environmental policies. It is unclear that these issues are being faced adequately.

INDEX

PICTURE CREDITS

t = top, b = bottom, l = left, r = right

Alamy: 22, 81, 108, 125, 154, 158b, 163b, 164, 176

David Woodroffe: 153, 185

Getty Images: 6, 23, 26, 31, 32, 34, 37, 43, 45, 54, 58, 64, 68 (x2), 73, 74, 75, 79b, 82, 83, 84, 88, 91, 93, 96, 100, 104, 106, 117, 118, 122, 128, 135t, 136, 138, 139, 140, 141, 144, 156, 159b, 161, 168 (x2), 170, 171t, 183, 184, 186, 187, 189, 193, 194t, 196, 198b, 202, 204, 206, 208, 211, 217, 221, 224, 226, 227 (x2), 228, 230, 231b, 232, 236, 239, 241, 244

NASA: 18

National Museum of the US Air Force: 195t

Shutterstock: 12, 14, 17, 27, 28, 29, 30, 33, 35, 36, 46, 49, 52, 56, 57, 60, 62, 63, 67, 72, 78, 85, 86b, 87, 90, 92, 95, 98, 102, 105, 112, 115b, 124b, 127 (x2), 129, 130, 131, 132, 134, 137, 146, 147, 150, 151t, 152, 155, 160, 162, 171b, 175, 178, 180, 182, 209, 212, 215, 220, 222, 233, 240, 242, 247, 249, 250,

Topfoto: 11, 41, 59, 61, 76, 99t, 145b, 158t, 165, 167, 169, 188, 197, 203, 207

Wellcome Collection: 69

Wikimedia Commons: 8, 9, 10, 16, 19, 20, 21, 24, 25, 39, 40, 42, 44, 47, 48, 51, 55, 65, 66, 70, 71, 77, 79t, 80, 86t, 89, 94, 97, 99b, 103, 106, 107, 109, 110, 111, 114, 115t, 116, 119, 120, 121, 123, 124t, 126, 135b, 143, 145t, 149, 151b, 159t, 163t, 166, 172, 174, 177, 191 (x2), 192, 194b, 195b, 198t, 199, 201, 214, 216, 218, 219, 223, 225, 229, 231t, 234, 235, 238, 245, 246, 251